PHILOSOPHY OF LIFELONG EDUCATION

CROOM HELM SERIES IN INTERNATIONAL PERSPECTIVES ON ADULT AND CONTINUING EDUCATION

Edited by Peter Jarvis, University of Surrey
Consultant Editors: Chris Duke and Ettore Gelpi

PHILOSOPHY OF LIFELONG EDUCATION

Kenneth Wain

CROOM HELM
London • Sydney • Wolfeboro, New Hampshire

© 1987 Kenneth Wain
Croom Helm Ltd, Provident House, Burrell Row,
Beckenham, Kent, BR3 1AT

Croom Helm Australia, 44 Waterloo Road,
North Ryde,113, New South Wales

British Library Cataloguing in Publication Data

Wain, Kenneth
    Philosophy of lifelong education. —
    (Croom Helm series in international
    adult education)
    1. Continuing education — Philosophy
    I. Title
    374.'.01 LC5215

    ISBN 0-7099-3675-3

Croom Helm, 27 South Main Street,
Wolfeboro, New Hampshire 03894-2069

Library of Congress Cataloging-in-Publication Data

Wain, Kenneth.
    Philosophy of lifelong education.

    (The Croom Helm series in international adult
education)
    Revision of thesis (Ph.D.) — University of London,
1984.
    Bibliography: p.
    Includes indexes.
    1. Continuing education — Philosophy. 2. Humanism.
I. Title. II. Series.
LC5215.W28 1987   374'.001   86-24321
ISBN 0-7099-3675-3

Printed and bound in Great Britain by
Biddles Ltd, Guildford and King's Lynn

EDITOR'S NOTE

The Croom Helm Series in International Adult Education brings to an English-speaking readership a wide overview of developments in the education of adults throughout the world. Books have already been published, or are planned in this series of four different types:

(a) about adult and continuing education in a single country;
(b) having a comparative perspective of two or more countries;
(c) studies having an international perspective;
(d) symposia from different countries having a single theme.

This book by Kenneth Wain is a major theoretical analysis of the concept of lifelong education, a recent development in education which has been espoused by Unesco. However, the theoretical development of this phenomenon has been sparse and pragmatic, so that this philosophical analysis is an important addition to the literature on the subject.

Kenneth Wain is a senior lecturer in the Faculty of Education of the University of Malta.

Peter Jarvis
Series Editor

To Lina and the Children.

CONTENTS

INTRODUCTION

1. THE PHILOSOPHICAL PARADIGM

2. LIFELONG EDUCATION

3. HUMANISM

4. HUMANISM IN CURRENT EDUCATIONAL THEORY AND
   LIFELONG EDUCATION

INTRODUCTION

The idea that education is for life is a popular one
today. Not everyone knows, however, that the name
`lifelong education' can be attached to a body of
literature that has grown in consistency over the
past couple of decades into a theory, with which it
is also possible to identify a nucleus of theorists
who have made the most significant contributions to
it.

This book, which is a radical re-writing of the
author's PhD. thesis submitted to the University of
London in 1984, departs from two perceived needs
with regard to that theory. First, there is the
need to render it into a `programme' (in the tech-
nical sense of the word described in Chapter 1).
Second, what is currently called philosophy of education in the English-speaking world makes no space
for a phenomenon like a lifelong education programme. For many years the predominant paradigm
within the discipline was that of analytic philosophy. But even in the current post-analytic era
there is virtually no awareness of the fact that
lifelong education can be presented as a challenging
programme to the liberal or Marxist ones.

So the first chapter of the book defines a paradigm
for philosophy of education within which it makes
sense to assess the lifelong education programme as
a *competing* programme with others. The next task is
to describe the extant lifelong education theory
critically (clarifying, in the first place, the term
itself, which is subject to several ambiguities and
which is commonly understood as a more sophisticated
word for `adult education'). The rest of the book
is devoted to the attempt to find the right

philosophical expression for the theory, ie. one that would turn it into a coherent programme, in different philosophical positions; humanism, existentialism, liberal philosophy of education, and pragmatism.

Eventually, Dewey is considered the best choice, and it is suggested that the key concepts and principles of the theory could be rendered most coherent within the framework of his philosophy where they have a natural home. Meanwhile the consideration of the other positions becomes a critique of their principles and concepts from the perspective of the theory itself. From this point of view the critique of liberal philosophy of education in Chapter 5 derives particular importance from the fact that its programme rationalizes the dominant educational practices operational in much of the Western world.

In brief, the strategy of the book is to describe the philosophical paradigm mentioned above and the current state of the lifelong education theory in the first two chapters. Chapter 3 examines whether humanism, the declared ideology of the lifelong education theorists, can be rendered a coherent philosophy, while Chapter 4 looks at what is currently called humanistic educational theory and which has pronounced 'existentialist' overtones, and sees whether there is a comparable position in the lifelong education literature and if so, what its value for the programme could be. Chapter 5, as we said, examines the relationship between lifelong education as an idea and as a programme respectively, and liberal philosophy of education, while Chapter 6 does the same thing for lifelong education and Dewey's philosophy of education. Finally, the last chapter considers the concept of a 'learning society', which is projected as the formal embodiment of the lifelong education programme. At the end of the book there is a small section on 'justification'.

Chapter One

THE PHILOSOPHICAL PARADIGM

BACKGROUND

A number of articles have appeared in recent years
in different journals describing the history of
philosophy of education since it established itself
as a discipline in the 1950s when it was brought in
line with mainstream analytic philosophy.[1] That
beginning is frequently referred to as the 'revolution', since it took philosophy of education out of
the 'undifferentiated mush' that currently passed
for education theory into the light of day.[2] It
was launched with unbounded optimism at the time, in
the power of the new philosophy to improve practice
considerably by virtue of its very academic rigour,
but within less than two decades began to suffer an
opposite reaction as different grounds for
dissatisfaction with it both as a philosophical
programme and as an aid or guide to educational
practice began to be voiced. Both classes of complaints have also been extensively aired and do not
call for any elaboration here.[3] As a matter of
fact, the cracks in the analytic edifice had begun
to appear long before Edel described its programme
as being 'at the crossroads' in 1971.[4] Indeed the
criticism of analytic philosophy in general began to
manifest itself even before the new philosophy of
education made it its dogma, which raises questions
whether, looking back in hindsight, it was a wise
choice to make even at the time. But the 'second
revolution' in philosophy of education did not really get under way before the 1970s and then its aims
were very straightforward ones; in true counter-
revolutionary fashion, it sought to reverse the
programme of the 'first revolution' and to return
the philosopher to the 'cave' which his analytic

1

colleague had scorned with such impunity and abandoned with such confidence.

What exactly had the philosophical programme of the new analytic philosophy of the first 'revolution' been? A succinct answer to the question is available in an article Israel Scheffler, one of its earliest pioneers, wrote in 1954 called 'Toward an Analytic Philosophy of Education'.[5] In it Scheffler outlined the analytic programme in terms of : (1) a greater sophistication as regards language, and the interpenetration of language and inquiry; (2) an attempt to follow the modern example of the sciences in empirical spirit, in rigour, in attention to detail, in respect for alternatives, and in objectivity of method, and; (3) the use of the techniques of symbolic logic brought to full development in the previous fifty years. In sum, the intention was to bring to the study of education a 'union of scientific spirit and logical method applied towards the clarification of basic ideas'. [6] The horizons of analytic philosophy had been set by the early Wittgenstein; philosophy was 'to leave everything as it is'; it was to *explain* the world rather than to try to change it. It would therefore, 'have no truck with ideology'. Its interest would be in 'second-order' questions. It was also declared, not as an afterthought but as an article of faith, that everything else was not 'philosophy'.

With such a programme, as Mary Anne Raywid has emphasised, the decontextualizing of philosophy was more than a mere matter of emphasis; it was not simply the devaluing of context that it implied but *the very denial that the context is pertinent*.[7] She distinguishes two outstanding problems related to this strategy originally indicated, she says, by John Dewey. One, in Dewey's own words is that:

> When the context is suppressed .... elements become absolute, for they have no limiting conditions. Results of inquiry valid within specifiable limits of context are *ipso facto* converted into sweeping metaphysical doctrine. [8]

The other, in Raywid's own words this time, is that conceptual analysis 'serves up a kind of atomism ..... by denying empirical connection in the establishment of a concept'.[9]

The Philosophical Paradigm

The intention of the counter-revolutionaries was to reverse all these three trends; mainly to return the debate to the `human circumstances' from which the analytic philosophers had so violently `ripped' it in their anxious search for a `scientific' detachment from the world that would enable them to pronounce truths about it that are value-neutral.[10]

The `decontextualization of the spoken and written word' referred to by Raywid was the means by which they strove to achieve it. The counter-revolutionaries proposed to recontextualize the language of philosophy in the real world and to keep philosophy of education open to resolution into different paradigms according to the intentions and requirements of the philosopher. This latter pluralism was recently expressed by Robert Dearden who declared:

> I do not myself think that philosophy of education stands in need of a single paradigm. Its patterns and strategies of argument should be tailored to the subject matter under discussion, which is normally certain general concepts, principles, positions or practices. [11]

With the recontextualizing of philosophical debate, the context is what is pertinent. For a recontextualized philosophy it is within a particular spatio-temporal, or historical, situation that we define our concepts and choose the issues we want to discuss; it is by referring to and being related continuously to the context of their employment that concepts avoid `atomism' or taking on a quasi-metaphysical status.

Analytic philosophy of education was from the beginning the chosen paradigm of liberal thought, and immediately became its domain. It held out to the liberal philosopher that promise of `objectivity',of `value-neutrality',that has always been the dream and ideal of liberal scholarship. And it was the discreditment of the notion of `scientific objectivity' in philosophy of science, with the advance of the `theory-ladenness thesis', that opened analytic philosophy itself to criticism from different quarters. Since the `theory-ladenness thesis' denies the possibility of `detachment', of adopting an a-theoretic standpoint with regards to the phenomena being investigated. If it is true, then there is no way of avoiding ideology; science *is* 'ideology'. The whole base of analytic philosophy therefore crumbles with this thesis, and the objections that were aimed against it as a result were not merely epistemological but political also, as Marxist philosophers have cashed in quickly by accusing their liberal counterparts of using the analytic paradigm to hide their real value commitments.

Nor is this criticism lost on the new post-analytic wave of philosophers. Brenda Cohen, in fact, reflects the sentiments of many when she urges her fellow liberal philosophers of education to abandon 'the unattainable idea of neutrality in the direction of more conscious commitment to values and ideals', thereby depriving Marxists of a facile political advantage.[12]

From the background of a recontextualized view of education emerges an important consequence for the way in which we come to define the concept itself. Thus, within this paradigm, the appropriate question to ask is not the generic one, 'What is education?', but the contextualized one; 'What ought education to mean given conditions X ?', if what is required is a *normative* or philosophical statement, ' What does education actually mean in conditions X ?', if what is required is a *descriptive*, or sociological statement. This is a vital point I am making, as such it merits further elaboration and emphasis, for the form that any educational programme takes is determined largely *by the way we define education itself initially*. For the manner of the question will indicate the form of·response required and, further, what directions the inquiry that will answer it will take and how that answer will be justified. From this point of view philosophers·of education have been right in insisting all along that the question of what we *mean* by education has logical priority over other subsidiary questions, though they have not always been in accord with this suggestion about how it can be answered.

The· context with and within which philosophy of education will work, the 'cave', is the world of educational practice. This could mean that a recontextualized philosophy of education reverts to the Deweyian thesis that education must be for some particular kind of society, which is itself the context for educational activity. Since the openness to different paradigms it implies amounts to the concession that there are different ways into the `cave` and different ways of describing it.

Liberal philosophers of education in general, however, not simply the early analytic ones, have tended to assume that education occurs in schools and is the business of teachers, and have granted education no other context. And this is true also of orthodox Marxist philosophers of education, like Matthews and Harris for example,[13] who are mainly concerned with a critical analysis from their own ideological viewpoint of the practice of schooling in liberal-democracies, the objections they raise are often presented as negative evaluations against `education`. To the extent that Harris, for instance, whose book illustrates this point perfectly, writes of the need to oppose `education` with `anti-education` in these societies. In short Marxist philosophers tend to assume, in their criticism of liberal philosophy of education, the same equivalence of education with schooling as do liberal philosophers. What they tend to object to, besides the ideology that guides the liberal theory of schooling and that is supportive of the general political order which they evidently oppose, is the disguised function of analytic philosophy itself as `supportive rhetoric` for that ideology and order, and the status analytic philosophers claim for their conclusions, which they project as *the definition* of education. A standard example of the Marxist argument is presented by Anthony Skillen, where he makes the point in the following manner:

> Conceptual deference is not of course peculiar to politics, higher entities abound in all areas of thought: theology has `God`, psychology has `self` and sociology has `society` and philosophy of education treats the state school as the one locus of education. Like the state and unlike God and the immortal soul, the school is real enough. What is mythical is its presentation as, essentially and specifically, that-which-educates. It becomes difficult, then, for a student even to entertain the proposition that such institutions, far from solving the problem of freedom and reason in society, are themselves an important part of political and educational problems. If, as Peters says, it is only in a stretched sense that a visit to a brothel can be said to be `an educa-

tion' (*Ethics and Education*) it is certainly
only in a cramped sense that an education is
gained from the schools so dutifully rationalized in contemporary 'philosophy of education'.
[14]

The sensitivity of post-analytic liberal philosophers of education to this and other criticism of the
same kind has provoked some sharp reactions not
merely to the analytic programme in general, as was
stated earlier, but also to the employment of
conceptual analysis itself as a tool of definition.
Few however can be described as sharper, in this
respect, than John White's:

> Let me stipulate that education is simply up-
> bringing .... Objectors may want to pick a bone
> over the term 'upbringing', some arguing that
> it is broader in application than education,
> others, bearing such things as adult education
> in mind, that it is narrower. But I have lost
> whatever passion I may have had in the past for
> conceptual joustings of this kind. At an oppos-
> ite pole from those who cannot stay to examine
> their implicit beliefs about aims in their
> haste to worry away at their concepts, I am
> anxious — some might say *too* anxious — to leave
> concept analysis behind me and proceed to my
> main business as soon as possible.[15]

White is, of course, only interested in that aspect
of 'upbringing' that concerns schooling for, from
his point of view, it is only that that counts for
education. And since this standard assumption within
philosophy of education that education and schooling
refer to one and the same thing is a crucial one as
far as we are concerned, much more will need to be
said about it in a further chapter where we will
also need to return to this statement and others
about lifelong education that White makes in his
book.[16]

There are some comments however that need to be made
immediately about his attitude toward his definition
of education as 'upbringing' because this is relevant to the present chapter. Thus one feels sympa-
thetic with his feelings about 'concept analysis',
which are substantially those of all the post-
analytic philosophers, but his polar reaction is an
unjustified one; mainly for the reasons that he
himself anticipates in the passage, namely that

others with different conceptions of education to his own, such as the one that is the subject of this book, will want to contest his definition. Nor is his excuse for it acceptable, for it is not clear that a defence of his definition need involve him in 'conceptual joustings', unless his opponents are analytic philosophers, and even then, he need not consent to fight them on their own ground. In cavalier manner he says, by way of explaining his choice of definition, that it is enough for him that 'upbringing' is how parents, teachers and citizens look at education since it is the upbringing of their young that interests them most. And there can, of course, be no objection to this; there is no doubt that he has the right to set his own programme. If it is the upbringing of children that he is mainly interested in, then this is what he should write about, and it is only right that, if he does, he should address himself to the interested parties. But he has also written a *philosophical* book, and as such he is also inevitably addressing himself to philosophers besides the people he mentions. This being the case he cannot, therefore, ignore whatever predictable criticism he may anticipate from this quarter and decline to defend his view against it.

One can go further and say that his attitude towards definition is not only unacceptable to philosophers, it cannot be of much help to the people he mentions either. This is because they will also be addressed by other philosophers and theorists besides himself with alternative proposals, and for those of them who are reflective (if they are not, they are not going to be interested in educational theory or in his book anyhow) his unsupported stipulation that education means 'upbringing' will not help them much to make up their minds. Besides, the way people think about something cannot be the determinate criterion for 'adopting it as a definition of what a thing really is, even less of what it ought to be. The perceptions of people with regards to education are, more often than not, as badly based and informed as they are frequently dogmatic. One, again, sympathizes with what may be White's underlying motive of bringing theory and practice together by making the former more accessible to a wide range of people. But such an exercise does not necessarily mean making theory *supportive* of practice; theorists may want to polemicize with those in practice or with parents and other citizens concerned with it. White would answer this last point by pointing to his statement that he himself *agrees* that education is about upbringing. If this is the case, however, his agreement must surely rest on grounds other than unreflective conformity with the current opinion of these people. It is these grounds that are interesting to his fellow philosophers who will want to assess them and his defence of them in competition with their own. Surely this is what the philosophical 'game' is about, *and* surely this is what all the interested parties parents, teachers and other citizens will want to hear; particularly those other citizens who are policy-makers of some description.

Taking into account the general philosophical paradigm with which we shall work in the coming pages, a paradigm which takes full account of the principles of recontextualization and is faithful to the epistemology to be described in the coming section, the general matrix within which the answer to the question of meaning should be framed takes something like the following form: education is a *response* of kind X to a set of conditions which will include real or ideal (according to whether the intentions of the definition are descriptive or normative) conceptions Y about what constitutes, in general, a betterment of the quality of human life within a context Z which is historical. Philosophical definitions of education, therefore, presuppose a justification of Y and a description of Z before they can be deemed satisfactory.

PRAGMATISM AND PHILOSOPHICAL HERMENEUTICS

Recontextualizing philosophical language in the world, epistemologically achieves its most complete form in the pragmatism of James and Dewey. Rorty describes the programme of pragmatism as follows:

> My first characterization of pragmatism is that it is simply anti-essentialism applied to notions like 'truth', 'knowledge', 'language', 'morality', and similar objects of philosophical theorizing ....Those who want truth (etc.) to have an essence .... want to be able to use their knowledge of such essence to criticize views they take to be false .... Rather, the pragmatists tell us, it is the vocabulary of practice rather than theory , of action rather than contemplation, in which one can say something useful about truth ....

(So) a second characterization of pragmatism
might go like this: there is no epistemological
difference between truth about what ought to be
and truth about what is, nor any metaphysical
difference between facts and values, nor any
methodogical difference between morality and
science .... For the pragmatists, the pattern
of all inquiry — scientific as well as moral —
is deliberation concerning the relative attractions of various concrete alternatives ....

Let me sum up by offering a third and final
characterization of pragmatism: it is the doctrine that there are no constraints on inquiry
save conversational ones — no wholesale constraints derived from the nature of the objects,
or of the mind, or of language, but only those
real constraints provided by the remarks of our
fellow-inquirers.[17]

This programme, in turn, finds its fullest expression in philosophical hermeneutics, which turns it
into a culture as well as a methodology.

Philosophical hermeneutics emphasises the *historicality* of philosophy; it views philosophy not as an
ongoing timeless debate ('footnotes to Plato'), but
as the setting up of projects responsive to the
demands of differing historical situations. It falls
within a tradition which, as Rorty points out,
besides John Dewey, has its other great representatives in Heidegger and in the later Wittgenstein
and which is carried on into contemporary philosophy
by successors like Quine, Sellars, Putnam, and, of
course, Rorty himself.[18] In its essence it is
opposed to what Rorty calls the 'foundationalist'
project in philosophy which casts philosophy into
the role of guardian of culture. The 'foundationalist' project supposes that because philosophy's
ultimate epistemic concerns are with the nature and
basis of truth claims, then it is in a privileged
position to adjudicate between the different knowledge claims that constitute culture, rather than
being part of that culture itself. Contrary to this,
a recontextualized hermeneutical philosophy departs
from the rejection of this central 'foundationalist'
supposition since it does not share the latter's
confidence that philosophy can be so distanced from
the rest of culture in order to take up this meta-
critical role.

The Philosophical Paradigm

Rorty points out that the 'foundationalist' project was inherent already in Descartes and Locke, and that it reached its completion with Kant. But the notion that underlies it, of truths that are certain because of their causes rather than because of the argument brought for them is of more ancient stock. Rorty describes it as the fruit of what he calls the 'Platonic principle'. Within this principle, knowledge is modelled on perception, since it treats 'knowledge of' as grounding 'knowledge that'. Modern philosophers, Rorty argues, have not only inherited the Platonic metaphors, they have, moreover, failed to recognise their nature as *optional* and have instead made them *definatory* of 'philosophical thinking'. In doing so they have failed to understand the essential historicality of these metaphors. The exceptions, such as Dewey, Heidegger and Wittgenstein have differed precisely in the possession of this awareness and in their determination to express themselves within a historical perspective. The three, having identified the provenience of foundationalism, were able to return tranquilly to where the Sophists were before Plato brought his 'principle' to bear on philosophy, Rorty says, by looking for 'an airtight case rather than an unshakable foundation'.[19]

Hermeneutics, Rorty points out, in restoring philosophy to culture, takes the form of an epistemological holism involving all the diverse sources of knowledge and forms of interpretation familiar to mankind even the most marginal, idiosyncratic and esoteric. It sees all these different sources and forms as constituting an ongoing *conversation* contextualized in social practice, which lies open to history and is also the outcome of historical interpretation. The critical premise of the hermeneutical outlook, which subsumes the pragmatic, is that we understand knowledge when we understand the social justification of belief, and thus have no need to view it as accuracy of representation; knowledge is something negotiated in social practice rather than an attempt to 'mirror nature'. If we view it in this way we are unlikely to envisage the need for a metapractice which will be the critique of all possible forms of social practice.

It is evident that the hermeneutic view of knowledge also challenges the foundationalist conception of justification. This no longer remains a matter of a special relation of correspondence between ideas or words and objects, but a matter of acceptable social practice.

A good deal is condensed into this account, but, in general, at the bottom of the hermeneutic culture Rorty sees the rejection of what he describes, using Caird's metaphor, as a 'mirror of nature' model of epistemology and scientific inquiry, one which rests upon our supposed ability to state the 'facts' as they are, unmediated by anything, by normative or mataphysical incursions.[20] Within the 'mirror of nature' model the presupposition is that it is possible to demarcate the 'scientific' from the 'non-scientific' in the strictest terms and to set up special canons for the purpose. These canons are supposed to constitute the a *priori* conditions of scientific inquiry and are themselves taken to be as timeless as the objects they pursue; the 'facts' that are the constituents of experience. The philosopher who adheres to this model sees himself, supposedly like the scientist, as being in systematic pursuit of the truth, the definition of which requires the rejection of 'irrelevant' data or material. The hermeneutic approach to philosophy, on the other hand, rejects the very model of science with which the 'foundationalist' works. It goes even further than that, it starts by rejecting the basic notion that the physical sciences constitute some superior paradigm or form of theorizing which sets the standard for other fields of inquiry, continues by rejecting the idea that these can arrive at the same 'certainties' by adopting a positivistic approach to their subject matter and ends by rejecting the view of the individual researcher as one engaged in a monological relationship with a 'fact' or its equivalent within his chosen field of discourse.[21] In its place it recognizes the Kuhnian notion of science which has

> redirected the focus from the internal development of the cumulative growth of knowledge towards the socio-historical embeddedness of science and the occurance of gestalt-switches which underlie major redirections in the conceptualization and investigation of the object of science. New conceptual frames form different language games which allow not only the discovery of new facts but also the reinterpretation of previously established ones. New theories do not 'speak the same language' as previous ones and contain different standards

of rationality. The normative function of paradigms precludes the possibility of judging
their superiority from the outside since that
would only constitute the unwarrented application of external standards originating in a
different language game.[22]

The contrast between the pragmatic-hermeneutic conception of philosophy and the programme outlined for
analytic philosophy of education by Scheffler is
evident enough not to require much elaboration; the
latter has all the qualities of the 'foundationalist' project, with its preoccupation with second-
order questions its emphasis on rigour and objectivity, its methodology of 'detachment', its conservative conception of educational theory as essentially
a debate about timeless aims, values and qualities.

RELATIVISM

Liberal philosophers of education who have moved
away from analytic philosophy have, in general,
found it difficult to accept the 'relativistic'
consequences of hermeneutic philosophy. For relativism must be the logical outcome of a viewpoint
that rejects the possibility of an objective commen-
suration between different programmes, between
different knowledge-claims, which rejects the traditional facts-value distinction, and so on, and relativism is an uncongenial frame of reference for
philosophers raised in the empirical/analytic tradition. Rorty foresees the charge of relativism and,
indeed, points out that it has frequently been levelled against Heidegger, Wittgenstein and Dewey.
Holistic theories appear to philosophers of the
empirical/analytic tradition to threaten the whole
basis of rational discourse, they

> seem to license everyone to construct his own
> little hole - his own little paradigm, his own
> little practice, his own little language-game
> and then crawl into it.[23]

Thus philosophers have never been comfortable with
relativism, because it appears to many of them to
encourage skepticism and anarchy. Another popular
argument is that it must be wrong because it is
counter-intuitive. Both forms of objection are brought against it, for instance, by Roger Trigg [24].
Both are standard complaints, although there are

others.[24]

Trigg can be answered, as far as these objections
are concerned at least, with the observation that he
tends to concentrate his arguments on reasons why
relativism must be impossible or unacceptable rather
than prove that it *is* so by providing a coherent
account of a foundationalist theory of the world. In
fact, none of these reasons sticks. A perfectly
straightforward and facile reply to the charge that
relativism is counter-intuitive, can be made by
referring to the relativist argument that what appears to be counter-intuitive can be explained historically, and ought so to be explained. While the
charge that, in the moral sphere, it leads to permissiveness or anarchy can be answered with the argument which Rorty makes, drawing on Sartre, that the
acceptance of relativism implies an acceptance of
moral responsibility, while the search for 'objective' moral and other values implies a preparedness to
surrender that responsibility and hence a reluctance
to exercise one's choice.[25] There are certain
arguments against relativism that are harder to
shake off.

For instance there is the equally, perhaps the most
popular charge, levelled against it by most of its
opponents, including Trigg, that relativism involves
a paradox. Relativism's own claim that the truth is
relative, it is claimed, is not *itself* taken to be a
relative truth; thus the theory, *ipso facto*, contradicts itself, since it appears to be asserting what
it denies, namely that there can be any absolute
truths, by declaring that there is at least one
truth that is absolute, which is that there can be
no absolute truths. We will return to this 'paradox
shortly. Before doing so we need to take up a
distinction Trigg makes in the earlier part of his
book between 'relativism' and 'subjectivism' to
make clearer a point about hermeneutic philosophy.

Trigg points out that, although they are alike in
what they deny, namely the conception of something
being the case apart from either a community or an
individual thinking that it is, the two approaches
nevertheless differ in that whereas the subjectivist
believes that the truth is in the mind of the think-
er, the relativist believes that it arises from *collective agreement*, as it is embodied in some culture. The hermeneutic understanding, ascribes a
different epistemic role to the subjective, in the

way implied by the combined realities of the `double hermeneutic`, and of the `hermeneutic circle`, while holding that our knowledge criteria have a social origin. [26]

With this important point made, we can return to our `paradox`. One reply to it is made by F.C. White who points out that:

> If its argument convinces anyone, it will convince only the already committed non-relativist. For only the latter is likely to accept that a claim intended to be universal in its application cannot be relative in its truth.[27]

Also, as Jonathan Lear points out, there need be no reason why relativism should be held in such `vulgar form` as that described.[28] He describes, for instance, a `more sophisticated, and coherent form of relativism`, such as is to be found in Bernard Williams' book on *Moral Luck*. There is no need to enter here into any prolonged discussion of the different forms relativism can take. The points being made are: that relativism can be interpreted variously, and that even in the form assumed by those who detect a `paradox of relativism`, the supposed `paradox` is not an effective argument against it. The first observation takes us back to Trigg, who while agreeing that this appears to be the case argues at the same time that any interpretation of relativism must, in fact, eventually collapse into the one form which he calls `conceptual` relativism. Thus, although he accepts the existence of what he refers to as `ordinary` relativism, he argues that, in effect,

> conceptual relativism, is not just one form of relativism, but is itself the logical outcome of any form of it.[29]

The conceptual relativist holds, according to Trigg, that since different cultures have different concepts their members must therefore *see* the world differently; there is therefore no *right* way of seeing the world, and no one society's understanding of things is the *correct* one. It thus, according to the relativist, becomes impossible to judge other cultures at all, since our own conceptions always get into the way. There can be no neutral way of describing the world against which every conceptual system can be measured. Thus, Trigg concludes, *the*

relativist passes from the fact that it is logically
impossible to step outside every conceptual system
to the doubtful inference that we are logically
imprisoned within our own system.

Now the argument that all forms of relativism collapse logically into 'conceptual' relativism is essential to Trigg, because what appears to distinguish
'ordinary' relativism from 'conceptual' relativism
('at first glance', he says), is precisely that part
of the latter's characterization that is italicized
above. It is that whereas 'conceptual' relativism
makes understanding, communication, or translation
outside a given 'form of life' *impossible in principle*, 'ordinary' relativism *does not envisage any
difficulty of this kind.* And it is vital to Trigg's
major arguments against *relativism in general*, that
it should hold this view of mutual incommunicability
which he ascribes to 'conceptual' relativism because
these depend heavily on the evident absurdities to
which this position leads.

Clearly, if Trigg were right, his argument would
make the whole hermeneutic project, as described in
the preceding pages, impossible, or at least unintelligible, on its own a *priori* relativistic grounds.
It is important however, to observe that his own
'conflation' argument depends on his reading of
Wittgenstein's notion of a 'form of life' (since he
attributes the paternalism of 'conceptual' relativism to Wittgenstein) which he attempts to reduce a*d
absurdum.*

Wittgenstein's view, with regards to how we hold
moral and other 'truths' is that 'What has to be
accepted, the given, is - one could say - forms of
life'.[30] Wittgenstein himself describes a 'form of
life' as a community of those sharing the same concepts criteria of evidence and accredited routes to
knowledge. As a 'community' those sharing a form of
life can also be described as sharing the same views
of salience, routes of interest, feeling of natural-
ness, etc., to which as members they are committed.
[31] On the other hand, basic conceptual disagreeme-
nts between people demonstrate a difference of commitment to different forms of life.

Trigg attacks the concept 'form of life' as vague
and imprecise, and proceeds to draw absurd interpretations to which it could, he says, lend itself.
Without going into detail, which would be impossible

here, it can be pointed out in reply to this criticism that *none* of his interpretations are necessary ones and that, more importantly, numerous philosophers have, since Wittgenstein, used the concept profitably without encountering any difficulty at all. Even within philosophy of education O'Hear [32] and Hamlyn [33] for instance have found it useful. In sum, if there are possible absurdities to which the term could lead, absurdities similar or different from those Trigg points out, it need not be conceptualized in terms that render it liable to these absurdities. Besides, the most ludicrous of these absurdities are those taken to follow from the supposed mutual incomprehension and incommunicability that holds between different 'forms of life'. These are so evident, however, that it is patent that Wittgenstein could not have held his thesis in this form.

But, at any rate, whatever the form in which Wittgenstein held it, no particular concept of a 'form of life' need be forced on the relativistic position in general. Margolis, for instance, rejects a relativistic position held by Harman which states that:

> every principle by which 'moral' judgements are to be confirmed or disconfirmed subtends its own set of appropriate judgements, and plural principles share no overlapping sectors of such judgements.[34]

and which bears close similarities to the 'conceptual relativism' which Trigg attacks, in favour of 'more interesting forms of relativism' which

> one way or other, acknowledge a shared practice of judgement within which disputes and contested claims arise, but, *in which* claims incompatible within certain normal contexts may actually be satisfactorily defended — jointly, without contradiction.[35]

Margolis describes his own position as a 'robust relativism' and the account of it he gives evidently concurs with the relativistic component of the hermeneutic dimension.

The point I want to enforce is that the existence of different relativistic accounts like Williams' account of a 'sophisticated' form of relativism, Margolis' conception of a 'robust' relativism and so on, indicate that *relativism can be held in different forms*, and this contradicts Trigg's assertion that all forms of relativism collapse into `conceptual relativism', as *he* describes it. In fact he never really makes a case for it since his argument besides the attempted *reductio* just described, is an evident example of *petitio principii*, or question begging, as the italicised part shows. The offence is clear enough to speak for itself:

> If one group of people call `red' a totally different set of objects from those we call `red', we expect that they are just using the word differently, and we might think we could look at the way they used it to see what they mean. This itself presupposes an objectivist view of the world, by imagining that we can in principle pick out the same differences between objects as others do. It even presupposes that objects are the same for them as for us. *A relativist can make neither assumption but has to accept that if a group of people use a word in what seems an odd way, we cannot hope to know what they are talking about.* We must just recognise that they think in a way which we are logically barred from understanding. This is clearly to espouse conceptual relativism.[36]

But why can a relativist make neither assumption? It is only Trigg's `conceptual relativist' who is open to this form of objection because this is how Trigg has chosen to define his position. It is not necessary that the `ordinary' relativist for instance, should hold the absurd thesis that we are *imprisoned* by our `prejudices' in this way. The only defining premises of all forms of relativism is that which commits them to the view that all our judgements about the world are made from a cultural viewpoint since there are no viewpoints and, especially, no courts of appeal external to all cultures. And this is not incompatible with the view that several of our beliefs, values, and dispositions happen to be held cross-culturally. This fact, in effect, explains the *possibility* of communication and translation between cultures and traditions.

The hermeneutic understanding does of course recognise the existence of obstacles to mutual understanding. Betti describes them as follows: (a) the conscious or unconscious resentment towards ideas and positions which differ from the more common ones, and especially from those held by the observer, which leads (b) to their denigration and distortion; (c) the attitude of self-righteousness which sees issues in terms of black and white and is unaware of the dialectics between good and bad; (d) the conformatism towards dominant conceptions and the pharisaic acceptance of 'conventional bias' in judging others; the lack of interest in other cultures, as well as intellectual and moral narrowness or laziness - which shows itself in the growing tendency to shirk from sincere theoretical discussions and an open exchange of opinion in general.[37] But it does so and emphasises their existence precisely because, contrary to Trigg's 'conceptual relativist', it actively presupposes and is, as a theory, itself intimately dependent on, the possibility of understanding and communication, on 'openness' to the other. There is nothing in the account of the world that it gives that makes this presupposition incompatible with its relativistic premises, neither does Trigg's argument minimally threaten that compatibility. On the other hand no foundationalist project has hitherto proved these premises wrong.

TOUCHSTONE THEORY

The denial that relativism need necessarily involve the kind of philosophical solopsism of which its critics frequently accuse it, involves a neccesary undertaking   to describe how one can evaluate different programmes competitively while continuing to assert that as *distinct forms of life* they are essentially incommensurable. Also, we need to explain on what basis supporters of the different programmes could communicate. With reference to the second undertaking one vital principle needs repetition; i.e., that 'incommensurable' does not mean 'untranslatable'. This point is one that has been made as forcefully as possible in the preceding discussion of relativism where it was seen that the anti-relativist would translate the one into the other. What incommensurability means is only that philosophy of education cannot be brought under a supervening set of rules 'which tell us how rational agreement can be reached on what would settle the issue on every point where statements seem to conflict'.[38] At the same time hermeneutic philosophy encourages us to view the different programmes as

strands in a possible conversation, a conversation which presupposes no disciplinary matrix
which unites the speakers, but where the hope
of agreement is never lost so long as the conversation lasts.[39]

The question is, what would be the terms of reference of such a conversation? One suggestion is 'touchstone theory'. The possibilities of touchstone have
recently been well explored by J.C. Walker and C.W.
Evers [40] who express their support for the hermeneutic philosophical position through their criticism
of what they describe as the widespread, virtually
uncritical, adherence to a foundational epistemology
currently dominant in the study of 'Education', and
through their support instead for the kind of holistic epistemology supported by hermeneutics. In accordance with this epistemology they necessarily go
for a *coherence* account of evidence as against that
of correspondence with a 'fact', with the implication that justification is mainly an internal matter
to begin with. This means that the programme itself,
while engaging the philosopher in different kinds of
internal concerns, with criteria of theoretic coherence, simplicity, comprehensiveness, elegance and
explanatory power, also supplies him with the basis
of truth and evidence.

Touchstone theory is 'theoretical machinery common
to rival theories', a way of bringing rival programmes together under a common theoretical perspective
from within a substantially similar theoretical
background.[41] The authors describe some examples
as elementary logic, most mathematics, and a theory
of semantics. These tools of touchstone 'enable(s)
us to assess knowledge claims (i.e. competing theories) and therefore (since they are equivalent)
justification for action'.[42] The underlying assumption is that since the competing theories address
themselves to the solution of common problems and
are therefore contextualized within the same broad
area of practices, they are therefore liable to
comparative examination of a formal, and possibly
empirical, kind, and are therefore open to the relevant inter-disciplinary approaches since, for this
reason, they are bound to contain 'vital overlaps'.
[43]

But over and above the formal approaches of touchstone theory, hermeneutic philosophy itself explains
the possibility of translation and inter-theoretic,

or programmatic, understanding by its own characterization of theory as 'edifying discourse'. There is no wish, within this understanding, as Rorty says, to close off the 'conversation', indeed the value of a plurality of voices is what it recognizes and gives value to. It is in this sense that Gadamer in contrast to Trigg, emphasises the necessity and usefulness of our 'prejudices', a concept that features prominently in his hermeneutic philosophy. In his understanding of the word our 'prejudices' are not, as Trigg characterizes them, some prison that would isolate us from the rest of the world, from the new or the different, but a particular starting point from which understanding advances:

> The historicity of our existence entails that prejudices, in the literal sense of the word, constitute the initial directedness of our whole ability to experience. Prejudices are the basis of our openness to the world.[44]

The task of a hermeneutical form of inquiry directed towards widening the understanding rather than the discovery of 'knowledge', is the proper preliminary understanding of the 'horizon' of prejudices which are brought to bear on the inquiry by the inquirer rather than the engagement in a futile attempt to avoid it. Coming to understand one's own prejudices implies, first and foremost, coming to understand one's historicity, coming to understand the context of knowledge as a cultural project to be understood with reference to a particular point in time and space and to consider that knowledge itself as the fruit of the collective activity of a community. This, in itself permits that 'openness to the world' on which the hermeneutical discourse depends, since the very recognition of our own historicity enforces upon us that ideal attitude of tolerance of the other that is presupposed by any ongoing form of discourse, and therefore opens the way for the 'fusing' of other horizons with one's own.

THE MAKING OF AN EDUCATION PROGRAMME

It is now time to turn to the question of how an education programme is itself to be described, and a better model for such a programme could scarcely be found than in Lakatos' evolutionary model of science.[45] Very roughly, Lakatos' model of scientific inquiry is characterised by its 'methodological falsificationism'. The scientist decides to make unfalsifiable or unproblematic, on the basis of appropriate criteria, a basic 'core' of background knowledge made up of singular statements with spatio-temporal reference, to which is given 'observational status' and which is hence not treated as 'theory'. At the same time it is recognised that the 'privileged' status of these statements is so *relative to the theoretical framework itself*; they therefore have no absolute or a-theoretic status or privilege, as is the case with the privileged statements of foundationalist projects. This 'hard core', according to Lakatos, is what guides research both negatively and positively by stipulating which areas must not be challenged and by suggesting guidelines for profitable development. The 'hard core' is itself, in turn, surrounded by what Lakatos calls a 'protective belt', which is what bears the brunt of testing, what sorts out anomalies within the programme, and what is constantly modified or adjusted in order to protect the 'hard core'.

Lakatos further points out that science, represented in this model as a hard core-protective belt complex, should not itself be thought of as 'a theory', for this would be to make a category error. Rather (in accordance with its evolutionary nature, provoked by its falsificatory methodology) it should be thought of as a series, or an ongoing research programme. In sum, Lakatos' viewpoint is that scientific explanation does not constitute the evaluation of a 'theory' but the appraisal of research programmes on the basis of whether they are 'progressive' or otherwise; i.e., on the basis of whether they are able to achieve what he refers to as 'progressive problem-shifts' or not. A series is 'theoretically progressive', he says, if each new theory has 'excess empirical content' over its predecessor.

Theories meeting this condition constitute 'theoretically progressive problem-shifts'. Theoretically progressive problem-shifts are also empirically progressive if they explain the previous success of their predecessors; if all the unrefuted content of the predecessor is included in them, and if some of their excess content is corraborated. Finally, a problem-shift is 'generally progressive' if it is *both* theoretically and empirically progressive, otherwise it is degenerant. In conclusion, in Lakatos' terms, a theory in a series is falsified only when a progressive problem-shift is achieved, that is when it is superceded by another theory with higher corroborated content; and it is this very procedure that also provides the grounds for commenting critically on the whole research programme under consideration.

Lakatos' research programme model refers only to the general paradigm of science, and is essentially a description of the state of affairs within the physical sciences, where his evolutionary characterization is relevant because these have acquired a 'maturity' which has long taken them beyond the 'conflicting schools' stage which currently characterizes the social and the moral sciences (which are therefore still, technically, in accordance with his characterization, at a 'pre-paradigmatic' stage). Philosophy of education did, in its early years as a discipline, enjoy a period of relative stability where, as was mentioned earlier, it was dominated by a single paradigm, but that stability was a sign of immaturity rather than otherwise, and it is evident that the unity of the discipline could not have been maintained for long once the theoretical and methodological base of the programme came under serious attack and philosophers began to appear with ideological viewpoints different than that of the liberal. But the model *can* be used to describe the state of affairs *within* a particular distinct education programme in conflict with others.

Evidently the 'hard core' of an education programme viewed as one undergoing ongoing research cannot be, as in the physical sciences, some set of singular statements with spatio-temporal reference. Indeed, the statements that can be taken as unfalsifiable, since, in fact, they are of their own nature not open to falsification, not being true-false or propositional statements, are those that express the *ideological* beliefs that guide the programme. These will be beliefs about the *meaning* of education expressed in translation of the variables Y of the general matrix described in the final paragraph of the first section of this chapter, *and about an ideal way of life*. The 'protective belt' will be the set of *operational* conditions that define how the ideological core will express itself in practice or respond to its historical context.[46] These conditions will therefore be entirely empirical and, consistent with the falsificationist methodology, will be continuously tested accordingly - as problem-solving devices that permit a more successful attainment of the conditions identified in the core against the pressures and requirements of the environment or historical context; they will, therefore, correspond to variable Z of the same matrix.

According to this model, then, the operational definition of any particular programme comes between the ideological objectives of that programme and the set of historical conditions within which it must work and which constitutes a continuous test for it. The operational definition is therefore what will bear the brunt of the challenges to the programme. Furthermore, from the interaction of the operational definition with the ideological presuppositions of the core will emerge the general guidelines for practice which the theoreticians will ideally negotiate with the practitioners themselves. The most urgent negotiation will evidently need to occur at points where the operational definition comes into confrontation with the context, wherever it may be; the classroom, community, ministry,etc. The philosopher's own specific contribution to the process will be that of synthesizing the knowledge that comes to the operational belt from the other theoretic approaches to the programme into the belt itself. This synthesizing activity has been well described by Spencer Ward, it requires the philosopher to:

(1) aim for a style and organisation of writing which is conducive to being read by other researchers and practitioners;

(2) utilize a broad range of literature relevant to the topic addressed; and

(3) actively involve practitioners and researchers from relevant disciplines in review and revision of frameworks and in explication of implications for practice and policy making.[47]

Openness to the historical context is what enables the programme to pursue 'progressive problem-shifts' that are empirically valuable, while the continuous interaction of the extant operational definition, which defines the empirical state of the programme, with the permanent ideological core, is what makes the programme 'theoretically progressive'. In fine, a programme will be generally progressive if, on the one hand, the successive operational definitions explain the historical context or environment better

than the ones they replace, and, on the other hand,
as greater theoretic success is obtained in relating
the operational definition with the ideological
core.

IDEOLOGY

Brenda Cohen's recommendation to her fellow liberal
philosophers that they should concern themselves
with ideology and express their commitments in the
same way as the Marxist philosophers, referred to
earlier, represents a revolt against a demarcation
line which had hitherto been held as sacrosanct
within liberal analytic philosophy of education;
that between 'philosophy' and 'ideology'. Analytic
philosophers have always held that the former should
never be confused with the latter, that it could and
should be held pure from the latter by establishing
that rigorous 'objectivity' and detachment from the
world which they supposed to be typical of the physical sciences by sticking to explanation, to the
'facts', and steering away from the 'values'. In
other words, the analytic philosophers have tried to
draw the same distinctions between 'philosophy' and
'ideology' as were once traditionally drawn between
'science' and 'ideology' by making philosophy itself
'scientific'.

This belief that the physical sciences enjoy a dis-
tinctiveness, a privileged epistemic status of the
sort presupposed by this sort of distinction is part
of the doctrine of 'scientism'.[48] 'Scientism' is
the basis of the foundationalist project in philosophy. Set against it is the contrary hermeneutic
belief that there is no possibility of achieving the
standpoints it demands. This is because of the existence of the 'hermeneutic circle' referred to earlier, which is inevitable and which imposes its
conditions on all our theoretic practices, which,
therefore, only become truly enlightened with its
due recognition. The 'hermeneutic circle' is another
way of stating the thesis that all our judgements
about the world are 'theory-laden', not free and
neutral. From this viewpoint the very distinction
between science and ideology becomes fictitious.

For the philosopher working within a hermeneutic
culture, or for one who at least accepts the
'theory-ladenness' thesis, nearly universally ac-

cepted in the philosophy of science, there is no
controversy over the claim, expressed in the the
previous section, that an education research programme must have an *ideological* core if it is to
function coherently; i.e., if it is to lead to consistent policy and practice. But, it must be admitted, the word 'ideology' still has an ambiguous
meaning in most other settings, so the need to make
it more precise in the present context presents
itself. And the   appropriate first step in this
direction, perhaps, is to indicate the sense of
ideology which is not meant. This is the Marxian
sense in which the connotations of the term are
derived from a class analysis of society and which
therefore describes ideology as the apparatus resor-
ted to by the dominant class for *distorting* reality
by using techniques of duplicity and 'mystification'
in order to keep the subjugated classes in thrall.

But using a non-Marxian understanding of ideology
still creates problems for philosophers of education. This is because, for historical reasons
already described, the concept has had its home, as
far as educational theory is concerned, outside
philosophy and, usually, within Marxian-inspired
social science approaches. Notwithstanding Cohen's
exhortation, Harris, to my knowledge, is the only
philosopher to have brought the term sharply to bear
in philosophy of education with the intention of
using it not in order to reject its relevance, and
Harris' perspective is also distinctly Marxian.[49]

This refusal on the part of liberal philosophers of
education to recognise the inevitability of ideology
and hence to take up the problems it presents
further explains the conservative nature of the work
they have produced hitherto and its tendency to
structure inquiry within a taken-for-granted educational context which they regard as unproblematic.
Marxist philosophers, on the other hand, have long
recognised the real derivation of the customary
conceptions and have always, therefore, insisted on
their ideological nature. This has caused them to
specify two senses of the term: the *descriptive*
which refers to the sense in which ideological ex-
planations *do* reflect the historical and cultural
conditions that they describe, and the *analytic* in
terms of the other Marxist meaning of ideology from
which I disassociated myself above, and which refers to a description of the 'negative' conditions
that prevail in liberal democracies, and which

therefore carries normative presuppositions. Harris
employs the term in both these senses, though eventually he becomes more interested in its analytic
employment as his work disappointingly evolves into
the customary diatribe against 'education' in liberal democracies. Then what comes to the forefront is
Marx's traditional pejorative understanding of ideology as anti-scientific rather than its descriptive
usage. In effect what happens in Harris' book is
that he begins with a descriptive understanding of
ideology consistent with the epistemology he describes in the first part of the book but then for-
sakes this understanding in his critique of liberal
education which lapses instead into evaluations
that are couched in the usual jargon.

In order to avoid misunderstanding it needs to be
explained that a descriptive definition is not one
that is theory-neutral; the theory-ladenness thesis
proscribes such a possibility. It is one based on a
theoretical understanding which does not *directly*
colour the context of its use. Thus a descriptive
definition of ideology is one based on a theory
which is sociological, it is a theory about the
meaning of a term within the language game of
sociology not of politics. Consequently it becomes
just a way of collecting together certain facts
about the world according to that meaning, not, as
with the analytical sense of the word, a tool for
evaluating that world normatively.

Eventually, Harris' indiscriminate use of the two
understandings of the term embroils his discussion
in contradiction in several different ways. Examining them presents itself as a tempting detour that
must be resisted. Instead recourse can simply be
made to his compact and useful account of ideology
made in the earlier part of his book. Here, after a
critique of epistemology and of scientific explanation and evaluation, he makes Feyerabend's claim
that ideology can be accomodated as theory on the
same lines of science. Ideology, Harris says at this
stage of his book, can be loosely defined as:

> a set of theoretic stances, involving
> attitudes, values and habitual responses (which
> are embodied in definite social practices) and
> which seek to maintain the *status quo* or to
> bring about a changed set of social relations
> and social formations.

The interesting part of the definition is the last part because it indicates that the term 'ideology' need not be reserved only for the *dominant* or 're-ceived' political perspective of a given group or society, it can also be taken to define the stances of an alternative, revolutionary, dissident set. In fact, according to this descriptive interpretation of ideology the name applies to *any* more or less coherent set of theoretic stances, even the utopic. It is therefore convenient, within this sense of the word, to make a still further distinction between 'lived-ideologies' and ideologies simple; the former referring to stances not explicitly stated but read into social practices, the latter to explicitly stated theoretic stances.

It is clear that when Harris is defining ideology in this way he is expressing a meaning of the term common in the social sciences in general. In the non-Marxian social sciences the word ideology simply stands for a general social phenomenon which, in its concrete form, as Daniel Bell puts it, manifests itself in 'the conversion of ideas into social lev-ers'.[49] And, in fact, Harris continues to attrib-ute qualities to it that are consistent with this description.

Within the descriptive understanding of ideology ideological thought is also necessarily 'political', since its point is to rationalise and legitimise action, and this could be seen, Harris argues, as one sense in which ideology *does* differ from scien-tific thought. Another is ideology's concern with the effectiveness with which it converts into ac-tion, an effectiveness that frequently requires 'simplification'. Ideology can also frequently draw support from different sources of legitimation, including myth, legend, and tradition, for example. There are still other less evident differences but, Harris quickly points out, these distinctions bet-ween the two are not conceptual but practical ones, and he refers, in support of this contention, to Kuhn, Popper, Tranoy and Feyerabend who also share the view that scientific theories themselves possess an ideological status — philosophers, scientists and academics in general have their own professional ideologies, and science itself is just one of the many ideologies that propel society and should therefore be treated as such. In short, considered descriptively as 'sets of theoretic stances' or 'total belief systems' which are equally socially

based, Harris, rightly, sees no difference in kind
between science and ideology. And this is what makes
it legitimate to take over the Lakatosian model of
science and adapt it to a different theoretic framework.

On the basis of Harris' descriptive account of ideology, which is also in accord with hermeneutic epistemology, one would have expected the rest of his
book to proceed as an argument in support of his own
programme, or 'critical preference' according to
specified criteria, or simply, and more consistently, to set up both his project and the liberal one
as rival programmes and leave the rest to the reader
after he had made the case for both. This is what
his preparatory discussion of epistemology in the
first part of his book prepares one for. Instead, in
the very next chapter following on his discussion of
the descriptive sense of ideology, titled 'ideology', he opens with the famous quotation from Marx's
A Contribution to the Critique of Political Economy,
in which *ideology is contrasted negatively with
science*. The quotation is preceded, very oddly in
the light of what went forward in the chapter preceding, by this explanation;

> The purpose of this chapter is to indicate in
> greater detail the way that ideology functions,
> and to outline certain conditions whereby ideo-
> logy necessarily projects and presents distor-
> tions and misrepresentations, and disguises the
> real nature of the existing state of affairs.
> [50]

While the chapter that follows is titled 'Attacking
Ideology', by which time the initial descriptive
account of ideology has long been forgotten and
Harris is launched on his attack on the 'ideological
distortions' of capitalism.

In fine, in describing the inner core of an education programme as ideological reference is being
made only to the descriptive sense of the term, and
there is to be no confusing this fact when it is
used, as it frequently shall be, in the pages to
come. This definition of ideology as a set of 'theoretic stances' etc., that are or could be 'embodied
in social practices' of whatever sort, precisely
reflects the meaning intended, for this is how the
relationship between the ideological core of an
education programme and its operational definition

is to be envisaged.

CONCLUSIONS

The coming chapter will consider lifelong education
as a programme; as a set of principles based on the
understanding of education as lifelong process but
otherwise expressing the preferences of a group of
theorists who have worked on the concept and come to
an agreement about them. Such an approach evidently
does violence to the idea that education is an
"incontestable concept" and that its meaning or
programme has nothing to do with agreement between
people but is something that can be read into the
concept itself.[53] On the other hand it is
compatible with a view of education theory as an
arena of competing programmes adherence to which
constitutes the basis of agreement or disagreement
between philosophers and educationalists who support
one or the other, but who are also ready to enter
into ongoing conversation with each other on the
merits and demerits of their respective programmes.
This means that they are also ready to keep their
'prejudices' permanently open to touchstone, and
this is what renders such conversation 'rational'.
On the other hand, touchstone theory, where a
practical activity like education is concerned, must
consist of criteria that are both formal and
empirical, or historical.

Again, this way of resolving disputes, or at any
rate putting them to the test, will be rejected
outright by subscribers to a 'transcendental' theory
of justification,[54] or by those who argue that
what is justified for inclusion in an education
programme is only knowledge that is intrinsically
valuable, for these will dismiss the relevance of
history or context altogether. Against these one can
do no more than hold up the 'theory ladenness'
theory of knowledge which opposes both the thesis
that theory can be neutral or 'value-free', and the
theory that there is knowledge which is intrinsically valuable, and holds up a pragmatic alternative to both in their stead. If the thesis fails
to convince them, then they will also reject the
theoretic approach we are adopting altogether. But a
convincing case against the 'theory-ladenness' thesis
has yet to be made, and it does not seem that any
such can exist.

Our approach then, being a valid one, the programme
it indicates is clear: we have to work out a

coherent lifelong education programme, which is
internally consistent according to the description
of internal consistency described in this chapter
(that there are the proper relationships between the
different components of the programme)' and according to the formal rules of touchstone,and empirically relevant because it responds adequately to
the pressures and demands of historical context. The
next chapter which, as we have said, describes the
current lifelong education programme, will establish
whether such coherence already in fact exists, by
looking specifically at the question of internal
consistency. Evidently, the answer is presupposed
already, since there would be no justification for
writing this book if it did, so we shall really be
searching for the causes of non-coherence rather
than establishing whether coherence is already
there.

NOTES AND REFERENCES

    1.   For example: Dearden, R.F. 'Philosophy of
Education, 1952-82', *British Journal of Educational
Studies*, Vol. xxx, No. 1, Feb. 1982; Wilson, J.
'Philosophy and Education: retrospect and prospect',
Oxford Review of Education,Vol. 6, No. 1, 1980;
Wilson, J. 'The Future of Philosophy in Education',
British Journal of Educational Studies, Vol. xxxi,
No. 1, February 1983; Gilroy, D.P. 'The Revolutions
in English Philosophy and Philosophy of Education',
Educational Analysis, Vol. 4, No. 1, 1982.
    2.   The expression is R.S. Peters' (*Ethics and
Education* (1966), London, Allen and Unwin)
    3.   Thus, for instance, from the philosophical
viewpoint, Carr argues that 'since its inception,
'conceptual analysis' has been criticised so severely that its claim to define the nature and scope of
philosophy are (with the notable exception of the
philosophy of education) no longer taken seriously'.
(Carr, W. 'Philosophy, Fantasies and Common Sense',
p. 94 review article in *Journal for Higher Education*, Vol. 4, No. 2, Summer 1980) While a good example of the complaints of practitioners with analytic
philosophy is Allen Graubard's contribution to the
symposium on J.F. Soltis' (ed.) book *Philosophy and
Education: Eightieth Yearbook of the National Soc-*

Graubard says: 'Philosophers of education are considered relevant to the people who are required to
take their courses, the future primary and secondary
school teachers. Once these people become teachers,
the number who look at the kinds of essays collected
in this volume is, I would estimate, smaller than
the average classroom size.... No attention is paid
in these essays to the actual problems of teaching
in elementary grades, where the issues are not esoteric discussions of the number of ways to slice up
knowledge. Nor do the contributors debate the basic
issues of socialization and indoctrination, the
relationship of school to the world of work, systems
of motivation and discipline, and other practical
questions that plague thoughtful school teachers.
Perhaps the reply of the profession is that these
considerations are not relevant to philosophy of
education; they are psychological or political or
cultural issues. So much the worse for philosophy of
education'. p. 425, *Harvard Educational Review*, Vol.
51, No. 3, August 1981.
    4.   Edel, A 'Analytic Philosophy of Education
at the Crossroads', in: Doyle, J.F. (ed.) (1973)
Educational Judgements (London, Routledge and Kegan
Paul)
    5.   Scheffler, I. (1954) 'Toward an Analytic
Philosophy of Education', in: Scheffler, I. (1973)
Reason and Teaching (London, Routledge and Kegan
Paul)
    6.   ibid., p. 10.
    7.   Raywid, M.A 'More Criticism of Analytic
Philosophy of Education', *Philosophy of Education*,
1980.
    8.   op. cit., p. 26. The quote is from
'Content and Thought', Bernstein; R.J. (ed.) (1960)
On Experience, Nature and Freedom p. 96 (N.Y.
Liberal Arts Press)
    9.   ibid., p. 26.
    10.   The expression is of Van Cleve Morris.
'Living Without Bridges', p. 20, *Philosophy of
Education*, 1980
    11.   Dearden, R.F. (1982) op. cit., p. 66.
    12.   Cohen, B. 'Return to the Cave: New
Directions for Philosophy of Education', p. 99, *Educational Analysis*, Vol. 4, No. 1. 1982. Cohen's full
statement is: "Indeed, considerable advantage is to
be gained from a conscious shift within a liberal-
empiricist approach to philosophy of education from
the unattainable ideal of neutrality in the direction of more conscious commitment to values and
ideals. That only Marxists should appear to have a

defined position on substantive moral matters -- and this while repudiating objective morality altogether -- is an unfortunate consequence of the excessive austerity and deliberate avoidance of moral commitment which has characterised the analytic tradition until recently'.

13.   Matthews, M.R. (1980) *The Marxist Theory of Schooling: a study in epistemology and education* (Sussex, Harvester Press), and Harris, K. (1979) *Education and Knowledge* (London, Routledge and Kegan Paul)

14.   Skillen, A. (1977) *Ruling Illusions*, p. 3 (Sussex, Harvester Press)

15.   White, J. (1982) *The Aims of Education Restated*, pp. 5-6 (London, Routledge and Kegan Paul) A more moderate statement along the same lines was made earlier by Warnock who expressed the view that 'a great deal of time has been spent, and I suspect, largely wasted, in an attempt to define education. Is it an activity? Is it a commodity which can be dispensed in smaller or greater quantities to clients or consumers? Is it necessarily goal-directed?' (Warnock, M. (1977) *Schools of Thought*, p. 12 (London, Faber and Faber))

16.   See Chapter 5.

17.   Rorty, R. (1982) *Consequences of Pragmatism*, pp. 162-165 (Sussex, Harvester Press)

18.   Rorty, R. (1980) *Philosophy and the Mirror of Nature* (Oxford, Blackwell)

19.   op. cit. (1980) p. 156.

20.   Caird, referring to Kant, said that the earlier philosophers 'were metaphysical while he isn't; they made assumptions and submitted their own ideas for the teaching of experience, while he has simply make his mind into a mirror of nature, and stated the facts as they are'. (Quoted in Rorty, ibid., p. 41)

21.   Bleicher defines 'scientism' as a set of attitudes which reflect the view that 'science deals with 'facts' given independently of the researcher; the empirical-analytical method is the only valid mode of knowledge acquisition; that this method should be extended to all spheres of cognitive activity; that its results are the only true form of knowledge'. in: Bleicher, J. (1982) *The Hermeneutic Imagination*, p. 14, (London, Routledge and Kegan Paul)

22.   Quoted in Bleicher (1982) op. cit. p. 36.

23.   Rorty (1980) op. cit., p. 317.

24.   Trigg, R (1973) *Reason and Commitment* (Cambridge University Press)

25.   Rorty (1980) op. cit., p. 361.

26.   The 'double hermeneutic' is described by Bleicher (op. cit., 1982) in Dilthey's terms as the recognition that 'the first condition for the possibility of a science (of history) consists in that fact that I myself am a historical being; that he who researches into history is the same as he who makes it'. (p.80), while the 'hermeneutic circle' can be described as 'the realization that the subject *shares* the world with his objects, and has a pre-understanding of them which guides his subsequent methodical inquiry'. (ibid., p. 36)

27.   White, F.C. 'Knowledge and Relativism I', p. 5 *Educational Philosophy and Theory*, Vol. 14, 1981

28.   Lear, J. 'Ethics, Mathematics and Relativism', p. 55, *Mind*, Vol. XCII, 1983.

29.   op. cit., p. 25.

30.   Wittgenstein, L. *Philosophical Investigations*, p. 226 (1972 edition, translated Anscombe, G.E.M., Oxford, Blackwell)

31.   The description occurs in Lear's article (1983) op. cit., p. 45.

32.   O'Hear, A. (1981) *Education, Society and Human Nature* (London, Routledge and Kegan Paul) while disagreeing with relativism finds the concept a perfectly coherent and useful one.

33.   Hamlyn, D.W. (1978) *Experience and the growth of understanding*, (London, Routledge and Kegan Paul)

34.   Margolis, J. 'The Reasonableness of Relativism', pp. 92-93, *Philosophy and Phenomenological Research*, Vol. XLIII, No. 1, September, 1982.

35.   ibid., p. 93.

36.   op. cit., p. 86.

37.   Betti, E., in Bleicher, J. (1982) op. cit., p. 65.

38.   Rorty, R. (1980) op. cit., p. 316.

39.   ibid., p. 318.

40.   Walker, J.C., and Evers, C.W. 'Epistemology and Justifying the Curriculum of Educational Studies' *British Journal of Educational Studies*, Vol. xxx, No. 2, June 1982.

41.   op. cit., p. 220.

42.   ibid., p. 221. It is important to note, as the authors point out, that 'Touchstone is not made up of epistemically favoured statements. It is merely the (shifting) amount of theory that is shared by rival theories and/or theorists'. (p. 220)

43.   ibid., p. 222.

44.   Gadamer, H.G. *Philosophical Hermeneutics*,

p. xv (1976, translated Linge, D.E., University of California Press)

45.   Lakatos, I., and Musgrave, A. (eds.) (1970) *Criticism and the Growth of Knowledge* (Cambridge University Press)

46.   Cropley describes an `operational definition' as one obtained by `trying out ideas in practice, rejecting them, refining them and trying again, or even accepting them as the case may be'. (Cropley, A.J. (ed.) (1979) *Lifelong Education : a stocktaking*, p. 13 (Hamburg, UIE Monographs 8)

47.   Ward, S.E. `The Philosopher as Synthesizer', p. 72 *Educational Theory*, Winter, Vol. 31, No. 1, 1981.

48.   Bleicher, J. (1982) op. cit., p. 3, also defines `scientism' as a view of science as `a supra-historic, neutral enterprise and as the sole mode of acquiring true knowledge'.

49.   Harris, K. (1979) *Education and Knowledge* op. cit.

50.   ibid., p. 47.

51.   Quoted in Cotgrove, S. (1968) *The Science of Society*, p. 201 (London, Allen and Unwin)

52.   ibid., p. 63.

53.   See Wilson, J. `Concepts, Contestability and the Philosophy of Education'. *Journal of Philosophy of Education*, Vol. 15, No. 1, 1981.

54.   Peters, R.S. (1966) *Ethics and Education*, op. cit., p. 164.

Chapter Two

LIFELONG EDUCATION

THE MOVEMENT

Since about the middle 1960s there has come into
being a new movement in the world of education.
That new movement has expressed its presence through
a body of reports, through conferences, through
publicity, and through experiments carried out in
its name; lifelong education.[1] There is no claim
that the guiding principle of the movement, the idea
that education be viewed as a lifelong matter, is
new, indeed it is acknowledged to be very old indeed.   What is claimed to be new is the movement
itself.   Accounts about how it came into being are
to be found in the introductory pages of almost
every book or article written about lifelong education in recent years.   The relevant fact for our
purposes is that the movement, as distinct from the
idea, was born within UNESCO; it was born from the
decision taken by this organization in the early
1960s to make lifelong education the `master con-
cept' for all its educational planning.[2]   Since
then a considerable bulk of literature has appeared,
linked mainly with UNESCO initiatives, aiming to
clarify the concept and study its implications for
educational practice.   The movement has thus come to
acquire a programme — or has it?

During this time perhaps the most influential and
widely read report was the Faure report, *Learning to
be*, produced in 1972.[3]   The report ended with a
list of principles of lifelong education with
subsidiary recommendations about how they should be
read.   Not too long afterwards, in 1975, R.H. Dave
published a list of `concept characteristics' of
lifelong education that were meant to synthesize the

extant literature into a programme and define its
meaning accordingly.[4]   At the same time Paul
Lengrand, who was strongly involved in the initial
acceptance of the lifelong education principle by
UNESCO, published a book called *An Introduction to
Lifelong Education*,[5] and this was followed very
soon afterwards by another book by Dave called
Foundations of Lifelong Education which had the
declared scope of providing an initial exercise in
constructing the theoretical foundations of lifelong
education for a clearer understanding and effective
implementation of the concept,[6] by establishing
'binding threads' through an interdisciplinary
synthesis.[7]   The feeling was, in fact, expressed
by both Lengrand and Dave that the concept had
hitherto been inadequately defined, even if the
practice of lifelong education had advanced apace.
Then in 1979 Cropley produced a book called *Lifelong
Education: a stocktaking*[8] which was meant to
report progress in this direction and which, like
Foundations of Lifelong Eduction, was a cooperative
effort by a more or less settled body of theorists
whose names and those of others were coming to be
connected with the movement.

Among the latter, although he contributes to none of
the works named above, one should mention the name
of Ettore Gelpi, which, in many countries, partly
because of his position as chief of the lifelong
education division of UNESCO in Paris, and partly
due to his publications, has become synonymous with
lifelong education.[9]   Gelpi, in fact, is the
individual who stands out most prominently among the
theorists on lifelong education and recently his
name has been linked with that of Illich and Freire
as 'among the most important contributors to
educational debate especially as it has influenced
discussion of adult and lifelong education'.[10]
The writers and the views expressed in these books
can accurately be considered to represent the
theoretical orientations of the movement and can
therefore be turned to, in addition to some
supplementary sources for the articulation of its
programme such as it is.

It will be recalled that in the previous chapter the
general theoretical structure of any education programme was described as having two broad constituents; an ideological inner core and an operational
belt.   It was also claimed that the strength or
weakness of such a programme depends essentially on

four factors: (1) the clarity and coherence of its
ideological core; (2) the clarity and coherence of
its strategy; (3) the compatibility of its strategy
with its ideological core; (4) the relevance of its
strategy to current world conditions on the cultural
and socio-economic front. The first paragraph of
this chapter closed with a question which began as a
statement, 'The movement has thus come to acquire a
programme -or has it?' The question reflects doubts
about whether one could properly speaking refer to a
lifelong education programme, doubts that take the
form of two subsidiary questions: is there properly
speaking a lifelong education *programme* in the sense
defined? And, is there properly speaking a, one,
single programme of lifelong education or several?
These are the preliminary questions to be considered
before any critical assessment of concept or movement is engaged in. The first to be tackled is the
second question.

SEMANTICS AND PROGRAMMES

The nearest attempt approaching the formal statement
of the lifelong education programme is Dave's 'concept characteristics':

(1) The meaning of the concept of lifelong educa-
     tion is based on the elemental terms - 'life',
     'lifelong' and 'education'. The meaning att-
     ached to these terms and the interpretation
     given to them largely determine the scope and
     meaning of lifelong education.

(2) Education is not to be seen as restricted to a
     particular period of life. It is a lifelong
     process which covers the entire life-span of
     the individual embracing and unifying all
     stages of education - pre-primary, primary,
     secondary, tertiary and adult education. It
     views education not as a fragmented spectrum of
     individual parts but in its totality - as in-
     tegrated whole.

(3) Lifelong education encompasses those sectors of
     education commonly described as formal, non-
     formal and informal. This flexibility allows
     for varied patterns and forms of acquiring
     education.

(4) Education is not confined to formal institu-

tions of education. Whilst they remain important as one of the agencies of lifelong education they no longer enjoy a monopoly on education. Indeed the family is seen as exerting a crucial influence on the initial and continued development and learning of its members in a truly lifelong dimension.

(5) Lifelong education is rooted in the community which performs an important educative role. Life itself is seen as the major source of learning.

(6) Lifelong education seeks integration at its horizontal and depth dimensions at every stage of life.

(7) Lifelong education also seeks continuity and articulation along its vertical dimension.

(8) Lifelong education represents the democratization of education. It is based, not on an elitist principle but on the universalist principle of education for all at all ages.

(9) Lifelong education is a dynamic approach to education which allows adaptation of materials and media as and when new developments take place. Learning tools and techniques, content and time of learning are flexible and diverse.

(10) In lifelong education the learning process is the key to all education.

(11) There are two broad components contained within lifelong education - general and vocational - which are interrelated and interactive in nature.

(12) Lifelong education provides individuals and society with opportunities not only to adapt to change but also to participate in change and to innovate.

(13) Lifelong education provides an antidote to the shortcomings of the existing formal education system.

(14) The ultimate goal of lifelong education is to maintain and improve the quality of life.

(15) There are three major prerequisites for lifelong education — opportunity, motivation and
educability.

(16) At the operational level lifelong education is
an organising principle providing a total system for all education.[11]

How is one to assess them as a programme? Cropley,
without specifying he was referring to this but
using the same word 'characteristics' as Dave and
probably having it in mind, says that the lifelong
education programme contains:

> Characteristics which are essential and crucial
> to lifelong education (without which it would
> not be lifelong education at all), those which
> might well be necessary characteristics, but
> are not inevitably linked with lifelong
> education and would not mean that what remained
> was not lifelong education if they were absent,
> and those which are best seen as happy outcomes
> of the implementation of the ideas of lifelong
> education. These latter characteristics largely
> encompass values which are regarded as
> desirable by many educational theorists, but
> are not uniquely related to lifelong education,
> since they would be important features of any
> acceptable approach to education.[12]

Thus, according to Cropley, an analysis of the programme reveals three different levels of statement:
the necessary, which refers to those features of the
concept without the inclusion of which one could not
properly be taken to be referring to a *lifelong
education* programme, and the contingent, which he
subdivides into two levels containing, respectively,
those characteristics which are not 'inevitably
linked' with lifelong education, in the sense that
one could still be referring to a particular programme as a *lifelong education* programme in their
absence, and those characteristics 'which are best
seen as happy outcomes of the implementation of the
ideas of lifelong education'. The contingent characteristics, Cropley points out, are no more than
prescriptive statements reflecting the values and
understanding of the theorists contributing to the
programme.

In effect, the only statement in the list that unambiguously defines conditions that are necessary

features of any programme of lifelong education is the opening one of 'characteristic' (2) which says that from the point of view of such a programme 'Education is not seen as restricted to a particular period of life. It is a lifelong process which covers the whole lifespan of the individual'. The statement, in fact, amounts to no more than a tautologous re-statement of the same idea of lifelong education. Otherwise everything else is contingent, including the end piece to the same 'characteristic' (2), which says that the programme views the educational process as an 'integrated whole'. This is because, as 'characteristic' (1) indicates, the bare view that the education should be seen as covering the entire life-span of the individual is open to different kinds of understanding and different kinds of strategic solutions of two broad kinds; either it could be taken to mean that the educational process is to be conceived of as *continuous and uninterrupted* throughout the individual's life, or it could be conceptualized as a stop-start process, one that does continue regularly throughout the individual's life but *at intermittant periods* interspersed with other activity which is non-educational.

The difference is partly reflected in different terminological usages that translate the *idea* of learning for life variously through the adoperation of such names as 'continuing education', 'recurrent education', and *'education permanente'*. But the frequency with which these terms are used inter-changeably among themselves and with the term 'life-long education', conceals this fact and creates not a little confusion in the field even among educa-tional theorists themselves,' not all of whom are suitably discriminative. The problem for the general public is, moreover, further complicated by the fact, to which reference was made in the Intro-duction, that the term 'lifelong education' is fre-quently used, particularly in the United States, as simply another name for adult education. The con-fusions that have accompanied this loose usage of the terminology have not, to put it mildly, cont-ributed towards the programmatic clarity of the *con-cept* of lifelong education featured in the move-ment's literature, and have urgently needed sorting out for a long time.

One way of achieving a suitable discrimination bet-ween the terms is to tighten their usage according

to their semantics. One immediate advantage of this
strategy is evident; it becomes absurd to exchange
'adult education' for lifelong education', for the
former, like childhood education clearly refers to a
particular period of learning in life, while the
latter refers to learning spread over the whole of
life. Again, by recourse to the semantics of the
different terms one can also mark a crucial conceptual factor about the term 'recurrent education',
this is that it implies a programme of discontinuous
or intermittent education, or education alternating
through life with periods of non-education. For this
immediately suggests that the term 'recurrent education' represents a different kind of lifelong
education programme from that characterized by Dave
and the other UNESCO-based theorists we have referred to. Since, as we have seen, they take lifelong
education to refer to an understanding of education
'not as a fragmented spectrum of individual parts
but in its totality — as an integrated whole ('concept characteristic' 2). And this means that it must
be taken to include formal, non-formal and informal
learning (3) integrated in a manner that affords
continuity and articulation at different points
between learning and life.[13] The accurate characterization of 'recurrent education' would therefore
be as one way of conceptualizing the idea of learning for life. But the fact that that way is a distinctively different one from that theorized about
by Dave and the others does not emerge from semantic
considerations.

Nor is this conclusion about 'recurrent education' a
standard one. Other writers have defined it differently and have made different distinctions between
the different terms. For Kallen, for instance, 'recurrent education' is the primary concept, while all
the others, including 'lifelong education', he lumps
together as 'affiliated policy concepts'. [14]
While, more recently, Cross-Durant has argued that
while the terms 'recurrent education', 'lifelong
education' and 'learning society' can be grouped
together as signifying more or less the same things,
these collectively need to be distinguished from the
other alternative nomenclatures mentioned earlier,
since they

> differ from, say, *'education permanente'*, 'con-
> tinuing education' or the notion of alternance,
> in that the latter ideas suggest refresher and
> 'topping up' programmes (semantically, more of

the same, so to speak, implying formal education to a particular standard as a pre-requisite for continuing) and retraining, whereas
'recurrent education', or Boshier's 'learning
society', or 'lifelong education' suggests a
complete 'shift of paradigm' (Houghton and
Richardson 1974: ix). The approaches of *education permanente*' and of 'continuing education', even when they mean different things to
different people, usually imply a considerable
expansion of existing services which form part
of the general adult education provision, and
as such are concerned primarily with post-com-
pulsory education. They may be viewed as tin-
kering with an existing engine. The approaches
of recurrent education, a learning society or
lifelong education, on the other hand, involve
the fitting of an entirely new engine to drive
the educational bus.[15]

Cross-Durant is, in fact, employing two distinctly
different sets of criteria in making these distinctions; the semantic and the historical, both of
which are in fact valid ways of marking out the
conceptual territory of terms and deciding what they
denote. But, in strict accordance with the very
criteria of semantics, she is not right in setting
the concepts of *education permanente*' and 'continuing education' apart from the rest. At the same
time she is correct, if my earlier analysis of the
difference between 'recurrent education' and 'lifelong education' is right, in claiming with reference
to the former that it *can* be coupled semantically
with 'lifelong education' and the 'learning society'. But *the three terms cannot be taken together
to denote the same programme*. There are indeed very
close programmatic associations between the latter
two concepts, that of 'lifelong education' and that
of the 'learning society', but the triangle with
'recurrent education' does not close.

It is all the more surprising that Cross-Durant
should assimilate the programmes of 'lifelong education' and 'recurrent education' together since, in
fact, the programmatic differences denoted by the
two terms are tacitly reflected in the *definitions*
of 'recurrent education' used, though the clue to
them cannot be found in semantics and must therefore
necessarily be historical.Thus if one returns to the
OECD documents of the early 1970s where the expression was born, one finds 'recurrent education' de-

fined as:

> formal, and preferably full time education for
> adults who want to resume their education,
> interrupted earlier for a variety of reasons.
> [16]

This definition places 'recurrent education'
squarely within the class of concepts inhabited not
by 'lifelong education' or by the 'learning society'
but by *education permanente* and 'continuing
education', which similarly imply an extension of
extant education provisions to adults, and within
which concepts, therefore, as Cross-Durant points
out, no 'paradigm shift' is implied. Her own
definition of 'recurrent education' is not so narrow
as is this original OECD one. It is more consonant
with that in the more recent OECD literature over
the years. For her 'recurrent education' is, in
fact:

> a way of seeing *in toto*, with learning occur-
> ring at intervals throughout life, alternating
> with normal life activities; the unifying of
> all stages of education; accepting formal and
> non-formal patterns of education, and embracing
> education as an integral — not peripheral or
> separate — part of life.[17]

But although this new definition does bring the
concept closer to the ambit of 'lifelong education'
and the 'learning society', in that it similarly
views its programme as 'unifying all stages of education' and as 'embracing education as an integral
... part of life', the paradigm shift from the
traditional which it implies is not nearly so radical as that implied by the concept of 'lifelong
education' defined in the manner of the 'concept
characteristics', the reason being that the term
'recurrent education' cannot escape the law of its
own semantics. Thus Cross-Durant is obliged to define it so that it continues to mean 'learning occurring at intervals throughout life, alternating with
normal activities', which is crucially different
from the lifelong education concept which *includes*
these 'normal life activities' *as educative*.

Cross-Durant's historical criterion amounts to the
view that the meaning terms like 'lifelong
education' and 'recurrent education' come to have
depends strongly on the programmes with which they

are consistently identified. This is different from
the semantic criterion just described because it
makes differences between concepts depend not on the
semantic properties of the terms that represent them
but on the programmatic properties they separately
come to connote.

This distinction is an important one because the
term 'lifelong education' itself gives rise to some
additional ambiguity which can only be clarified if
reference is made to it. It will be recalled that in
our discussion about the semantic properties of the
term we concluded that adult education could not
conceivably be confused with lifelong education, but
that certain terms, like 'continuing education' and
'recurrent education' itself, could be described as
kinds of lifelong education because they satisfy the
temporal requirement implied by the word 'lifelong',
though in different ways; as the continuation of
schooling, as catching up or vocational updating
programmes, as a stop-start process alternating with
'normal activities', and so on. What creates the
problem is the fact that, as we have also seen, the
term 'lifelong education' is also made to stand for
the name of the particular programme characterized
in the way described by Dave and the other theorists
of the movement. This means that the term has two
meanings and can be used in either way. But when
reference is made to the *programmatic* differences
between 'recurrent' and 'lifelong' education it is
evident that these refer to the latter use of 'lifelong education', and it is evident that they cannot
be distinguished semantically, their origin being,
in fact, historical. This is what is meant when it
is claimed that there is no discrepancy between the
idea of lifelong education (which refers to its
semantics) and 'recurrent education' or any kind of
education programme that takes on a lifelong aspect,
though there are discrepancies, enormous ones sometimes, between the *programmatic* qualities of 'the
movement's lifelong education programme which they
call 'lifelong education' and the programmes signi-
fied by the other terms.

The historical criterion, in fact, appears to offer
a more promising way out of the terminological con-
fusions being discussed than the semantic, valuable
though the semantic criterion undoubtedly is. For it
is programmes not semantics that count in the world
of practice; semantic distinctions merely serve the
subordinate task of shedding light on the prog-

rammatic differences no more. Thus it seems more important to note that the lifelong education concept and 'recurrent education' have their homes in different organizations and have therefore evolved separately, the one within UNESCO the other within the OECD, as a way of making the relevant distinction between them.

Following this line of explanation Kallen in fact points out that the use of *education permanente* also indicates a different point of origin for this term from either; in the Council of Europe. While Jessup rejects the usage of the term 'continuing education' to describe the lifelong concept not for the semantic reasons that Cross-Durant suggests alone but on both criteria, because it tends to obscure the fact that lifelong education is compatible with discontinuous learning (and can therefore refer to a 'recurrent' programme) — the semantic criterion, and because it is used in North America to denote a particular type of continuing professional education — the historical criterion.[18] It is in fact for Jessup, as against Cross-Durant, this narrow programmatic association of the term with professional education that distinguishes 'continuing education' from the movement's concept of lifelong education rather than any semantic discrepancies such as may not exist.

On the same programmatic criterion Boyle suggests an even more interesting distinction between 'recurrent' and 'continuing' education. The two terms, he says, suggest *different social policies* advocated and defended respectively by the radical left and the liberal centre. He quotes Griffin on the main differences:

> The social policy of continuing education has evolved from the liberal-democratic tradition of adult education itself, and it is concerned that the education system should serve the lifelong needs of people in all sectors of society particularly those in relatively disadvantaged groups .... The social policy of recurrent education is much more of an alternative to the existing education system than a response to its inadequacies and failings: it is inclined to a political view of educational institutions, stressing the way in which they create and reinforce inequality.[19]

His own definition of 'recurrent education', which
he supports, is taken from Stoikov. It refers, he
says, to:

> a global system containing a variety of prog-
> rammes which distribute education and training
> of different levels (primary, secondary and
> tertiary) by formal and non-formal means over
> the life-span of the individual in a recurring
> way, that is, alternated with work or other
> activities.[20]

It is substantially in accord with the standard
definitions of 'recurrent education' referred to
earlier and further illustrates the compelling
semantics of the term, since he also takes it to
mean alternation of education with 'work or other
activities', though he does not use this point to
distinguish it from 'continuing education', as
Jessup does. Boyle's argument, in fact, is that the
crucial difference between the two concepts is an
ideological one, and it is this fact, he says, that
determines their programmatic differences. Thus the
general approach and the curriculum of 'recurrent
education' reflects a 'humanist' emphasis on
existentially authentic experience', while that of
'continuing education' has a ''positivist' emphasis
on rationality'.[21]

If, as Jessup argues, the expression 'continuing
education' tends to obscure the fact that a lifelong
education programme can be a 'recurrent' one, or one
that views education as discontinuous with life for
its programmatic purposes, this is because it tends
by virtue of the semantics of the term, to project
an understanding of lifelong education that rules
out alternation. This means, in effect, that
semantically 'continuing education' appears closer
to the meaning of education with which the UNESCO
lifelong education theorists work than does the term
'recurrent education'. If, however, one turns to the
historical associations of the term, as Jessup
describes them, then the difference between
programmes becomes immediately evident .

It is now time to ask what the crucial difference
between the understanding of lifelong education
within the movement's programme and that of its
closest associates, like 'recurrent education', for
instance, is. There are of course other differences
of detail and emphasis, but the really crucial dif-

ference appears to be the inclusion within the former's technical or formal definition of education of
informal learning processes, while the others include only the formal and non-formal. We in fact find
that the third defining characteristic of the programme identified by Dave elaborates the term education to refer to formal, non-formal, and informal
learning and therefore creates this crucial space
between itself and the other programmes.

It is important at this stage to render again explicit the point that the lifelong education programme of the movement reflects the *choices* of its
theorists, and this evidently includes the decision
to include informal learning within its technical
definition of education. This is because this way of
arriving at a programme has been criticized on the
grounds that it is *not* a satisfactory way of defining education by Lawson, who has expressed puzzle-
ment with the very concept of lifelong education on
this account.[22] For, because of the manner of its
construction, he argues, the meaning of the term
cannot be sorted out by conceptual analysis; he
therefore concludes that there is really no concept
of lifelong education at all. Or, more accurately,
he concedes (for this is not really a serious claim
to make in view of the fact that people *do* use the
term to mean something), it does exist, but only if
one is prepared to read it into the policy proposals
that, in actual fact appear under the name 'lifelong
education'. And this, for Lawson, is not satisfactory, and he goes on to show why; the policy proposals themselves, he says, are handicapped by the
absence of 'those finer conceptual distinctions'
that alone prevent confusion. And confusion, he
says, with regard to the lifelong education proposals, there certainly is; one clear proof of it is
the inclusion of informal learning as part of its
meaning of education. For this inclusion means that
the programme it gives rise to 'fail(s) to distinguish between the totality of formative influences
which determine our individuality and those influences which are intentionally chosen to form or influence us in desired and desirable ways'.[23]

Enough was said in Chapter 1 about the claims of
analytic philosophy and the worth of the 'finer
conceptual distinctions' recommended by Lawson, and
it is not proposed to go over the same ground again
here. The only point that requires recall because it
appears relevant to this criticism, is that which

established an intimate connection between analytic philosophy of education and liberal thought — the reader will remember the criticism that the former does no more than rationalize the latter under the guise of neutrality. So what 'conceptual distinctions' arrive at in this case is no more than the rationalization of liberal educational philosophy.

The connection between liberal philosophy of education and both the idea of education for life and the movement's lifelong education programme are the subject of a complete chapter later in the book, which will consider, among other things, the question whether a *liberal* lifelong education programme is theoretically possible in the sense that it would describe the main principles of the current liberal programme with a changed temporal dimension and the modifications required to accomodate it. But it is evident that such a programme would be a substantially different one from the movement's. This last point needs to be made because what Lawson is in fact doing, though evidently not consciously, is to criticize the movement's programme for this fact, for not being a liberal programme. Of course he does not *say* this, nor believe it, since like other analytic philosophers he evidently thinks that conceptual analysis will establish the *truth* about the meaning of education, not merely the beliefs of certain philosophers and others. But this is not a position we need accept, just as we have not accepted the philosophical programme from which it derives.

INFORMAL EDUCATION

Even apart from Lawson's criticism, however, the idea of including informal learning within one's definition of education is evidently a controversial one. It is therefore important to consider just what it means and what the criticism of it is about. In general informal learning is distinguished from other kinds of learning by the fact that it is non-intentional (a more precise distinction is rendered below). The usual tendency is therefore to *distinguish* it from education which is commonly taken to refer to intentional learning activities. The standard objection to the proposal to include non-intentional learning within its definition is that the move renders the term education meaningless. This is, in fact, one criticism often made against Dewey

by his opponents who accuse him thereby of having
made education indistinguishable from life. This is
because the meaning of a term, they argue, depends
as much on what it excludes as on what it includes.
If it excludes nothing then it includes everything
and consequently denotes nothing since it is left
with no distinct conceptual space of its own. A
definition of education that includes formal, non-
formal *and* informal learning processes includes
everything and excludes nothing. So, according to
the argument, it means nothing, or so its critics
would contend.[25]

This criticism of Dewey is particularly popular
with analytic philosophers of education, but it is
also shared by many others who are taken with this
argument and have made education stand for wholly
intentional learning activities involving teachers;
a position which naturally renders the informal
contrary to the educational, not part of it.[26] It
will be dealt with more fully in a later chapter
devoted to the relationship between Dewey's educational philosophy and the lifelong education programme which similarly shares Dewey's determination
to inter-relate education with life in the most
intimate way, and is therefore subject to the same
criticism if it can be made. With reference to the
analytic philosophers however, it is clear that our
assessment of their criticism must take into account
the fact that it comes from a theoretic outlook that
is obsessed with second-order questions or meta-
theory, with cutting up the language for fine conceptual distinctions. A theoretic outlook that departs from the assumption that the term education
stands for a free floating non-contestable concept
whose logical territory needs to be carved out of
the wider language for general use.

But this is a theoretic outlook which, to repeat the
conclusion of the previous section, lifelong education theorists implicity oppose, since their view of
education is a radically different one resting as it
does on the assumption that it is the name of a *con-
testable programme* not of a free floating concept.
Thus, while the concern of analytic philosophers is
to *exclude* from a concept all that can be distinguished from others, the opposing concern is for
what can be coherently and consistently *included*
within the particular programme that theorists are
interested in. This is why, for them, the programme
defines the term rather than the other way round -

Lawson's complaint about lifelong education theory, discussed earlier, shows a lack of appreciation of this point.

The more fundamental difference, of course, between Dewey and the lifelong education theorists on the one side and analytic and liberal philosophers of education in general, who insist that all *educational* learning must be intentional, on the other, lies with the fact that whereas the former are more concerned with the 'process' aspect of education and are therefore basically interested in locating education in the learner, the latter are more interested in the activity of teachers and are therefore more interested in what teachers should transmit and how, so that they locate education in pedagogical activity.

If education is viewed as process, then, evidently (since it is difficult to imagine where it could be located except within 'life' itself and life is a unitary thing), the potential collective effect of all the forms of his learning on the learner's life is what counts and is what is of interest to the theorists and the educator. For isolating one kind of learning away from the others is not only, from this point of view, unrealistic, it also makes a true understanding of the others impossible; this is the sense of the contention that education cannot be separated from life. If, on the other hand, education is defined as what is learned directly or indirectly through the activity of teachers, then informal learning, indeed all learning from experience or life, is irrelevant to education.

To conclude, the subject of informal education cannot be left off without some important elucidations relative to the meaning of the terms formal, informal and non-formal themselves as they qualify education. The first is that many educationists do not recognise the non-formal at all as a category in its own right; the usual distinction being between formal and informal education. This is the case, for instance, with Dewey who asserts that:

> one of the weightiest problems with which the philosophy of education has to cope is keeping the balance between informal education and schooling, the more incidental and the more intentional modes of education. [27]

but makes no reference at all to non-formal education as a distinct category from the two he mentions. This is not because non-formal learning is not recognised as education but because the tendency is to bury the non-formal within the catagory of the informal. Theorists who recognise the only proper distinction to be between the formal and the informal, in fact, tend to include within the latter class all learning that does not belong in the former. Thus, for instance, for Joe Park:

> By informal education is meant that planned or deliberate instruction a tutor may provide, or a parent may give a child, or a master impart to an apprentice. But more than that it includes the self education a person may seek through a planned course of reading in the library, or secure through conversation with friends, or obtain by travel or general observation or by use of one or more of several mass media now so freely at hand. Thus informal education may be planned or deliberately imposed on another, or it may result from self-motivation and be self imposed. Sometimes it may result more from chance than from design. What distinguishes it from schooling is that there is no institution especially provided in which it takes place, although informal education may occur in school even during regular class time.[28]

But, clearly, within this ponderous description, which scarcely allows any space for formal learning even, there is scope for sub-divisions that can be made coherently and effortlessly. Indeed the very ponderousness of the class of the informal as defined by Park cries for sub-division, and this is effected in a clear-cut and economic way by Chazan who furnishes the following technical definitions of each term that have the advantage also, in our case, of reflecting, more or less, the distinctions worked with within the lifelong education literature:

> Formal education: the hierarchically struc-tured, chronologically graded 'education sys-tem', running from primary schools through the university and including, in addition to gener-al academic studies, a variety of specialised programmes and institutions for full-time tech-nical and professional training.

> Informal education: the truly lifelong process whereby every individual acquires attitudes, values, skills and knowledge from daily experience and the educative influences and resources in his or her environment — from family and neighbours, from work and play, from the market place, the library and the mass media.

> Non-formal education: any organisational activity outside the established formal system — whether operating separately or as an important feature of some broader activity — that is intended to serve identifiable learning clienteles and learning objectives.[29]

One final remark about the relationship of informal learning defined as in Chazan (a definition which will continue to be upheld throughout the book) and the lifelong education programme. The link between the programme and the idea of a 'learning society' is, as Cross-Durant claims, a conceptual one *because* of the inclusion of informal learning within the technical definition of education of the former. Since this inclusion makes the very social environment in which we live educationally relevant.

CONTINGENT 'CHARACTERISTICS'

Cropley, while specifying, in agreement with our previous analysis, that the only 'characteristic' of lifelong education into which the concept can be 'unambiguously defined' (because it alone is 'essential and crucial') is the temporal idea of education 'being available at all ages', distinguishes further, within the conceptual area of its contingent 'characteristics' referred to earlier:

> two major ideas which, while not falling clearly into the first category just described (the 'essential and crucial') are central to theorizing about lifelong education, and are not simply characteristics of the second kind ('those which, while necessary, are not definitive attributes of lifelong education')[30]

The first is the understanding 'embraced by the idea that systematic and purposeful learning is not confined to schools'; the understanding just discussed of education as involving non-formal besides formal patterns of learning, and as including, therefore, deliberate self-education and possibly the participation of institutions and systems or networks other than the school, in the community (as described in nos. 3-7 of Dave's 'characteristics') [31]

The other is the understanding that lifelong education implies a 'humane' approach to learning which would avoid coercion and concentrate on building into learners in the early stages a positive motivation to learn, against other possibilities.

But, although he groups them together, it is clear that the two ideas, major or otherwise, are not derived from the idea of lifelong education with the same logical force. The first does indeed follow as a legitimate assumption on *practical* grounds, since it is questionable whether the extension of education in a lifelong sense could effectively be realised without some broadening of our understanding of education to include other learning agencies than the formal. It is, however, only a practical assumption that logically has other alternatives, for it is perfectly possible to conceptualize lifelong education *without* the inclusion of non-formal agencies; there is nothing in the bare idea of lifelong education itself that prevents it from being understood as lifelong *schooling*, the extension of formal education for life. This is precisely the fear of Illich and Verne (and, to an extent, of John White too [32]), who express misgivings about the determination of lifelong education theorists to institutionalize the concept. For, they say, the institutionalization of lifelong education could serve to *suffocate* all the learning initiatives that are currently 'spontaneous' and would turn society itself into a 'global classroom'.[33]

How is this criticism to be met? Before venturing an answer to this question, a little more needs to be said about the statement that the lifelong education theorists are determined to institutionalize the concept. This would in fact already appear to follow from the simple fact that its elaboration is being referred to as a programme. But this is not so, for programmes need not be intended for this purpose; they can be theoretically defined then left to the initiative of individuals without any claim that institutions should respond to them. So it is important to stress that lifelong education theorists do indeed intend their programme to be institutionalized. Not only, they intend it to be so in the most far-reaching way, so much so that in `concept characteristic´ (16) Dave distinguishes lifelong education as `an organising principle providing a total system for all education´ based on `the universalist principle of education for all at all ages´. (8) Hence, apparently, justifying Illich and Verne's fears.

Not only, lifelong education theorists actually consider the proposal to institutionalize the idea of lifelong education to be the *distinctive feature* of the movement's programme. Otherwise, as we stated in the opening page of this chapter, and as critics who dismiss the current `fuss´ about lifelong education point out, the idea itself is an old one. To such criticism in fact Kallen replies in a manner that is typical of the theorists:

> Every major idea can with some good will and much artisanship be traced back to antiquity ...., there is great merit in this demarche, as it allows us to see the continuity in human needs and in human thinking, (but) as long as ideas do not become the focal point for policy and action, their political relevance is not obvious. In order to play this role, ideas need to be developed into models that can serve as the basis for policy-making.[34]

And this is precisely the case with lifelong education. While Hawes, with the same intention as Kallen's in mind but replying to the more specific observation that in early cultures and in primitive civilizations lifelong education was actually a way of life, points out that `the activities described were conceived piecemeal as a response to particular needs and not as part of a perceived educational philosophy.´[35]

In sum, then, the intention to institutionalize lifelong education is not only specified in the lifelong education programme, it is also considered to be a distinguishing feature of the programme. So, to return to the question, how is the criticism of Illich and Verne to be met? The answer must be sought in the programme itself, and this is where the importance of the technical definition of education with which it operates comes yet again to the fore. For the fears of Illich and Verne would be justified only if this definition of education restricted the meaning of the term to formal learning (the assumption that education means formal learning also lies at the back of White's misgivings about lifelong education). In fact, as we have seen, the lifelong education understanding of education also includes non-formal learning activities, and the essence of the non-formal, as Chazan's definition shows, is that it refers to 'activity outside the established formal system'.

The second 'major idea .... central to theorizing about lifelong education', the 'humane' approach to learning it is supposed to imply, is not so closely tied to the idea of lifelong education as the first. For it is not obvious that the lifelong education idea need require any such approach either logically or in practice. This second 'major idea' would therefore seem to fall more squarely within the weakly contingent class of 'concept characteristics' identified by Cropley than within the strongly contingent, which, one supposes, would be the class to which the 'major ideas' should belong. This gives it the same status more or less, *qua* '*concept characteristic*', as the rest identified by Dave. For instance, it need not follow either, from the necessary temporal requirement built conceptually into the term lifelong education or from the requirements of practice, that the 'general' and the 'vocational' aspects of learning referred to in (11) should interrelate or interact together within the same programme. A conception of lifelong education governed by purely economic or instrumental considerations could, for instance, translate itself in purely vocational terms, while, from a different point of view, a conception of lifelong education translated into 'general' or 'cultural' terms would exclude the vocational element altogether.[36] Therefore, as with the claim with the 'humane' direction of the lifelong education programme, the principle that they should interact is a purely programmatic one reflecting a choice, pure and simple.

THEORETIC DIFFICULTIES

The use of words like 'movement' and 'programme', and the setting up of Dave's 'concept characteristics' as a synthesized version of the lifelong education programme will so far have conveyed the impression of a clear and well-ordered lifelong education theory, with well-defined concepts and a coherent structure of principles both operational and ideological. That impression is however quickly dispelled by Cropley's 'stocktaking' of the reaction to the lifelong education literature over the years:

> Much has been written about lifelong education in the last few years. The idea has been advocated with almost 'theological' fervour, as one writer put it (Elvin, 1975, p. 26). By contrast, it has been criticized as a meaningless 'elastic concept' (Pucheu, 1974, p. 375), a device for subverting educational reform or a 'trap' permitting perpetual control of people (Illich and Verne, 1975).[37]

Cropley also ventures his reasons why the same body of writing should provoke such contrary and contrasting views as the ones he quotes:

> The term is used in a variety of ways. For example, in one sense it refers to what Ruegg (1974, p. 7) called 'a utopian idea' which is, at best, capable of stimulating people to think about education, but is not itself a goal and does not provide guidelines for change. Long (1974) has discussed in detail what might be called the 'philosophical' conceptualization of lifelong education. At its most superficial level this approach reveals 'the mystique of education' (p. 7) according to which, since education is a good thing, more of it would be even better, and lifelong education would clearly be the best of all! As Long (1974, p.5) put it, the view is also sometimes taken that learning is almost synonymous with living, so that to talk about lifelong education (especially if this is taken to mean lifelong *learning*) is almost the same as talking about lifelong living, and therefore requires no further discussion.[38]

Criticism, in other words, is levelled at the programme at different levels. That of Ruegg and Elvin, for instance is aimed against the general theoretic approach in the literature which both describe as 'utopic'. But it is seen differently by Pucheau, who describes lifelong education, by contrast, as an 'elastic concept'. The criticism of the former refers, in effect, to the direction taken by the early literature of the movement and is an accurate description of that literature, as will be shown in the coming section where 'the state of the theory' will be discussed. The latter's criticism, on the other hand, probably refers to work like that of Long who, as Cropley says, attempted something like a conceptual analysis of lifelong education, with the results described by Cropley. Long's exercise in fact shows up the limitations of conceptual analysis where the terms involved are stipulative, revealing the programmatic prescriptions of a theorist or group of theorists, rather than concepts that evolved in the language, for the net result of his efforts is a vacuous tautology. Lawson, as we saw earlier, *ruled out* the possibility of any such analysis, though he considered this a deficiency in the concept rather than a limitation of analysis. The only possibility for conceptual analysis to yield any results in fact, in this case, would be, Lawson seems to indicate, to submit the concept of *education*, rather than lifelong education, to analysis, then prescribe the outcome for life. But this, we have said, is contrary to the implicit theoretic orientation of the movement's programme which defines education more broadly and is more interested in 'policy' than in 'conceptual truths', and would, in any case, produce an utterly different programme if one conceptualizes education in the manner described by analytic philosophy of education.

What is important, from our point of view, about the contrasting criticism of the lifelong education literature described in the previous paragraph is that it demonstrates that the literature is complex not unitary, embracing a plurality of theoretic approaches of which the utopic and the analytic may be but two, rather than representing a single paradigm. It is also clear that this pluralism creates problems for the theoretical presentation of a unitary programme for the movement, particularly if the theoretic approaches are contrasting as is the case with the two described.

The other difficulty that emerges from the criticism quoted by Cropley is one we have discussed already a few pages back. Is the lifelong education programme a 'trap' permitting perpetual control over people, as Illich and Verne contend? The possibility that it *could* be is frankly admitted by the representatives of yet another theoretic approach within the literature which we will refer to as the 'pragmatic' and which will also be discussed in the next section, who admit themselves preoccupied by it. Our earlier discussion of the problem concluded that the inclusion in the programme's technical definition of education of other than formal learning indicates that its itention is not to turn the 'learning society', which it speaks about, into a 'global classroom'. And yet the objection of Illich and Verne, and their general description of lifelong education theory as 'utopic' by Ruegg and Elvin, raise the question whether the normative aims of the programme, the part of its core that is politically ideological rather than educationally so, are sufficiently well defined to avoid ambiguity. The criticism does not indicate that they are.

In fact we saw earlier that Cropley claims a 'humane' direction for the programme. Our subsequent discussion of this claim however showed that, as the criticism above also indicates, it is not necessary that a lifelong education programme, defined in terms of its operational characteristics only, should be humane. One also notes among Dave's 'concept characteristics' the claim that 'The ultimate goal of lifelong education is to maintain and improve the quality of life' (14). There is not however any subsequent elaboration of what this means in more concrete terms. As a normative statement, therefore, it is about as enlightening as Cropley's.

Cropley's own more condensed version of Dave's list, which he similarly claims to be 'the comprehensive one implicit in the publications of UNESCO', serving it as 'an initial working definition' of lifelong education, contains an interesting if subtle development. The full version is as follows:

education should:

(1) last the whole life of each individual;

(2) lead to the systematic acquisition, renewal, upgrading and completion of knowledge, skills and attitudes made necessary by the conditions in which people now live;

(3) have as its ultimate goal the promotion of the self-fulfilment of each individual;

(4)   be dependent for its successful implemen-
      tation on people's increasing ability and
      motivation to engage in self-directed
      learning activities;

(5)   acknowledge the contribution of all avail-
      able educational influences, including
      formal, non-formal and informal.[39]

The fundamental points can, in actual fact, be seen
to be substantially those of Dave, though in more
economic form since the description limits itself to
the barest principles. The interesting development
referred to above, which naturally regards the normative statement of the programme, is point (3)
which announces that the 'ultimate goal' of the
programme is the 'self-fulfilment of each individual', as against the statement in Dave that it
is 'to maintain and improve the quality of life'.
Cropley adds that self-fulfilment depends on
'people's increasing ability and motivation to
engage in self-directed learning activities', which
is, again, a more specific re-statement of
'characteristic' (15) of Dave's list which says that
the 'three major requisites' for the individual's
lifelong education are 'opportunity, motivation and
educability'. What is conspicuously missing in
Cropley, as compared with the 'concept characteristics' is the distinctive social dimension added to
the concept by the latter in points (4) and (5) of
the list, particularly in the latter where Dave
states that 'lifelong education is rooted in the
community.'

Does it denote a change of direction, a shift of
emphasis in the interim between the publication of
the two lists, in the movement's ideological viewpoint? The question will be answered later. The
general picture that we require at the moment has
already begun to emerge. Although terms and expres-
sions like 'self-fulfilment', 'self-realization',
'self-direction', 'the quality of life', and, as we
shall see later, 'democracy', in particular, are
bandied about everywhere in the literature, more
often than not accompanied by rhetorical statements
in their regard, there is nowhere any attempt towards a deeper analysis of them, or any attempt towards integrating them into a coherent ideological
position which would give the programme an unambig-
uous normative direction. In short, the programme

appears to lack that philosophical underlay against which it could measure itself. This notwithstanding Cropley's reference to a readily distinguishable 'philosophy' which he claims it to have:

> The literature on lifelong education ... makes it clear that the majority of writers in the area have indeed accepted, implicitly if not always explicitly, certain beliefs about the nature of man, good, society and education. In this respect there is an identifiable 'philosophy' of lifelong education, if agreement between thinkers concerning goals and values can be said to involve a philosophy. This 'philosophy' is loosely humanitarian and humanistic in nature: in theory, at least, writers on lifelong education would therefore not accept that any and all practices that have the effect of extending education throughout life reflected the 'philosophy' of lifelong education.[40]

This is, one would agree, about right. There are indeed goals and values held in common within the literature, statements that appear repeatedly in the works of different writers, declarations about the value of individuality, the importance of self-realization as an educational aim, the indispensability of democracy as a measure of the quality of life. But they only qualify as a philosophy, as Cropley admits, in an inverted commas sense. Moreover, Cropley describes this 'philosophy' as 'loosely humanistic'. Humanism is already a 'loose' enough philosophy as it is, and as the next chapter will show; what does 'loosely humanistic' mean? Can a 'loosely humanistic' 'philosophy' define a suitable normative direction for an education programme? The fact that the lifelong education programme with its 'loosely humanistic' 'philosophy' gives rise to accusations like those of Illich and Verne, notwithstanding what Cropley says, indicates that it cannot.

THE STATE OF THE THEORY

Cropley distinguishes two distinct theoretic trends within lifelong education theory. The word 'trends' is actually Ireland's, who makes substantially the same analysis as Cropley's. It fits well Cropley's further assessment of the differences between them

as one of 'emphasis' rather than one that reflects
any deep, underlying, operational or ideological
disagreement.[41] The principles the two 'trends'
hold are, in fact, similar; they are the basic
principles of the programme outlined by Dave and
Cropley. What separates them, essentially, is their
different manner of theorizing about lifelong
education and of presenting the programme.

The difference can be expressed succinctly by
stating that whereas the one is more interested in
'the construction of detailed future models' of
lifelong education, and therefore reveals an
'optimistic and essentially utopic nature',[42] the
other is more interested in the practical
possibilities of applying the operational principles
of the lifelong education programme to different
existent societies. The outlook of the former could
therefore be described as 'utopic', while that of
the latter could be called 'pragmatic'.

It is important to note that, in point of time, the
'pragmatic' appeared after the 'utopic' and, largely, in reaction to the criticism levelled against
the early writing from different quarters. Some of
this criticism was discussed in the section before
this one, and the major point is summarized in Elvin's critical review of *Learning to be*, which is
perceptive in some ways and extraordinarily unfair
in others. Elvin attacks the report for its tendency to take refuge in rhetoric where some form of
normative commitment is demanded,[44] and our earlier discussion indicated this state of affairs as
symptomatic of the 'utopic' trend. The reaction of
'pragmatic' theorists to this criticism has not,
however, concentrated on rectifying this deficiency,
though, as was pointed out earlier, they are particularly sensitive to the 'dual potential' of an operational lifelong education programme to act as an
instrument of repression just as much as liberation.
Rather, they have limited themselves, as Cropley's
description implies, to proclaiming humanistic values, and have turned towards the 'neutral' social
sciences for their theoretic approaches. In this
way they avoid the charge of rhetoric and abstraction levelled against their predecessors while ref-
raining from any deeper ideological statement.

A primary example of this approach is Gelpi, who
believes that lifelong education practices will be

improved not by ideology but by sociological and
comparative work; particularly by analysis of the
obstacles that impede the operationalisation of the
lifelong education programme in localised and
international contexts. Gelpi, as was indicated in
the opening page of the chapter, is an important,
perhaps currently the outstanding, figure in the
lifelong education movement. This is partly because
of his position within UNESCO and partly because of
his prolific contribution to the theory of lifelong
education. The former means that he is extraordinarily well placed to monitor the lifelong education
programme at the international level and to engage
in the kinds of analysis just referred to. Gelpi,
in fact, is interested both in the problems that
inhibit the exchange of innovative views and practices at the international level and those that
hinder the lifelong education programme at a more
localised level, and he sees both aspects as closely
interrelated together. It is therefore important to
consider how he views the lifelong education programme which has germinated in the literature.

Clearly he adheres to its central strategic
principles and to the programme's technical
definition of the term education, but, at the same
time, in accordance with the outlook of the
pragmatic trend which he supports, for him, lifelong
education 'is based on a dialectic it is not an
absolute theory'.[46] In other words, for Gelpi,
within every society the concrete operationalization
of the concept is achieved by the dialectical interaction of the operational principles of the programme with the social forces at work, particularly
those that affect the productive sector. But although he sets such stock on the prevalent socio-
economic conditions, he does not, as Ireland points
out, share Vinokur's view that a classless society
is a necessary pre-requisite for the implementation
of the programme.[47] This is because Gelpi believes that in every society, no matter how repressive, there exists autonomy for educational action of
some kind however small, and that this autonomy is
expressed by the presence of 'progressive' individuals within it, even though he does not underrate
the political forces against their emergence and
subsequent influence any more than he underrates the
problems of exchange at the international level. It
is these individuals, Gelpi stresses, who need to be
attracted to lifelong education; they are the potential leaders of the 'long march through the institu-

tions' required to implement its programme.[48]
Gelpi is therefore against `imported models' of
lifelong education. By contrast he affirms the need
to bring the dialectical nature of the programme to
the attention of these people since they are likely
to be taken in by the current misrepresentation of
it as something belonging to the rich, technologic-
ally developed countries of the world, as is
currently happening with some of the more
`progressive' people in third-world countries who
are set against it.[49]

Finally, Gelpi makes it clear that the people he has
in mind his `progressive' educators, are not profes-
sional teachers, or at least not necessarily so,
they can, and often do, come from different walks of
life and can belong to any social group. Gelpi is
as conscious as the other `pragmatic' theorists of
the `dual potential' of the lifelong education prog-
ramme, and as sensitive to the fact that as pure
strategy it can be used by governments to create the
most efficient form of conservatism possible. Thus
he describes the tension it provokes theory-wise, as
between:

> an idealist approach (lifelong education as a
> new global answer to the educational and
> cultural needs of our society) and a negative
> moralist approach (lifelong education as a new
> form of manipulation) which is in fact also an
> idealist approach.[50]

The solution to such a tension lies with `a
sociological and historical approach to lifelong
education' which will give those struggling for
reform and innovation insight into the opposing
socio-political and economic forces already at work
in their society. Thus the dialectic of the
programme works as much against the conservative
forces within society as the reformatory; in this
sense the struggle to implement the lifelong
education programme cannot but be a political one.
But what about *political* ideology? Granted that the
struggle to effect educational change must be a
political one and that the dialectic described as
required will therefore not be anything but the
political forces at work involved in the struggle –
will the struggle itself over strategy not be
defined by the strugglers in terms of more concrete
underlying commitments of a political kind?

Gelpi, in point of fact, does state his own
political ideology in different places. Ultimately
he sees lifelong education as ideally 'part of a
process whose ultimate objective is the achievement
of a democratic egalitarian socialist society in
which everyone participates on an equal
footing'.[51] But at the same time he believes that
utopic visions of this kind need to be balanced by
hard realities which will fully expose the
difficulties in the way of progress towards the
ideal, and the dangers inherent in the lifelong
strategy itself.

The fact that he does identify a set of ideal
ideological principles for the lifelong education
programme in effect, means little, for their
systematic philosophical development is not part of
his theoretical research programme. One could in
fact say that his overt political beliefs are kept
in the background, but this is because underlying
his research programme lies a faith in the immense
power of educational strategy in itself to fulfil
human goals through the very democratization and
dissemination of knowledge which the lifelong
education programme implies and through the very
growth of the number of individuals committed to it.
A similar optimism may be why theorists of the
pragmatic 'trend' in general, tend to be satisfied
with an ideological commitment to humanism and to
'humane' educational practices without feeling the
need for any deeper specification of what this
means.

But there are other reasons that could be just as
compelling for adopting humanism as an ideological
position. One would be Lengrand's, who argues that
the established ideologies, liberalism, Marxism
etc., as well as the leading religions, are
currently in crisis and are therefore both incapable
and unqualified to guide individuals living in times
when the very beliefs and values they possess are
constantly challenged. The other, very different,
one could have to do with Elvin's hypothesis about
the lack of ideological commitment of the Faure
report:

> The necessity of abstaining from overt critic-
> ism of the social and political regimes within
> which, and often against which, educational
> reformers have to work, has meant that M. Faure
> and his colleagues could not go into their

> problem as thoroughly and penetratingly as an
> independent scholar might.[52]

In other words it could, as this criticism says, be
an imposition on the movement forced on it by its
UNESCO sponsorship. Another reason still could be
the need to present a broad homogeneity of outlook
within the movement, which would not be a 'movement'
otherwise, which could only, perhaps, be obtained by
adopting an ideological underpinning for it that is
permissive enough to embrace nearly everything.

We could only speculate which of these and other
possible hypotheses could be the right one. Certainly, the term 'humanism' has such a wide reference that it is capable of serving the purpose well
if it is adopted deliberately to avoid specific
ideological commitment. We have stated, however,
that, for this reason, it also tends to ambiguity of
different kinds, though what these are will emerge
clearly only after the next chapter. For before we
discard it too readily for this reason, we need to
see whether there are any advantages of a different
kind humanism offers, and to do that we will need to
look a little more closely into what it means. For
Lengrand's point, above, is a valid one, and so is
the last suggestion made in the previous paragraph,
that humanism has the permissiveness that suits an
international movement. It may be, therefore, that
a more specifically defined humanism, by which I
mean a narrowing down of the options to a particular
'philosophy of man' among all those that currently
fall under its umbrella, in a manner which is consistent with the programme, will do the trick. The
difficult problem, in this case, will be seen to be
that of resolving the tension between permissiveness
and dogma that worries many self-declared humanists.

CONCLUSIONS

The main task of this chapter has been to make a
very preliminary evaluation of the programme of the
lifelong education movement gravitating around UNES-
CO. It has been assumed that Dave's concept characteristics constitute an accurate representation of
it on the basis of the fact that Dave's source was
the extant writing on lifelong education over the
years which his 'characteristics' synthesized.
Reference was also made to the UIE definition of
lifelong education reproduced by Cropley in succinct

form and holding tenets similar to those of Dave.
The subsequent discussion of Dave's 'characteristics' and of the terminological ambiguities affect-
ing the state of the theory brought the following to
light: (1) the term lifelong education is itself a
potentially ambiguous one, for apart from the
necessity that it should refer to education
spreading over the life-span of individuals, there
are different alternative views about how this
condition can be fulfilled; the main difference
being between the view that education should
alternate with other phases and activities over the
individual's life-span, and the view that it should
be viewed as continuous with life itself. It was
seen that the difference is reflected in different
nomenclatures used instead of lifelong education,
all of which are designed to capture the underlying
idea of education for life but with this and other
programmatic differences in mind. (2) The difference between programmes is in fact mainly owing to
the technical definition of education with which the
movement's lifelong education programme works and
which includes informal learning besides non-formal.
This inclusion has far-reaching consequences because
it also makes necessary the inclusion within the
programme of some conception of a 'learning
society'. (3) The 'learning society' itself can,
in fact, be seen as the embodiment of the programme's determination to so conceptualize education
that 'at the operational level lifelong education is
an organising principle providing a total system for
all education'. (Dave's 'characteristic' 16). This
means that lifelong education theorists want the
concept institutionalized; indeed it was seen that
they consider this aspect of their programme and the
operational recommendations to which it gives rise
as their distinctive contribution to educational
thought. But not institutionalized in the sense
feared by Illich and Verne where it becomes a 'trap'
and an excuse to suppress all 'spontaneous' initiatives.

It would be accurate to say that these three points
include the main operational principles of the
movement's lifelong education programme. There is
also substantial agreement about many of their
subordinate principles some of which are included in
Dave's 'characteristics'. Among these perhaps the
most important are: that which places 'learning-to-
learn', or the objective of self-directed learning,
as the foremost goal of formal or institutional,

education, and that which emphasises the educational value of the social environment itself. The first implies that value is placed on *autonomous* lifelong learning, the second reacts to the threat of a 'schooled' society and of domination or oppression through lifelong education mentioned above, the third reacts to the traditional isolation of the school from life and to the prevailing belief that schooling and education mean the same thing, both of which prejudices undermine the lifelong education programme especially in its embodiment as a 'learning society'.

It was seen that much of the earlier theorizing about lifelong education tended to be utopic, concentrating on *abstract models* of a 'learning society' and presupposing a common fate towards which existent societies are inexorably advancing; that of becoming a 'global community'. The criticism levelled against this approach was, as we have seen, extensive and varied; for one thing it makes the concrete application of the operational programme to actual societies well-nigh impossible mainly because both the models themselves, and the principle that such models should be adopted, are unacceptable to many. The contrary reaction has been to emphasise the lifelong education programme not as a global model but as a set of principles working dialectically with the actual conditions, social, economic and educational, of different societies. The second major criticism concerns the lack of normative commitment of the movement's programme.

It is true that the Faure report and Lengrand, for instance, stress the fact that lifelong education can only reach its full expression in a democracy, while Suchololski similarly maintains that it is unattainable under certain social conditions that encourge 'alienation'. There is also explicit commitment in the Faure report to 'scientific humanism' as the guiding light for educational reform [53]. But there is little further examination of these terms to be found, or elaboration of what they imply in specific socio-political and economic terms. At the same time the very ambiguity of a term like 'humanism' could be a convenient reason for using it since its ambiguity is allied with its being, like 'democracy', a 'hurrah-word', a word which evokes positive responses when it is used since it is assumed, by virtue of its very meaning, to signify something valuable. The theorists of the 'pragmatic' trend, reacting to their 'utopic' predecessors, have been inclined to retain the commitment towards humanism while, at the same time, shifting their methodological sights from conceptions of a 'learning society' as model, to sociological analyses of extant societies with the view of assessing their disposition towards the operationalizing of the programmatic principles of the movement, and to work of comparative analysis. Both could be ways of avoiding entering more deeply into normative questions while at the same time facilitating the dialectical approach.

NOTES AND REFERENCES

1.   The first to refer to a 'movement' of lifelong education, to my knowledge, was Yeaxlee (Yeaxlee, A.B. (1929) *Lifelong Education; A Sketch of the Range and Significance of the Adult Education Movement* (London, Cassell). In 1934 a 'Center for Continuing Education' was founded at the University of Minnesota. 'The idea was that education should not come as a break in people's lives, in the form of recapitulation and continuation courses, but that education should, instead, be considered as being permanently in progress'. (Gestrelius, K (1979) 'Lifelong Education - a New Challenge', *European Journal of Science Education* p. 278, Vol. 1, No. 3. But the 'movement' did not gain consistency and widespread polularity before it became associated with UNESCO.

2.   The origin of the term 'lifelong education' is unknown but it first appeared in an official document in the 1919 *Final Report of the Ministry of Reconstruction, Adult Education Committee* (London) which emphasised the necessary role of education in modern life and stressed that such education be kept permanent and lifelong. It first appeared in UNESCO reports in the 1962 *Draft Programme and Budget for 1963 - 64.* In 1965, the UNESCO *International Committee for the Advancement of Adult Education* discussed a paper by Paul Lengrand on the concept of continuing education and subsequently recommended that UNESCO embrace the principle. In the planning for International Education Year 1970, lifelong education appeared under the 12 major objectives listed in Resolution 1-112 of the General Conference. And by 1973 it was recognized as the

'master-concept' for all of UNESCO's educational planning.

3.   Faure, E., et al., (1971)   *Learning to be* (London, Harrap)

4.   Dave, R.H. (ed.) (1975)   *Reflections on Lifelong Education and the School* (Hamburg, UIE)

5.   Lengrand, P. (1975)   *An Introduction to Lifelong Education*, (London, Croom Helm)

6.   Dave, R.H. (ed.) (1976)   *Foundations of Lifelong Education* , p. 12 (Oxford, Pergamon)

7.   ibid., p. 353.

8.   Cropley, A.J. (ed.) (1979) *Lifelong Education: a stocktaking* (Hamburg, UIE Monographs 8)

9.   Gelpi's most   recent publication is *Lifelong Education and International Relations* (London, Croom Helm, 1985), but his first book, *World History of Education* appeared in 1976, and over the past years his contributions   to different aspects of education have been many.

10.   Griffin, C. (1983) *Curriculum Theory in Adult and Lifelong Education*, p. 172 (London, Croom Helm)

11.   Dave, R.H. (ed.) (1975) *Reflections on Lifelong Education and the School*, op.cit., p. 55

12.   op.cit., p. 14.

13.   Thus Lengrand, for instance, defines lifelong education as 'education in the full sense of the word, including all its aspects and dimensions, its uninterrupted development from the first moments of life to the very last and the close, organic interrelationship between the various points and successive phases in its development'. (op.cit., pp. 20 - 21)

14.   Kallen, D. 'Recurrent Education and Lifelong Learning: definitions and distinctions', in: Schuller, T., and Megarry, J. (eds.) (1979) *World Yearbook of Education, 1979*, p.45, (London, Kogan Page).

15.   Cross-Durant, A. 'Lifelong Education in the Writings of John Dewey', *International Journal of Lifelong Education*, p.115, Vol. 3, No.2, 1984.

16.   Kallen, D., in: Schuller, T., and Megarry, J. (eds.) op.cit., p. 47.

17.   op.cit., p. 115.

18.   Jessup, F.W. (ed.) (1969) *Lifelong Learning* (Oxford, Pergamon)

19.   Boyle, C. 'Reflections on Recurrent Education', p. 12, *International Journal of Lifelong Education* Vol. 1, No. 2, 1982., p. 12. Reference is to Griffin, C. (1978) *Recurrent and Continuing Education - A Curriculum Approach*, p.3 (Association for

Recurrent Education Discussion Paper 3)

20. ibid., p.8. Reference is to Stoikov, V. (1975) *The Economics of Recurrent Education and Training*, pp. 2-5. (Geneva, International Labour Office)

21. ibid., p.13.

22. Lawson, K. 'Lifelong Education: Concept or Policy?' *International Journal of Lifelong Education*. Vol.1, No. 2, 1982.

23. ibid., p.97.

24. In effect, Lawson defines education as follows: 'What we call 'education' can be regarded as planned, intentional preparation, it is an aid to coping a way of short-circuiting personal experience by drawing upon the accumulated experience of others'. (p.103)

25. Lawson's own criticism is that the total account of learning that characterizes the lifelong education programme's technical definition of education actually makes it 'loose and lacking in 'cutting edge'', and therefore counter-productive policy-wise (p.103). This, however, does not follow since such a total account does not necessarily sacrifice the *effectiveness* of specific and intentional intervention, it merely says that such intervention cannot be all that education means.

26. Lawson's own argument runs as follows: 'If all experience is to be counted as part of an individual's 'development', the argument becomes quite circular and we are the product of circumstances, and there is a sense in which we are what life makes us', (p.103) and life could make us in undesirable ways. Education should therefore be viewed more as a *corrective* of life than as being at one with it. This is, in fact, the typical liberal view , as will be seen in Chapter 5.

27. Dewey, J. (1916) *Democracy and Education* p.9 (New York, Free Press, Macmillan, 1976 edition)

28. Park, J. 'Education: Schooling and Informal' *Philosophy of Education*, 1971, p. 9.

29. Chazan, B. 'What is Informal Education?', *Philosophy of Education*, 1981 p. 242.

30. op. cit., p. 15.

31. The principle is referred to in the lifelong education literature as that of 'horizontal integration' which, Cropley says, explains the 'relationship between education and life' (ie. the wider life. In fact in making the same claim theorists refer to the 'life-wide' aspect of lifelong education) (Cropley, A.J. (1977) *Lifelong Education...a psychological analysis*, p. 16 (Oxford,

Pergamon)). On the other hand, the concept of `vertical integration', as Parkyn points out, explains the `lifelong' component of the term lifelong education. (Parkyn, G.W. (1973) *Towards a Conceptual Model of Lifelong Education* (Paris, UNESCO)). Both terms are implied in Dave's `characteristics' (6) and (7).

32. White, J (1982) *The Aims of Education Restated* (London, Routledge and Kegan Paul). . The criticism White makes of the concept of lifelong education is dealt with in detail in Chapter 5.

33. Illich, I., and Verne, E. (1976) *Imprisoned in the Global Classroom* (Montreal, Writers and Readers Publishing Cooperative).

34. op. cit., p. 46.

35. Hawes, H.W.R. (1974) *Lifelong Education, Schools and Curricula in Developing Countries*, p. 27 (Hamburg U.I.E. Monographs, 4).

36. Referring to the `dual potential' of a lifelong education programme to act as an object of oppression rather than freedom, an aspect that will be discussed in the next section, Furter says that it `can just as well favour the professional and social enhancement of the worker's status as justify forms of exploitation which increase still further the need for productivity. One has to learn more, not to live better, but to produce more'. (Furter, P. (1977) *The Planner and Lifelong Education*, p. 13 (Hamburg, Unesco)) A conception of lifelong education which is utterly instrumental could indeed render itself in such terms, while the dislocation of education from work affects the attitude individuals and societies hold towards work adversely; Lengrand considers the dichotomy between work and culture that it creates none the less oppressive (op.cit., p.13 and ff.).

37. Cropley, A.J. (1979) *Lifelong Education: a stocktaking,* op. cit., p. 8.

38. ibid., p. 12.

39. ibid., p. 3.

40. ibid., p. 102.

41. Ireland, T.D. (1978) *Gelpi's View of Lifelong Education* (Manchester Monographs 14, University of Manchester).

42. Ireland T.D. op. cit., p. 21.

43. ibid., p. 25.

44. Elvin, L, `Learning to be...', *Education News*, 15, 1975. Elvin says that as a consequence of its rhetorical approach, the report ultimately presents a `very low level of discourse, whether judged intellectually or practically' (p.26) This judge-

ment is in fact entirely unfair and as overstated as Kallan's utterly opposite estimation of it as representing ` for the first time a coherent philosophy, about man, education and society to which the idea of lifelong learning was related'. (op. cit., p. 52) *Learning to be*, as Kallen continues to say, `adopts an optimistic view about human nature and about the power of education to change society'. (p.52), and therefore belongs in spirit to the utopic trend in the lifelong education literature; as a consequence it also shares the defects of the trend. At the same time its very rhetoric makes it provocative, and, in many places the reader is struck by the truths it expresses about the defects educational systems around the world currently share. Moreover its own alternatives always stimulate reflection because they are sometimes so radical. Although these qualities may not be considered valuable to an Anglo-Saxon mind.

45. Huberman (Michael), author of the 1975 UNESCO report *Understanding Change in Education* is quoted by Richmond as having said `I think that the whole issue (of lifelong education) is very badly defined. It has become the province of philosophers and politicians who have confused it beyond recognition'. (Richmond, K `The Concept of Continuous Education', in Cropley, A.J. (1979) *Lifelong Education: a stocktaking*, (op. cit., p. 74) Richmond complains that the literature of UNESCO, the OECD and the Council of Europe about their different affiliated concepts of lifelong learning, is invariably `highly theoretical and it is by no means clear how they (policies) are to be implemented. Moreover, much of the literature in the emergent field tends to be so highflown and turgid as to invite the criticism that it is guilty of wishful thinking'. `Rhetoric', he continues, echoing Elvin, `is no substitue for rational argument'. (p. 72 – 73) Also of interest in Richmond's article is his suggestion that the term `continuous education' (to be distinguished from `continuing education') be brought in to settle the ambiguity over the term lifelong education discussed earlier in this chapter. What is attractive about this suggestion is that it would seem to capture the opposition of the `lifelong education' programme to the attitude towards lifelong learning as a discontinuous programme without involving the associations of `continuing education' referred to by Jessup.

46. Ireland, T.D. (1978) *Gelpi's View of Lifelong Education*, op. cit., p. 27.

47. Reference is to Vinokur, A. 'Economic Analysis of Lifelong Education', in Dave, R.H. (1976) *Foundations of Lifelong Education*, op. cit.

48. Ireland (op. cit.) uses the expression, quoted by Gintis and taken from Rudi Dutschke.(p. 32).

49. See Gelpi's article on 'Lifelong Education and International Relations', in: Wain, K. (ed.) (1985) *Lifelong Education and Participation* (Malta, The University of Malta Press).

50. Ireland. T.D. (1978) *Gelpi's View of Lifelong Education*, op. cit., p. 38.

51. ibid., p. 41.

52. Elvin, L. 'Learning to be' (1975) op. cit., p. 15.

53. These points are developed and discussed in the next two chapters.

Chapter Three

HUMANISM

BACKGROUND

There has always been a so-called humanist tradition
in education. Names come easily to mind; Socrates,
Erasmus, Comenius, all the 'great educators' were
moved, at the very least, by a common concern for
humanity and by a common faith in the potential of
human beings to achieve progress through education.
To that extent their creed was 'humanist'. But when
it comes to assessing this common faith against the
education programme which unfolds from it, when
education is brought to terms with metaphysics or
with   the   dictates   of   different   ideological
positions,   i.e.,   when humanism is defined as a
'philosophy of man' and humanist education as a
programme   reflecting   this   philosophy,   then   the
problem of meaning becomes manifest.

Plato,   for   instance,   is   described   by   some   as   a
'scientific humanist' (though not in the sense to be
described later) because he believed that human
being could be made the proper subject of scientific
study.   But how does this description square with a
philosophy that is otherwise decidedly other-worldly
in its orientation, and with a view of science that
distrusts   human   experience   and   is   structured   on
deductive inference from first principles? Does an
education programme which defines its ultimate aim
as the attainment of metaphysical knowledge and of
moral   perfection   qualify   as   humanist,   where
perfection means the transcendence of the human?
Perhaps Plato's educational philosophy can be cited
as the paradigm case of what it is *not* to be
humanist?

Can we turn to Aristotle instead for our true humanist? For Aristotle, of course, scientific study meant something altogether different from Plato's deductive metaphysics, it involved active participation in the world. But, on another plane, for Aristotle, as for Plato, the philosopher, from both a moral and an intellectual point of view, is essentially one who aims for uniqueness and self-sufficiency. On the moral side, Aristotle's attitude towards ordinary civic virtue is contemptuous in a manner similar to Plato's, the philosopher's proper attitude towards the inferior, towards the bulk of humanity, that is, being one of magnanimity. Man may be by nature, and therefore unavoidably, social, but the function of others in the self-sufficient individual's life and hence their worth as far as he is concerned, is their indispensable contribution towards the exercise of his own personal virtue. Moreover, for Aristotle, as for Plato, there is nothing intrinsically valuable about human being since the order of things is such that nature can make the individual a slave as much as a free person. As slave he has no greater moral value than his utility as a tool or object to his master, and justice demands that he be treated as no more than such. The virtue of magnanimity, on the other hand, which properly marks the master, is bred from that same self-sufficiency, and its hallmark is intellectual pride. The education programme that will give the magnanimous man these qualities recognizes, as with Plato, the ultimate epistemic and moral worth of 'contemplation' rather than social interaction or discourse:

> Again, the quality that we call self-sufficiency will belong in the highest degree to the contemplative activity. The wise man, no less than the just one and all the rest requires the necessaries of life; but, given the adequate supply of these, the just man also needs people with and towards whom he can perform just actions... but the wise man can practice contemplation by himself, and the wiser he is, the more he can do it.[1]

Contrary to popular commentary, therefore, there is no fundamental dislocation of belief between the philosophers of the polis and those who belonged to the Hellenistic schools that sprouted with the polis' demise. Withdrawal from the world was as much the central objective of the ones as of the others. What bound the former to society was, basically, their perception of the deficiencies of individual human nature which made living with others essential; a far cry from the Periclean view of the community as the individual's greatest good, participation in its life his ultimate fulfilment. Indeed, for Plato, it is the cultivation of the proper sense of duty that ties the philosopher with social life, while for Aristotle, as we have seen, it is the impossibility of *complete* self-sufficiency. The difference in spirit and attitude which led Pericles, on the one hand, to emphasise the value of *participation* in social life, and the philosopher of the polis on the other to emphasise the value of *function*, is plain to see, for the one reflects an outlook on human life which is clearly optimistic, and hence democratic, while the other reflects pessimism, and is hence oligarchic.

With the Hellenistic philosophers the march of historical events drove their pessimism to a stage where the sense of duty itself became an empty virtue, and, with the same stroke, made its allied ideal of self-sufficiency through social involvement a remote and unattractive one. The death of 'society', of the community, of the polis, meant the temporary loss of the first and the distortion of the second, since the ideal of self-sufficiency came to acquire novel, anti-social connotations for these philosophers which drove some of them to the excess of anarchy. The virtue of duty was returned to its central role among the virtues by the Stoics who also restored to Western culture the Aristotelian ideal of self-sufficiency interpreted in such a manner, however, that it could accomodate the role of duty in moral life. The novelty lay in the fact that the Stoic's ideal of intellectual and moral self-sufficiency was also accompanied by an understanding of human society as part of the established or Divine order of things. The task of the virtuous individual, it came to be thought, must be, in some way, to come to terms with this fact rather than seek to escape it; hence the restoration of the sense of duty as a central virtue. Philosophical wisdom for the Stoic, in effect, lay in the understanding of one's destiny and in the acceptance of one's station in life. The individual, within this viewpoint, comes to be seen simply as an element within an inscrutable universe so ordered by God; his virtue lies in cooperation with it. Surely this cannot be what humanism is about either!

Underlying this early Stoic ideal there lies the same struggle to effect a synthesis between a standpoint 'that invites us to stand *against* the world of physical and political circumstance' rather than within it, and a standpoint that regards human beings as essentially social by nature or vocation that confronted the philosophers of the polis, and its solution was predictably similar to theirs also, since the Stoic divided the world into the community of the wise and the herd of fools.[2] The model is of clearly Platonic origin, but it was subsequently taken over by Christianity (which substituted the community of the 'wise' with that of the 'saints', and the herd of 'fools' with that of 'sinners'), and its cultural strength, backed by the formidable might of these historical roots, has entrenched it within the Western way of life where its modern heir, as MacIntyre points out, is the bureaucratic type; the dispassionate, efficient Weberian specialist, possessed of technical and professional skills that make him, self-consciously, a member of an elite, and imbued with an ethic which demands that he hold the world at arm's length while acknowledging his responsibilities towards it. In short the bureaucratic type possesses:

> a spirit of formalistic impersonality, 'sine via et studio', without hatred or passion, and hence without affection and enthusiasm. The dominant norms (for this type) are concepts of straightforward duty without regard for personal considerations. Everyone is subject to formal equality of treatment in the bureaucratic situation, that is in the same empirical situation.[3]

Again, it is doubtful that the elements of a humanist outlook can be identified with this type. At the same time it needs to be noted that the general education programme to which the Weberian specialist belongs and the kind of social organization he implies is tied is the Platonic one also. There is in fact no fundamental divergence of viewpoints between Plato's educational principles and those that animate modern meritocracies. As with the meritocracy, Plato emphasized the importance of equalizing early educational opportunities for the *maximum* of efficiency in the tapping of 'natural' resources, then using a common curriculum for the purposes of socio-political and vocational selection, the ultimate aim being to select technically qualified elites.

Later revisions of Stoicism, however, brought into focus ideals other than those of resignation to an impersonal fate, the suppression of feelings and emotions, an unconditional obedience to the dictates of duty, and a strictly formal efficiency in carrying it out. With time in fact, and under historical and theoretical pressure, the emphasis in Stoicism turned, more and more, away from the ideal of self-sufficiency while the civic element grew in its conception and superceded the early elitism of the Stoic school postulating instead the ideal of a *common human community* bound together by the common possession of a rationality shared by *all* human beings. The revolution lay in coming to conceive of reason as a common human property rather than one that distinguishes certain people as an elite and bundles the rest together as a common herd.

The significance of this change, culturally, politically, and educationally, can hardly be over-emphasized. The early Stoics had used the rational quality in human being, like Plato, to draw distinctions between classes of human beings and to justify the leadership or domination of one class over the other, the later Stoics used it to unite the whole of humanity into one moral, if not intellectual, community. Contemporaneously with this development, in fact, one traces the overthrow, theoretically at least, of the other ancient root of discrimination; the old Greek one which postulated the view that some human beings are inferior to others 'by nature'. Henceforth the theory embodied in Plato's philosophy even before Aristotle's that human beings are essentially non-equals and that nature backed up by education divides the world into wise man or master, and slave, sinner or fool, was challenged by the cosmopolitan notion of a humanity rendered *one* by that very nature that gives all men their reason and therefore makes them brothers.

This later Stoic outlook has been described as the first expression of a truly humanist viewpoint. Usally this distinction is in fact reserved for Protagoras who announced that 'Man is the measure of all things, of things that are that they are, and of things that are not that they are not'.[4] But Protagoras' meaning is, in general, taken to be epistemological rather than moral. It has been ex-

pressed in its full implications in more modern
times by F.C.S. Schiller who, taking it as his point
of departure has argued that:

> Humanism is merely the perception that the
> philosophic problem concerns human beings
> striving to comprehend a world of human
> experience by the resources of human minds...
> It demands... that man's complete satisfaction
> shall be the conclusion philosophy must aim at,
> that philosophy shall not cut itself loose from
> the real problems of life by making initial
> abstractions which are false and would not be
> admirable, even if they were true.[5]

But it is evident that, given this kind of
epistemological backing, humanism turns into an
utterly secular philosophy of life which was not
really, as such, given its first cultural form
before the Renaissance and which only attained its
high point with the philosophy of the Enlightenment.
The distance travelled in fact from the later Stoic
position to the Enlightenment's faith in reason, and
in its conception of rationally intuited natural
human rights that demand a political response to
them is not a far one. If the postulate of a common
rationality is, on the other hand, joined on to the
further belief in the basic natural goodness of
human beings, the way is open to the conclusion that
education presents limitless opportunities for
reforming the world. For if *all* human beings are *ab
initio* equally good and equally possessed of the
power of reason, then they are *all*, and not simply
an elite minority of them, equally educable. At the
same time we are led to two fundamental conceptions
of education: one of education being a right for all
on the simple qualification of being human, two, of
education as a limitless tool for individual and
social reform which can break down all differential
barriers between people, including the national.

The cultural success of the Enlightenment, then,
brought into prominence ideals other than the
technocratic to which MacIntyre refers. For one
thing, set against the technocratic emphasis on *duty*
one finds a contrary emphasis on the intrinsic worth
of human being born of a notion of *rights* held
against all kinds of human institutions, even the
typically technocratic ones. This latter emphasis
could, in turn, tend towards the conception of human
institutions themselves, including societies, as

'fictitious entities', the individual alone being 'real' — the duty relationship is therefore inverted, political duties derive from society to the individual rather than the other way round;[6] the rejection of the philosophy of the polis, in fact, coming full circle once more with this notion of individual rights and with the cosmopolitanism of the Enlightenment. Which meant that henceforth, as Rousseau quickly perceived, within one tradition at least, it would be the collective that would come under pressure as these new waves tended to destroy the meaning and value of the community in people's eyes. Rousseau's own forlorn struggle to save it, as is well known, itself took the form of a theory which sought a synthesis between an ideal of individual feedom and the political demands of communal life, one of his major fears being that the new cosmopolitanism would destroy that freedom rather than enhance it.

Rousseau's objections to the conception of the whole of humanity as a single community were many.[7] His argument, in succinct form, was that the ideal of a universal human community is self-contradictory; for this reason it is also illusory, a 'veritable chimera'. This is because, he said, humanity in its totality can never possess the elements of a true community. For one thing, he argued, mere likeness of kind does not create a community; being a community entails the holding together of certain cultural possessions, such as a common language, a common interest and well-being etc., which cannot be attributed to a collective humanity. At the same time, however, Rousseau's own conception of community, like Kant's later, views it as a 'moral person', represented politically, for the former, by the 'general will', which is the common possession of all by virtue of the fact that it expresses for them their 'enlightened' self-interest. Rousseau was, in effect, back in spirit with Pericles and on the opposite side of liberalism for which political position it is the individual not the group that decides where this self-interest lies.

The difficulties with Rousseau's general defence of the community against the enlargement of individualism through the conception of the 'general will' are famous; its epitaph is enshrined in the paradox that within its conception the autonomous individual must be 'forced to be free'. His attempt to combine personal autonomy with a theory of the communal that

would make both sovereign contemporaneously had
become a defence of collectivism. This failure, in
turn, opened the way to different kinds of reaction
that also engineer a compromise of some description
with cosmopolitanism; one to an affirmation of individual freedom that reaches it peak first with
romanticism and later with existentialism, and which
expresses itself morally as a theory of ethical
voluntarism underpinned by a subjectivist epistemology; another to the affirmation of an 'enlightened'
individualism that sprang originally, like liberalism, from Locke's philosophy, an individualism that
sought to minimize the role of the collective while
claiming its rights from it, and at the same time
embracing a philosophy of cosmopolitanism expressed
mainly in economic terms through the operations of a
free market; another still a reaffirmation of the
political project which the later Stoicism, revisions and all, had never succeeded in exorcising —
the old Platonic ideal of the 'kingdom of the wise',
of an enlightened elite class which, interpreted in
Marxist-Leninist terms, would take upon itself the
mantle of the collective will and, in its name and
interest drive, first, a particular society, then
the whole of humanity, inspired as it is by its
spirit of cosmopolitanism, towards utopia; the last,
welfarism, is a hybrid which recognises the mutual
responsibilities of individual and collective alike,
which emphasises the element of both individual and
community worth at the same time, but which has a
question mark over it — whether it has not effectively destroyed individual freedom by its philosophy
of 'assistentialism', whether it has not merely
substituted naked repression with domestication.

IN SEARCH OF A DEFINITION

Which of these different directions is meant when
reference is made to humanism? Each, in some way,
presupposes a 'philosophy of man'. It will be noted
that no definition of the term has been attempted so
far, though queries have been raised about the
credentials of some of the positions outlined in the
previous section to qualify as humanist. This is
because there is none that is meaningful and at the
same time commands common support. Indeed any
attempt to define humanism would confront one with
so many formidable problems as to make its success
appear well-nigh impossible. This is not only
because, although it occurs within all modern

European languages, its meaning changes from one to
the other, but also because within the same language
its meaning can fluctuate 'Thus the meaning of
'humanism' has so many shades that to analyse all of
them is hardly feasible'.[8]   So that, in the
absence of any definition humanists have sometimes
been classed, in the blandest way possible, simply
as people who have 'invested their best energy and
talent to improve the condition of humanity',[9]
while humanism itself has been described, perhaps
even more blandly, as '(all that) has to do with the
improvement of human beings'.[10]

Disagreement about what this means is so wide that
not even the Protagorean dictum referred to earlier
is granted general accord, notwithstanding the fact
that it is regarded by most as a kind of minimal
condition for humanism linking it with secular doctrines about life, at the least, and ruling out theo-
centric philosophies of the human condition.   So
much so that self-styled 'religious' humanists not
only distinguish themselves from secular humanists,
they even regard the doctrines of the latter as not
authentically humanist at all, describing secular
humanism as no more than a Renaissance-inspired
aberration from the authentic classical form of
humanism which, they claim, was theo-centric in
character.[11]   Further, and to add to these complications, contemporary secular humanists themselves distinguish between the more traditional
'anthropo-centric' humanism which places human being
squarely at the centre of life, and 'bio-centric'
humanism which admits of no special status ethical
or otherwise for human being.

In general the situation is, in effect, very much
like that described by Neville, one of Sartre's
interlocutors following the latter's delivery of his
essay identifying existentialism as a humanist
philosophy:

> In these days, unfortunately, humanism is a
> word employed to identify philosophic tenden-
> cies, not only in two senses but in three,
> four, five, or six. We are all humanists to-
> day, even certain Marxists. Those who reveal
> themselves as classical rationalists are human-
> ists in a sense that has gone sour on us, der-
> ived from the liberal ideas of the last cen-
> tury, a liberalism refracted through the con-
> temporary crisis. If Marxists can claim to be

humanists, the various religions, Christian, Hindu, and many others also claim above all that they are humanist; so do the existential-ists in their turn and, in a general way, all the philosophies. Actually, many political movements protest no less that they are human-ist. What all this amounts to is a kind of attempt to re-instate a philosophy which, for all its claims, refuses in the last resort to commit itself, not only from the political or social standpoint, but also in the deeper philosophical sense.[12]

The current situation, in fact, is such that all the continental philosophies and ideologies, or nearly all, would call themselves humanistic, in much the same way as they call themselves democratic, when what they are after is not so much a political as a moral content for their doctrines. In Britain, on the other hand, though not in the United States, humanism is not a term in much theoretic use, and its philosophical potential, such as it is, has attracted few takers if any. This may be because time has not solved the semantic ambiguities of the term by attaching to it determinate doctrinal qualities; there is still no readily identifiable body of theory called humanism, nor does the adjective humanistic applied to the different ideol-ogies appear to denote any common property among them that could constitute its meaning. The 'Concise O.E.D' (1982 edition) defines humanism as:

> A moral or intellectual system that regards the interests of mankind as of supreme importance, in contradistinction to individualism or theism.

But these distinctions would be deemed arbitrary and would be rejected by existentialists and 'religious' humanists.

In point of fact humanism, as philosophical term as distinct from concept, seems to have made its first appearance in France in the second half of the eighteenth century, and was subsequently introduced into Germany. Feuerbach's philosophy with its emphasis on the humane and with its reduction of the divine to the humane, was termed humanism or 'humanistic realism'.[13] But humanism was first given a consistent 'though utopian and simplistic' philosophical embodiment in Marx's writing where humanism in considered the final stage of communism

and the ultimate realization of progress, while the
social and economic conditions prevalent in capitalist societies are described as 'dehumanizing'.[14]

Describing   particular   social   conditions   as
dehumanizing is, evidently, saying that they are
contrary to the humane. Marxists have characterized
dehumanizing conditions in terms of different forms
of alienation which describe the varying kinds of
relationships into which individuals are conditioned
to enter as a consequence of living within capitalist socio-economic conditions.   And opposition to
these conditions constitutes one form of expression
humanism takes in the lifelong education literature.
Theorists like Gelpi and Vinokur, for instance, and,
more especially, Bogdan Suchodolski, who claims that
lifelong education 'represents an entire philosophical system centred upon man and his creative
development', clearly take off from the Marxian view
that what is distinctively human about human beings,
namely their capacity to be creatively productive,
is thwarted under certain socio-economic and cultural conditions.[15]

Suchodolski who attempts a description of humanism
to back up the lifelong education programme, departs
from the declaration that 'Life in itself is not
valuable' - a life worth living requires effort, it
requires 'willingness to take risks, and sometimes
to fight'.[16]   It would in fact be a mistake to
equate it with continuous tranquillity. Rather it
should mean acknowledging uncertainty, even the
possibility of defeat.   In order to collocate this
mentality with the humanistic tradition, he says, we
have   to   go   back   to   Greek   tragedy   and,   more
specifically,   its   underlying   idea   that   'man's
greatness and freedom are founded on his courage in
taking decisions which seem to him right, even if he
knows   that   as   a   consequence   his   life   may   be
destroyed by gods or men'.   Christianity, Suchodolski says, undermined this Greek concept of 'tragic
guilt' and replaced it with a different principle of
guilt revolving around the idea of original sin and
requiring not 'the willingness to take risks, and
sometimes to fight', but 'penitance and redemption'.
In our modern secular societies, he continues, 'the
notion of guilt innate in the human race has been
replaced by the ideas of defeat, calamity and ill
luck'.   The new humanism, Suchodolski says, needs to
restore the Greek idea of tragic guilt, tied as it
is with the notion of freedom, to the centre of the

human stage, and this means that it must first teach human beings to accept responsibility for all their affairs. Such responsibility requires acknowledgement not only of the authorship of our actions but also of the consequences of decisions based on an act of selecting our particular way of life out of many other possible ways. For the human race in general, he says, what is required, on the other hand, is the acknowledgement of responsibility not only for the present but for the remote past, and the future also. In short, Suchodolski concludes,

> We are using the notion of Humanism in the modern sense. It is connected with the classical European tradition, but its essence consists in the conception of the world created by man for man.[17]

Its major enemy in modern life is, as we have seen, the differing forms of alienation human beings encounter in contemporary societies. It is for this reason that Suchodolski proposes 'a 'learning society' in which the whole existence of man would be centred on education' as a positive humanistic response.[18]

After Marx, a few scattered attempts were made by Hegelians to establish humanism as a new moral philosophy, but it was not until Heidegger's *Letter on Humanism* that the term was once more attributed real significance in German philosophy, and Heidegger's humanism is radically different from Marx's because both his philosophical perspective and his interests are different. His interest in humanism is also different to that of a fellow-traveller like Sartre. For Sartre, existentialism is a humanism first and foremost because of its atheism, because it sees man as abandoned in the world; a being who must create his own meanings and values. This was the position of Nietzsche also, but Heidegger's is sensibly different in that his stance is more open than that of both, as is shown by the following set of statements:

> The being whose manner of being is existence is man. Man alone exists. A rock is, but it does not exist. A tree is, but it does not exist. A horse is, but it does not exist. An angel is, but he does not exist. God is, but he does not exist. The sentence 'Man alone exists', in no way means that only man really is and that

all other beings are unreal or illusions or ideas of man.[19]

This makes his humanism less anthropomorphic than Sartre's and less 'existentialist' also, since according to his own statement, what interests Heidegger principally is not the question of man's *Existenz* (the question in its form first raised by Kierkegaard) but that of 'Being in its totality and as such'.[20] Yet at the same time the true meaning of human existence itself is to be sought in the realms of Being as a whole. So this means that Heidegger rejects, just as conclusively as every other existentialist from Kierkegaard onwards, the view that there is any human 'essence' to which we need to make appeal in our understanding of humanity; actual human existence is not for him, as it was for Marx, a description of an actuality that can be compared with an ideal, it is *the only actuality*. This is why, for Heidegger, 'it is not correct to speak about humanism in general, a term which philosophically lacks meaning and is something like a 'lucus a non lucendo''.[21] What we have to try to understand is the nature of the relationship between human being and the world, which is inevitably an historical one, engendered by the fact that he is 'thrown' into its arena and must strive within it for authenticity.

Science, Heidegger insists, together with the other existentialists, is not the way to study this relationship, since it itself is simply a manner of such being. Thus, not only can it not define human nature, it itself needs to be defined ontologically as a subordinate category in the *existential analysis of Dasein*.[22]

SCIENCE AND SCIENTIFIC HUMANISM

Existentialism, in fact, disclaims the value of science or any form of systematic theory: it therefore rejects any form of historical dialectic and pins its faith rather in ontology and phenomenological research as the way of coming to a proper understanding of human being. Marx, in contrast, described historical or dialectical materialism as 'scientific'. So also, in his view, is his definition of the human essence. Marxian philosophy therefore, in this sense as in many others is a recognizable off-shoot from the humanism

of the Enlightenment which, similarly, believed both
in the possibility of a science of humanity, and in
the possibility of rendering such a science into a
tool for utopia. But it is not only Marxists who
have shown this faith in these twin potentialities
of science. Indeed faith in scientific engineering
is so widely diffused that quite often, humanism
itself is simply equated with *positivism*. As such
humanism is frequently accused of projecting itself,
on the basis of the successes of the technological
revolution, as the new world religion; its dogma, as
a religion being science itself, while its 'core' is

> a supreme faith in human reason — its ability
> to confront and solve the many problems that
> humans face; its ability to rearrange both the
> world of Nature and the affairs of men and
> women so that human life will prosper.[23]

So popular is this 'faith' said to have grown, and
so deep and wide has it penetrated our mentality
that it is said to lie at the heart of our modern
civilization, being subscribed to, even if unconsciously, by all developed countries alike and by
most of their members. It is further claimed that
this very confidence in the all-conquering power of
science has produced under the name of humanism an
attitude towards life that is arrogant, manipulative
and exploitative.

This is an important criticism since, in *Learning to
be*, we are told that any educational action, in
order to be democratic, must lay stress on:

> A common conception of what may be described as
> 'scientific humanism'. It is humanistic in
> that it is mainly concerned with man and his
> welfare as an end in itself; and it is
> scientific to the extent that its humanistic
> content remains defined — and thereby enriched
> — by the continuing new contributions of
> science to the field of knowledge about man and
> the world.[24]

The report, in fact, makes frequent reference to the
fact that the kind of humanism it envisages is a
'scientific humanism' (although it attempts no
further definition of the concept), and this may
partly explain its embroilment with 'utopia'.[25]
In point of fact the term 'scientific humanism' does
have an antecedent history of its own in the United

States, where humanism was affiliated with the emergent evolutionary science:

> `scientific humanism is rooted in the assurance that there is an understandable regularity behind the pattern of events, and that there is therefore sound hope of the ultimate achievement of a synthesis of knowledge to be reached by multiplying and co-ordinating our efforts and seeking the broad and long view of the processes in nature and society'. In the same way as all species evolved materially and biologically through countless generations, man evolved also spiritually and keeps evolving towards a higher realization of his being (one is tempted to use an Aristotelian term — entelechia).[26]

And this sense of the term was retained and further elaborated in the writings of Julian Huxley whose humanism was similarly provoked by the belief that science could, and eventually would, unite the whole of humanity in one faith and one global community. Storer quotes Huxley as writing in 1946, when he (Huxley) was working with the task force shaping the United Nations Organization:

> A world organization cannot be based on one of the competing theologies of the world, but must, it seems, be based on some form of humanism.... a world humanism...., a scientific humanism...., an evolutionary humanism.[27]

Storer continues to say that Huxley was quoted at the time as believing it possible `to establish a moral system which was purely scientific in inspiration and which would be capable of uniting mankind'.[28] And this belief, in effect, accorded with his assessment of the current state of human knowledge itself, as reflected in scientific achievement. For Huxley believed that through the unifying perspective of an evolutionary approach to life it was possible to harness the knowledge explosion of the previous hundred odd years or so since Darwin within one single unitary framework. Huxley was in fact convinced that though human knowledge is still highly incomplete it is at the same time comprehensive in its scope, in the sense of covering every aspect of reality, of the whole world of human experience. It thus, he further believed, gives humanity the tools it needs for a comprehensive vision of planetary evolution such as it has never before had, and such as makes the human management of the world possible.

There are no ambiguities about Huxley's ambitions for evolutionary science in this respect:

> Finally, the evolutionary vision is enabling us to discern, however incompletely, the lineaments of the new religion that we can be sure will arise to serve the needs of the coming era.... The emergent religion of the near future could be a good thing. It will believe in knowledge. It will be able to take advantage of the vast amount of new knowledge produced by the knowledge-explosion of the last few centuries in constructing what we may call its theology — the framework of facts and ideas which provide it with intellectual support; it should be able, with our increased knowledge of mind, to define man's sense of right and wrong more clearly, so as to provide a better moral support, and to focus the feeling of sacredness on fitter objects. Instead of worshiping supernatural rulers, it will sanctify the higher manifestations of human nature, in art and love, in intellectual comprehension and aspiring adoration, and will emphasize the fuller realization of life's possibilities as a sacred trust.[29]

And when he translates this vision into educational terms, the coincidence of his thinking with that about lifelong education, which is not all that surprising given his early involvement with the setting up of UNESCO, becomes very clearly evident. One could quote extensively, but two brief extracts from *Essays of a Humanist* will serve to give the reader an idea:

> education will acquire a new social dynamic: from being merely a preparation for life, it will become an integral part of life, an instrument of man's evolution.[30]

and,

> With the combination of more automation, compulsory leisure, and greater spending power, we shall soon be faced with the task of extending our educational system to meet the

needs of the entire adult population. Education in the ordinary limited sense seems destined to become only a part of a comprehensive and continuing process. Perhaps we should look forward to the establishment of a National Education Service.[31]

In effect, the attempt to combine the Huxlian brand of scientific humanism with the lifelong education programme is made most explicitly not by the report, but by Kirpal, who links this evolutionary vision with its natural correlate, a Hegelian metaphysical historicism. Thus for Kirpal, for whom civilizations are made and the course of history shaped by the 'spirit of man' acting out its diverse manifestations, there is currently a crisis in our contemporary civilization which arises from the fact that 'Man's technology and the social organization have far outstripped his spirit, resulting in a state of confusion and chaos, the loss of moorings and directions'.[32] Yet, at the same time humanity already possesses the tools and the disposition for its redemption:

The human spirit is now fortified by the attitudes and fruits of science and a new assertion of humanism. The humanism of the past was based upon man's discovery of himself, followed by liberation from taboos and dogmas accepted in fear and superstition. The humanism of tomorrow seeks to substitute love for power, stresses the brotherhood of man and his common humanity, and probes toward a new relationship of man with the cosmos. It aims at an act of transcendence which is within the reach of man, who is now more than ever the maker and arbiter of his destiny. The final aim of lifelong education is transcendence from the confused and troubled state of contemporary man to a new humanism, both human and cosmic, free, wise, compassionate and loving.[33]

Kirpal expressly states his belief that these objectives are imminent for mankind and that the key to them lies in Huxley's evolutionary humanism, which permits humanity, if it so wishes, to 'transcend itself, not just sporadically, in individuals here and there, but in its entirety, as Humanity'. [34]

Many humanists with a different orientation from the

scientific humanist do not however share the view
that humanism should take on, or has taken on, the
aspect of a world-religion. Kurt Baier, for instance, dismisses the very idea that it can be described as a religion or dogmatism of any sort; it is
not even a sharply defined philosophical position,
he claims.   In its modern form, he says, it is in
fact directly descended from Renaissance humanism in
that:

> Both emphasise man's capacity to improve his
> condition in his earthly life through his own
> efforts within the framework of suitable organ-
> izations.   Both oppose established and uncrit-
> ically accepted authority, including that of
> the church, and both accept the ideals of human
> dignity, autonomy and freedom.[35]

It cannot therefore be implied to support dogma or
to be itself dogmatic.

Still, it is clear that the identification of humanism with positivism is not unjustified, even if one
leaves out the claims of scientific humanism, since,
as we have already observed, the association of
humanism with science has a long intellectual history dating back to the Enlightenment. Positivism
is itself the fruit of this association; through it
humanism expresses its confidence in the methods of
science - the capability of science to ensure human
progress through the engineering potential of its
methodology in all the areas of human life: in economics, psychology and genetics, in demography, and
even in the human and moral sciences. Philosophers
like Hume and Hartley, Helvetius and Bentham, were
among those who perpetrated this confidence, though,
as Passmore observes, it formed part of the general
mental frame of most of the eighteenth century philosophers.[36] The philosophical success of positivism owed as much to the growing suspicion among
philosophers of purely deductive systems or of the
possibility of applied deductive reasoning to the
moral sciences (techniques that had engaged Hobbes,
Spinoza and Locke's confidence) as to the growing
faith in 'probable reasoning' which could also be
given mathematical form.

Nor did the positivist faith in the all-round
applicability of logical and mathematical forms of
inquiry and of the tools of science die with the
age. Its strength within the philosophical circles

of the early part of our century is well known and
its optimism has remained unabated up to our times.

Passmore says:

> In our own century the mathematical theory of
> games has aroused similar hopes. It has been
> recommended not only as a tool for understand-
> ing economic behaviour and international rela-
> tions but even as a reliable method of deter-
> mining   what moral policy it is best to adopt.
> [37]

In fact not only has positivism continued to be a
robust philosophy, it could also be argued that this
century, which has experienced a dramatic explosion
of scientific knowledge and technological expertise
hitherto unknown to human kind, has brought within
humanity's grasp many of the Enlightenment's more
ambitious engineering aspirations to an extent that
could even appear to make arrogance justifiable,
were it not for the sobering memories of two world
wars and of our harrowing experience of nuclear
warfare, for the accounts of degradation and murder
that have emerged and continue to emerge from
totalitarian countries where technological efficiency is ready at the disposal of oppressors, were it
not for the images of famine and death that imbue
one more with the feeling of helplessness than un-
limited power. Moreover, the nightmarish possibilities depicted in the writings of a Zamiatin or an
Orwell render fear as much as optimism a reasonable
attitude to adopt towards the technological revolution.

But fear of the consequences of positivism, justified as it may be, does not itself make the positivist's faith in the power of science an arrogant one.
Ehrenfeld's book tries to prove that it is.   It
develops accordingly into one account after the
other of different 'scientific' engineering attempts
in genetics, agriculture and so on that have come to
grief, usually with little publicity but at considerable consequent human cost. MacIntyre, for different reasons, does the same thing; he similarly
quotes examples from the social sciences to 'explode
the myth' that has grown around the supposed expertise we have acquired in 'human mangement' — the
belief in a 'science of efficiency'.   MacIntyre
recalls the Machiavellian concept of 'Fortuna', the
'bitch-goddess of unpredictability' in human life,

and argues, as Machiavelli did, that it is inelimin-
able from human affairs because its sources are
humanly uncontrollable.[38] MacIntyre shares Ehrenfeld's pessimism about our age, and, like Roberts,
who confidently predicts the demise of secular humanism, he believes that the source of the human
predicament, and therefore it solution also, is
ethical.[39] What mankind requires, he argues, is a
new moral project which restores *virtue* to the centre of the stage of human affairs, rather than science.

MANIFESTOS AND CONSENSUS

The convergence of humanism with positivism is,
however, a far from complete one. The true fact is
that, rather than demonstrate the unity of belief
and outlook that are characteristic of a faith held
in common,

> 'it is apparent that humanists today are almost
> as widely dispersed in moral standpoint as the
> 'community' of world religions'.[40]

According to Storer then, if one could properly use
the word 'religion' to describe the contemporary
state of humanism it would be to emphasise its
schisms rather than it acquisition of any unitary
outlook positivist or otherwise. In point of fact,
for Storer, humanists *do* share a number of
'emphases' in common, but being only emphases the
positions they share can only be stated very
generally, and to refer to them as emphases is to
make the point implicitly that they are not to be
regarded as dogmatic principles. These emphases he
itemizes as: concern for the importance of human
fulfilment, a measured freedom, the dignity of the
individual, a factor of situational relativity, and
a broad spectrum of human rights as cornerstone to
the structure.

Are there any grounds for optimism that these
emphases (many of which are challenged within
Storer's book itself) will, in some foreseeable
future at least, be developed into something more, a
tighter consensus, a more specific statement of
principles within a unitary ideological frame? The
closest explicit attempts in this direction are the
appearance of humanist 'manifestos'. The first of
these dates back to 1933, it was signed by thirty

four leading American personalities in the academic
and cultural world, and it included the name of John
Dewey. Its fifteen articles have been described as:

> a blend of tenets of 18th century Enlightenment
> and worship of reason, of utilitarianism a la
> Bentham of positivism and Darwinism, of 19th
> century absolute faith in the power of science
> and so on, not without a considerable touch of
> American pragmatism.[41]

The Manifesto, in fact, like Huxley, deliberately
refers to humanism as `a religion' where `religion
consists of those actions, purposes and experiences
which are humanly significant' (art.7), it being
understood that one's conception of the `signif-
icant' changes with time, though all religions, the
Manifesto says, have at least one common aim of
realizing the highest values of life, and all share
a common framework: a total environing situation
(theology or world view), the sense of values resulting therefrom (goals or ideal), and the technique
(cult) established for realizing the satisfactory
life.[42] At the same time, it asserts, `the nature
of the universe depicted by science makes unacceptable any supernatural or cosmic guarantees of human
values' (art. 5), and declares that `the distinction
between the sacred and the secular can no longer be
maintained', since `nothing human is alien to the
religious' (art. 7). Furthermore it continues to
consider the `complete realization of the human
personality' in the here and now of its existence to
be the end of life (art. 8). All associations and
institutions are therefore to be taken to exist
precisely to ensure such realization; this is `the
explanation of the humanist's social passion' (art.
8). And to this end `The intelligent evaluation,
transformation, control and direction of such associations and institutions with a view to the enhancement of human life is the purpose and programme
of humanism'. (art. 13) The Manifesto further declares its opposition to a `profit-motivated' so-
ciety and its contrary commitment towards a `social-
ized and co-operative economic order' for the
`equitable distribution of the means of life',
declaring as its final purpose, `a free and univer-
sal society in which people voluntarily and intelligently co-operate for the common good'. (art. 14)

Giustiniani, whose article I have used rather liber-
ally in this chapter, reacts to the Manifesto with

the comment that 'On the whole, the humanist *Mani-festo* claims to be rather a new brand of faith than a philosophy of man'. As a faith, he says, it even has a 'church' to go with it, the American Humanist Association with branches in Britain and elsewhere. These humanist associations and clubs, on the other hand, he continues to say, take different forms, and this is not surprising for what adherents find especially attractive is the very permissiveness of the Manifesto.[43] Indeed many self-declared humanists take this permissiveness to be its very virtue since it forestalls a hardening of its principles into dogma. Thus Paul Kurtz, the principle architect of a *Humanist Manifesto 2* argues that no tighter definition of a humanistic programme should be sought *because* this would immediately transform humanism into what its critics already say that it is and what, in fact, it should not be, namely a new dogmatism.[44]

The permissiveness of the humanist manifestos arises from the fact that a humanist ethics necessarily transcends both national and cultural borders. To be truly humanist it needs to apply to all persons in all societies, it needs to be an ethics of the human race. In short, it needs to assume the existence of a human community. And this fact returns us to the criticisms raised by Rousseau against any similar assumption, a criticism raised also in Storer's book by Schneider who observes that

> A humanist ethics and humanism in general aim at standards for mankind rather than local moralities. But this ideal of a morality for all mankind as a whole is still largely theoretical, for mankind is not a whole.[45]

And yet it is an ideal that is clearly not dead. Besides scientific humanism, the manifestos and the proliferation from them of societies and clubs that declare their allegiance to it, it is given expression in contemporary times, as Kolenda points out, in the shape of a number of international political and economic initiatives, in cultural organisations like UNESCO itself, and in an internationally accepted Charter of Human Rights which is, in effect, no more and no less than a manifesto of humanist ethics in its own right. Still it is an ideal which, Kolenda argues, continues to be as naive and abstract today as it ever was. People who continue to promote it, he says, do so because

they choose to ignore some crucial empirical facts.
Namely that:

> From all over the world we get signals that in
> its drive towards self-determination each
> region insists on making use of its own
> traditional experiences as embedded in social
> structures, economic patterns, art forms and
> religious beliefs.[46]

And, in his sense, he is undoubtedly right. The
contemporary signs are not that the ideological
frontiers are melting away, quite the contrary in
fact, one need only observe such political phenomena
on the international scene as the recent upsurge of
religious fundamentalism in Islamic countries like
Iran, Pakistan and Libya, for instance, or at the
current state of the ideological war between East
and West, to dispel this illusion.

Kolenda argues that the dream of a cosmopolitanism
breaking down not only cultural but also national
boundaries is not only unreal when confronted with
the political facts of life in contemporary times,
it is also dangerous in theory, however it is
achieved. For there is always the possibility that a
"world government" will fall into the wrong hands.
For these reasons therefore 'consensual pluralism'
is, he concludes, both a more realistic state of
affairs and a safer alternative to strive for, for
'In contrast to the vague, abstract code of world
unity, consensual pluralism is piecemeal and
concrete'.[47] Its strategy, he says, is in line
with Popperism extended on a world scale. It depends
on the willingness of the sides in the debate,
wherever it occurs, to be 'fully rational', in the
sense that they bring into the negotiations a review
of all the existing values and motivating principles
that are in play exposing their particular roles in
the game, that they lay on the table all the relevant rights, obligations, and potential benefits and
losses accruing to the different proposals, and,
finally, that they seek solutions in open deliberation.

Rationality, in this sense, Kolenda says, does not
exclude 'hard bargaining', but it does exclude
blackmail and ruthless pressure which, he says, work
directly against the key moral principle at stake;
the desirability of voluntarily embraced consensus.
Kolenda makes the important point that the objective

of building this kind of consensus depends on the
assumption that claims reasonably put forward by
parties seeking consensus have a *moral basis*.
Finally, though he rejects the likelihood or
desirability of an eventual cosmopolitanism, or of a
single human political community he retains enough
faith in consensual pluralism to suppose that:

> Consensus added to consensus will gradually
> help to build a comprehensive moral code for
> the entire planet, eliminating distrust and
> enlarging harmony.[48]

CONCLUSIONS

What emerges clearly from the discussion of the
previous sections of this chapter is not only that
humanism or, better, self-declared humanists, dis-
agree widely among themselves on points of belief,
principles and definition, but that within a more
narrowly defined humanism as a secular philosophy
opposed to the transcendental and stated in permissive terms, there are also problems of formulation
and strategy. The implication of Kolenda's article
is that any humanist manifesto must in fact be so
stated as to permit the cohabitation within it of a
pluralism of ideologies. But it is not clear that
Kolenda would support the need for any such manifesto. Indeed the very question whether manifestos,
in general, are good things to have or not is itself
hotly debated among humanists. Thus, in Storer's
book, while James, R. Simpson suggests that 'The
Humanist Manifesto II is accepted in its entirety as
a guideline for an international ethics of development'.[49] Alistair Hannay criticises its central
aim as misguided because it attempts to codify what
it describes as 'radically new human purposes and
goals', in order to replace 'traditional moral codes
and newer irrational cults' with them. In his opposition to this exercise Hannay argues that:

> Whatever faults the codes and cults may have, I
> cannot believe that moral codes can be
> generated by debate, or that having them
> endorsed by persons of academic standing and
> good will, or both, is the way to give moral
> directives effect. Or even that moral codes are
> good things.[50]

In fine, as analysis of the theories held by

humanists about humanism shows little agreement
about how it can present itself as a coherent
programme even where there is an agreement on
'emphases'. Should the humanist project be a
cosmopolitan one guided by the long-lasting ambition
of the global integration of the whole of humanity,
political, moral, or cultural through the possession
of a common ideology or faith in 'science'? Or
should humanists support a strategy of consensual
pluralism? Will the well-being of humanity be advanced by the communication of humanist manifestos,
or should humanists renounce having manifestos or
any separate ideological pretensions and simply
encourage the working of the 'humane spirit' through
other ideologies, as is the implied alternative to
the having of manifestos? These solutions have all
been variously proposed and contested by humanists.

The concept of a world community is a useful one to
hold even if it presents problems theoretically and
may be undesirable and far-fetched as a political
reality. For the acknowledgement of a body of *human*
rights to which it gives rise is both politically
positive in itself and a useful implement to bring
to bear on governments for the protection of
citizens, even those that may appear impervious to
moral pressure. Kolenda's argument that they can be
made substantial and effective by means of a
strategy of consensual pluralism has its difficulties and its limitations. To start with the latter,
it is clear that this pluralism suggested by Kolenda
can only be acceptable if the ideologies included
are compatible with broad humanist moral principles.
So the area of debate will be bound to be smaller
than the world to begin with, since some ideologies
at least will be excluded from the consensual debate
ab initio — fascism and different forms of racism,
for example.

More fundamentally, the very principle of
'consensus' when applied to moral as distinct from
political matters, is of questionable value. For it
is a well known principle, lucidly argued for by
Mill and others, that consensus over a thing or a
course of action does not itself make it either
right or good; if a thing or course of action is
right, etc., it must be so on grounds other than
consensus, though consensus is a desirable condition
for its politicization or adoption as socially
significant action. This means that the humanist
can only accept consensus as a desirable *procedural*

principle, for it is clear that, *prima facie*, consensus is always a preferable basis for civil or political practice than is force. But that is all; it cannot be the ultimate criterion of the good and the right. The limiting condition to its application from the moral point of view is that no humanist can, *qua* humanist (and therefore logically also), accept any course of action as legitimate, however supported or based, which directly or otherwise offends against the dignity of the individual person or which devalues the moral life of the collective, once it is assessed as so doing.

Yet at the same time whatever the defects of Kolenda's principle of consensual pluralism, it appears to be the only theoretically acceptable political procedure for the improvement of mankind, both at the level of international politics and at that of the national or local. Such procedure, as Kolenda points out, is compatible with the Popperian preference for 'piecemeal engineering'.[51] Also, the idea of letting the 'humane spirit' work informally through the established political ideologies is certainly a positive one; a humane Marxism is a more acceptable face on politics from a humanist point of view than what currently goes by the name of 'real socialism', while a humane liberalism is similarly preferable to a laissez-faire capitalism.

But is a body of human rights accompanied by the procedural principles of consensual pluralism a sufficient core for an education programme? It would be if the same procedural principles gave the body of human rights a well-defined substance that would qualify them as a set of normative commitments of a definite kind. But this is precisely where humanism fails to be of any help. We have, in fact, in this chapter, established some of the difficulties with pinning humanism down theoretically, either by considering it as a cultural project or as a 'philosophy of man', or by appealing to the usage of the term by self-declared humanists, or by turning to the history of philosophy itself. Sartre by describing existentialism as 'a humanism' implies that, rather than a theory or ideology in its own right, humanism is more of a defining property of other theories or ideologies. Others have tried to pin the concept down with a charter or manifesto without, of course, thereby imposing any copyright on the term. The Marxist manifesto, which takes up a well-defined ideological position, would, presumably, claim to *define* humanism (since its point of departure is a theory about what it is essentially to be human), while the Humanist Manifesto of the American intellectuals, by virtue of its very permissiveness, disclaims the view that humanism is an ideology, and this, subsequently, has been the line of many self-declared, non-Marxist, humanists. These have been inclined to hold that permissiveness is a good thing, and are content with having a manifesto, if at all, that is stated as a number of 'emphases' that most would accede to, rather than any ideological commitments.

We have seen how the Faure report declares 'scientific humanism' to be the culture of the lifelong education programme. But there is little or no explanation of what this means, although the evolutionary perspective and optimism that marks the history of the term itself and the work of Huxley, one of its major proponents, is found everywhere within it, and even more so in Kirpal's article. On the other hand we have seen how the permissiveness of the Humanist Manifesto seems to suit the temper of the lifelong education movement which, in fact, also shows this reluctance to express any definite ideological commitment and is more inclined to declare its general support for 'democracy' and individual self-realization and decry the conditions of 'alienation' in contemporary society and consumeristic cultures, while leaving the terms themselves politically imprecise. This does not mean that its theorists are not also politically active or that there are no political aspirations behind the practice of lifelong education. Quite the contrary in fact, the concept has attracted the interest of different associations, organizations and activists whose work in the field of adult education is intimately tied with political objectives that can be very definitely identified with the broad Left in the European political spectrum, though there are no similar political affiliations with the concept in the English-speaking countries where the tendency is to concentrate on the difficulties of bringing more learning to the adult population via new technologies and learning strategies. The contrast, in fact, between the outlook of adult educators in European and Third World Countries on the one side and the English-speaking ones on the other can be reduced to the fact that where the latter appear to view adult education as a commodity to be efficiently distributed in time and space, the former view it more as a cultural project demanding the active participation of the learner in face-to-face encounters, and it is this, last mentioned, perspective that is projected by the movement, whose sympathies reflect this strong orientation towards the political traditions of the Left in Europe, though this may be guarded because of the requirements of working within a UNESCO framework.

A consensual pluralism could, in fact, be the defining characteristic of the lifelong education movement's aim, as a movement. Its programme would thus avoid the excesses to which a scientific humanism is prone, given its utopic visions of the world and its openness to a form of dogmatism rendered the more dangerous by its very claim to being 'scientific'.[52] It would also facilitate the acceptance of pragmatism as the fundamental epistemic tool of the programme, and a hermeneutic philosophy as its culture. At the same time it would enable that same programme both to escape Power's warning that while it is easy to be misled by the pretensions of a vaguely defined humanism, it is even easier when humanism is not defined at all, [53] and to avoid the worst aspects of having manifestos; their necessary vagueness and permissiveness engendered by the requirements of universality which means that, in trying to be suitable for all contexts, they usually finish up by being relevant to none. But the problem of ideological commitment remains, since the formal principles that would define the substance of the body of human rights which the programme would protect are as yet undefined, although it exists already and is scattered as rhetorical statements through the literature. The evident choice of a philosophy to provide these principles while coordinating with the conditions just described, is one that is both pragramatic and hermeneutic and consistent with a 'participatory' democracy, central to the political ideology of the theorists mentioned above. The nexus of these conditions will be seen to exist already in one man's philosophy.

NOTES AND REFERENCES

1.   Aristotle, *Ethics*, Thomson, J.A.K. (ed.) (1979) p. 329 (Harmondsworth, Penguin)
2.   The quote is from   MacIntyre, A. (1981)

After Virtue, p. 157 (London, Duckworth)

3.   Quoted in Worsley, P. (1975) *Modern Sociology*, p. 269 (Harmondsworth, Penguin)

4.   Quoted in Giustiniani, V.R. 'Homo, Humanus, and the Meanings of Humanism', pp. 181 - 182, *Journal of the History of Ideas*, Vol. XLVI, No. 2, April - June 1985.

5.   Russell, B. *History of Western Philosophy*, p. 94 (London, Allen and Unwin, 1971 edition)

6.   This position is held in one form or other by all contractarian and liberal theorists; the theory being that society being the creation of individuals who come together from an original position (usually a 'state of nature'), it is therefore 'artificial'.

7.   Rousseau's criticism was meant as a reply to an article by Diderot on 'Natural Law' in the *Encyclopaedia* which reflected conventional ideas about the existence of a human community. Written for the *Social Contract* it was excluded from the final draft.   (Sabine, G.H. *A History of Political Theory*, p. 582 (London, Harrap, 1971 edition)

8.   Giustiniani, V.R. (1985) op. cit., p. 167.

9.   Power, E.J. (1982) *Philosophy of Education: Studies in Philosophies. Schooling and Educational Policies*, pp. 158-159 (New Jersey, Prentice Hall)

10.   Roberts, C. 'The Three Faces of Humanism and Their Relation to Problems of Science and Education', p. 168, in: Sloan, D (ed.) (1979) *Education and Values* (Columbia University, Teachers College)

11.   Roberts, C. (1979) op. cit.

12.   In Sartre, J.P. (1945) *Existentialism and Humanism*, pp. 62-63 (Harmondsworth, Penguin, 1982 edition)

13.   See Giustiniani, V.R. (1985) op. cit., p. 175.

14.   ibid., p. 176.

15.   Suchodolski, B. 'Lifelong Education - Some Philosophical Aspects', p. 77, in: Dave, R.H. (ed.) (1976) *Foundations of Lifelong Education* (Oxford, Pergamon).   Suchodolski claims that lifelong education must be 'deeply rooted in the social circumstances which determine the motives of human action'. Such circumstances must make it possible to view education as the most essential value of life. This cannot happen if 'man finds himself in surroundings that are hostile and alien to him,' for in similar surroundings 'education cannot be the dominating factor in life.' Suchodolski concludes: 'In philosophical terms, one might say that the indis-

pensable condition for the realization of the programme of lifelong education is to overcome alienation'. (pp. 71-72)
16. ibid., pp. 87-88.
17. ibid., p. 88.
18. ibid., p. 83.
19. These sentences from Heidegger's *Letter on
Humanism* are quoted in Macquarrie, J. *Existentialism*, p. 29 (Harmondsworth, Penguin, 1985 edition)
20. The quote is taken from a letter Heidegger
wrote to Jean Wahl (see: Passmore, J. *A Hundred
Years of Philosophy*, p. 483 (Harmondsworth, Penguin,
1972 edition))
21. Giustiniani, V.R. (1985) op. cit., p. 178.
22. Heidegger, M. *Being and Time* (Translated:
Macquarrie, J. and Robinson, E., Oxford, Blackwell,
1980 edition)
23. Ehrenfeld, D. (1981) *The Arrogance of Humanism*, p. 5 (Oxford University Press, Galaxy Books)
24. Faure, E., et. al. (1972) *Learning to Be*,
p. xxvi (London, Harrap)
25. There is a whole section in the report
entitled 'Towards a Scientific Humanism' (p. 146
ff.) which falls within Chapter 6 on 'Goals' but it
offers no further elaboration of the statement quoted in 24 and cannot be considered enlightening.
26. Giustiniani, V. R. (1985) op. cit., pp.
179-180.
27. Storer, M. B. (ed.) (1980) *Humanist Ethics*, p. 2 (New York, Prometheus Books)
28. ibid., p. 3.
29. Huxley, J. (1964) *Essays of a Humanist*,
pp. 91-92 (Harmondsworth, Penguin)
30. ibid., p. 134.
31. ibid., p. 149.
32. Kirpal, P.N. 'Historical Studies and the
Foundations of Lifelong Education', p. 98, in:
Dave, R.H. (ed.) (1976) *Foundations of Lifelong
Education*, op. cit.
33. ibid., pp. 106-107.
34. ibid., p. 108.
35. Baier, K. 'Freedom, Obligation and Responsibility', p. 75, in: Storer, M.B. (ed.) (1980)
Humanist Ethics, op. cit.
36. Passmore, J. (1970) *The Perfectibility of
Man* (London, Duckworth)
37. ibid., p. 202.
38. MacIntyre, A. (1981) *After Virtue*, pp. 99-
100, op. cit.
39. Roberts, C. 'The Three Faces of Humanism
and Their Relation to Problems of Education and

Science', in: Sloan, D. (ed.) (1979) op. cit. :
'Another great upsurge of human vitality can thus be
expected, but in contrast to that of the Renaissance
this rebirth will be ethical in nature. And we can
be equally sure that anthropocentric humanism will
not have the slightest chance of withstanding the
force of this pure theocentric thrust'. (p. 174)
    40. Storer, M. B. (ed.) (1980) *Humanist Ethics*, p. 3, op. cit.
    41. Giustiniani, V.R. (1985) op. cit., p. 178.
    42. The copy of the Manifesto quoted from here
is found in: Kurtz, P. *American Philosophy of the
Twentieth Century*, pp. 368-371 (London, Collier-
Macmillan, 1969 edition)
    43. op. cit., p. 179.
    44. Kurtz, P. 'Does Humanism Have an Ethic of
Responsibility?', in: Storer, M. B. (ed.) (1980)
op. cit.
    45. Schneider, H.W. 'Morality as an Art', p.
99, ibid.
    46. Kolenda, K. 'Globalism vs. Consensual
Pluralism', p. 108, ibid.
    47. ibid., p. 113.
    48. ibid., p. 114.
    49. Simpson, J.R. 'Towards a Humanist Consensus in Ethics of International Development', p. 131,
ibid.
    50. Hannay, A. 'Propositions Towards a Humanist Consensus in Ethics', p. 179, ibid.
    51. See Popper, K., *The Open Society and Its
Enemies* Vol. 1. (London, Routledge and Kegan Paul,
1974 edition) Popper contrasts 'piecemeal engineering' with 'utopian engineering'. The latter consists of the 'attempt to realize an ideal state,
using a blueprint of society as a whole'. (p. 159),
and the former will 'adopt the method of searching
for, and fighting against, the greatest and most
urgent evils of society, rather than searching for,
and fighting for, its greatest ultimate good'. (p.
158)
    52. Power, E. J. (1982) op. cit., p. 158.
    53. See Feyerabend, P. (1978) *Science in a
Free Society* (London, NLB). Feyerabend has a section called 'The Prevalence of Science a Threat to
Democracy'.

Chapter Four

HUMANISM IN CURRENT EDUCATIONAL THEORY AND LIFELONG EDUCATION

HUMANIST EDUCATIONAL THEORY

What we have not done yet is to investigate from a narrower perspective whether there is not a self-described humanist position in educational theory as such, and how, if there is, its orientations can be described. A suitable way to answer this question would seem to offer itself immediately through the other history of the term humanist than the one that has occupied our attention so far. From this alternative perspective it actually comes to describe both a kind of learning and the kind of scholarship related to this learning. The 'humanist' as a scholar was one dedicated to 'learning for learning's sake, *otium*, remaining within the limits of human knowledge, aimed at neither transcendence nor practical purposes'.[1] The 15th century 'humanista' in the Italian universities studied and taught *humanae litterae*. These usages of the term in its different derivations within the other European languages have remained constant since through the centuries that have followed, notwithstanding some temporary aberrations. One would therefore be pardoned the assumption that, even today, the traditional humanistic curriculum must constitute the central focus of any current self-defined humanist education programme if any exist. It therefore comes as some surprise to read the following comment:

> Humanistic education is more a diffuse and
> multiplex phenomenon than one that may be
> sharply caught and defined. Although in its
> own apologies it distinguishes itself quite
> dramatically from other educational systems,

> its rationale is elusive and the educationist
> must find his way through a series of exhorta-
> tions, general statements on education and
> life, anecdotes of personal success, and rec-
> ipes for particular methods. One rarely finds
> extended statements of educational theory that
> give enough detail and elaborated justification
> with which to concur or not.[2]

For it is immediately clear that the article from
which it is taken cannot be referring to the same
tradition.

In point of fact Williams and Foster, the joint
authors of the article, while making this
evaluation, cite as their point of reference an
entry that appeared in the 1971-72 *Education Index*,
where mention is made of a `new' humanism in current
educational thought.[3] Not only does this `new'
humanism show no continuity with this tradition, it
also shows no continuity whatsoever with that faith
in the power of human institutions to contribute
towards the betterment of life which Baier identified as part of the modern conception of humanism
inherited from the Renaissance. On the contrary it
is extremely sceptical, if not downright antagonistic, towards all forms of institutionalized learning, most especially schooling, and emphasises the
value of personal autonomy in its most radical form.
In fact, for the roots of the kind of theoretical
individualism suggested by the `new' humanism one
needs to go back to the anti-Enlightenment naturalistic philosophy of Rousseau's *Emile*, which similarly aligns itself `in favour of the individual as
an educational good in itself, and as prior to consideration of the individual's contribution to society'.[4]

Power, independently of Williams and Foster, writes
about `romantic' humanism as constituting a
distinctive if ill-defined trend in contemporary
educational theory. He also attributes to this
trend the same characteristics attributed to the
`new' humanism by the latter, distinguishing within
it the same kind of radical subjectivism and
eventually describing it as follows:

> what we shall call romantic humanism exudes an
> abundance of self-sufficiency and self-
> confidence. Tilting on the verge of arrogance
> it turns its back on the past, finds nothing of

much worth in tradition, and justifies the
motives of each person to find his own satisfaction in a face-to-face confrontation with
reality.[5]

It is interesting to note that the basis of the
`arrogance' identified by Power arises not from a
faith in science but in a faith in the self-
sufficiency of the individual. It denotes a courage
which was impossible for the philosopher of the
polis, who was firmly convinced that the very nature
of human being is social, and is unacceptable for
philosophers who present a communal ideal of man,
like Marx and Dewey. It was forced, briefly, on the
`skeptical' philosophers of the Hellenistic schools,
nearly conclusively buried by Christian theology,
and finally revived in a most resounding manner by
Nietzsche's pronouncement that `God is dead'; his
metaphor not only for the dissolution of religious
faith but for `the devaluation of our hitherto
highest values' - those of the Enlightenment as much
as any other.[6] Nietzsche's pronouncement, of
course, later became the point of departure of
atheistic existentialism.

Existentialists have consistently rejected the
notion that their analysis of the human condition
properly constitutes a `philosophy' in the usual
sense of the word where it applies to the
systematization of thought into the disciplined
formal expression of theories. Their position is
that no such systematization is possible, nor is it
required, to this extent they even reject the necessity of science. They argue that the generaliza-
tions to which systematization leads are necessarily
false, and this is a view that is tacitly echoed by
the `new' or `romantic' humanists (the second term
will be used exclusively from here on since it is
more significant and less likely to cause the reader
confusion). Both Williams and Foster, and Power, in
fact, observe the discomfort of `romantic' humanists
with philosophy, and Power confirms that their orientation instead towards the kind of psychology
connected with the personality theories of Rogers
and Maslow, is pursued at the expense of philosophy
which `scarcely gets a look-in'. The general situa-
tion in this respect is that

Few humanists are eager to shape any systematic
philosophy of education, and many of them worry
about the stultifying effect such systemat-

ization could have on educational aspirations.
[7]

For this reason one cannot properly speak of
'romantic' humanism as constituting a 'school',
though the word movement may not be inapt since it
allows for a greater degree of permissiveness in the
ranks, though even a movement needs some coordinating ideas and principles in order to be so defined
beyond the rejection of a systematic philosophy of
education. The radical writers identified with it
by the authors (Kozol, Holt, Silberman, etc.)
represent, in fact, a group brought together not by
any unified perspective on educational practice but
by their general dissatisfaction with 'school' and
other manifestations of institutionalized learning,
a dissatisfaction that, at times, borders on nihil-
ism. So the resemblances are clearly there, and it
comes as no surprise when Power suggests that if one
were to 'shop around' for a philosophical position
with which 'romantic' humanism could align itself,
the 'natural choice' would be existentialism, for,
as he says, it alone has the temperament that would
appeal to the new humanism's 'romantic' orientations. At the same time, however, we are also war-
ned by Power not to make too much of this fact because, he says, though 'romantic' humanists may eventually claim existentialism as their creed, this is
not the case at the moment, nor is any such align-
ment imminent judging by the actual state of the
movement.

EXISTENTIALISM

Richmond similarly says about lifelong education
that 'Philosophically, it might be designated as an
existentialist or phenomenological view' At the
same time a comment reminiscent of Power's about
'romantic' humanist education warns immediately that
'it seems advisable (however) to refrain from any
such pretentious labelling'.[8] It will also. be
recalled that when Cropley described humanism as the
'philosophy' of the lifelong education programme he
put the word 'philosophy' inside inverted commas,
and said that the programme in fact could only
'loosely' be called humanistic. Again, it needs to
be noted that when Richmond attaches the lifelong
education programme philosophically with existentialism he does so without making any further quali-
fications; it must therefore be assumed that he is

alluding not to some tendency within the movement but to the movement as a whole.

But it is clear that, on this last point, he cannot be right. This is because we have already uncovered different traits within the literature of the movement that have nothing to do with existentialism. Indeed critical reference has already been made in Chapter 2 to Cropley and Ireland's separate and independent identification of a `utopic' and `pragmatic' trait; neither author so much as mentions existentialism. And yet Richmond's observation is not wrong; it simply focuses on the literature from a different perspective to Cropley's and Ireland's. One recalls, for instance, in Cropley's own definition of lifelong education according to the UIE literature, that he refers to the ultimate aim of the programme as `the self-fulfilment of each individual'. The question was raised in that place as to how self-fulfilment could be conceived, in particular whether it can make space for the community, as Dave's lifelong education programme demands.[9] If self-fulfilment is conceptualized subjectively, then it will be the basis for a different lifelong education programme with orientations towards existentialism. Still, nowhere does one encounter any *explicit* statement of lifelong education as an existentialist programme. So Richmond can only be reading it into the movement's literature, just as it is only to be read into the `romantic' humanist educational theory. Or else the literature itself could be aligned with `romantic' humanist theory directly perhaps?!

Before any incursions are made into this possibility, however, it is first necessary to say a little bit more about the relevant aspects of existentialism as a philosophy. It has already been observed that its pregenitors are taken to be Kierkegaard and Nietzsche. The first was primarily concerned with the question `How can I become a Christian?' while the second asked the apparently contrary question how it is possible to live a Godless existence. The point of similarity between the two lies in what they both denied, namely the standard or conventional solutions to the problems they posed, insisting instead on complete subjectivity — each and every individual must come upon truth and come to terms with it in his own way unaided by the pronouncements of popular opinion. For both the standard sought is that of *authenticity*. Kierkegaard's individual

becomes authentic to the extent that his relationship with God is personalized, since although conformity with God's will is still the end of man, the
content of that will cannot be *known* to humanity in
the shape of universal principles. For Kierkegaard,
in fact, the individual as a particular is higher
than the universal and is justified against it not
the other way around.[10] While for Nietzsche authenticity lies in the pursuit of the *ubermensche*, of
that 'higher self' which 'does not however lie deeply hidden within you, but immeasurably high above
you, or, at least, above that which you usually take
as yourself'.[11] For both, the authentic person is
one who 'chooses himself', and authentic existence
is one based on faith and commitment to it, rather
than science and reason. This is how Passmore describes the convergence of their two philosophies
into existentialism:

> Both philosophers concern themselves passionat-
> ely, if diversely, with the human situation;
> they both reject as a delusion all abstract,
> objective, systematic, philosophy; for both of
> them 'life is more than logic'. 'It makes all
> the difference in the world', Nietzsche wrote,
> 'whether a thinker stands in personal relation
> to his problems, in which he sees his destiny,
> his need, and even his highest happiness, or
> can only feel and grasp them impersonally, with
> the tentacles of cold, prying thought'. That
> might be Kierkegaard talking — or any existent-
> ialist. Again, both Kierkegaard and Nietzsche
> see in 'essences' a device men use to tame the
> world, to reduce it to something indifferent
> and stable. The 'real' world, they tell us, is
> historical, 'existential', revealed as such to
> the courageous human agent, but lying beyond
> the understanding of abstract thought, which
> always, by its nature, deals in types. And
> Nietzsche, like Kierkegaard, bitterly attacks
> the Philistine, the mediocre man, whose highest
> ideal is to submerge himself — to do 'what is
> done', to be 'Man' as distinct from 'a man'.
> [12]

The more representative figures in existentialist
thought since have kept faith with this programme,
emphasizing the subjective element in human life and
relating it to the crucial questions of freedom,
decision and responsibility as they converge on the
problem of personal or authentic choice. Such

choice is rendered difficult, according to the existentialist, by our 'facticity'; by the fact that we are *thrown* into a world that predates our existence and is not of our own making. We are, furthermore, made to struggle within it because of the very nature of our own Being which is different from that of other beings also thrown into the arena of life in the sense that we alone are self-conscious about our own existential predicament. Or, put in another way, human beings are the only beings whose existence is an issue for themselves, they are therefore the only beings whose relationship with the world is typically that of 'care'.[13]   This means that choice is always a necessary condition of human life, it is always, to some extent, inescapable, but it is only authentic choice that enables us to 'stand out' as individuals.   Authentic choice, on the other hand, is the contrary of 'bad faith', and 'bad faith' consists as much in our failure to recognize our personal autonomy of choice as in our failure to recognize the significance of other moral consciousnesses in our lives besides our own.[14]

Macquarrie, in fact, says that probably all the leading existentialists pay at least lip-service to the truth that man exists as a person only in a community of persons.   But, at the same time, he continues to say: 'in the main they are concerned with the individual whose quest for authentic self-hood focuses on the meaning of personal being',[15] to the extent in fact that they find themselves involved in paradox.   This is because contrasting with their lip-service to the essential communality of human beings most existentialists retain a characteristic attitude to the 'Other' that is in accord with Sartre's, who views the 'Other' as one who, of necessity, by his very being, sabotages my possibility to make choices that are free. Within it the primordial relationship in which human beings stand to each other and to the rest of the community is one of *conflict*, as the 'Other' poses genuine limitations to the pursuit of personal authenticity. Furthermore, this latent antagonism between the individual and the rest is implied by the very fact of existentialism's subjectivism, from the very fact that each person is forced to pursue his own authentic life-project *ex-nihilo* and for himself.   Thus:

Since another human being cannot be the effort of transcendence that I am, and within which I experience and give meaning to my world, he can only *know* me and my world in the objective mode and this knowing collapses the properly evaluative dimension of my actions and leaves them stranded as so many natural events awaiting another evaluative interpretation which may or may not coincide with mine.[16]

Thus, the most common criticism levelled against existentialism from the point of view that is educationally significant is that it lacks any real social or moral explanation, and this is because existentialists are typically uncomfortable when it comes to measuring the criterion of authentic existence against the essential communality of human being.[17] Van Cleve Morris summarizes the content of the paradox as it presents itself to the existentialist as follows, quoting from Whitmarsh:

The problem which (existentialism) poses is a seemingly elementary one: Is not man thrown into a world which he did not create, confronted with obligations of a communal existence, forced to comply with the imperatives of an anonymous society, and continually faced with the inevitability of his own death – is not man, so conceived, incapable of justifying his own existence? [18]

The existentialist argues that reason seems to drive us to answer 'Yes', to this question, but the puzzle is, says Van Cleve Morris, that this answer is, at the same time, unacceptable to man; he is therefore haunted by this paradox which appears unconquerable by reason. The only response that remains to him lies in the 'blatant thrust beyond reason' towards a zone where values are created in the act of an individual living a life. Morris says that in such a situation, 'To encourage the young to invade this zone and stake out their own plots there – this is an Existentialist education'.[19]

LIFELONG EDUCATION AND 'ROMANTIC' HUMANISM

A comparison between the characteristics of the educational theory of 'romantic' humanism, as identified by Williams and Foster, and Power, and certain prominent aspects of the lifelong education literature reveals some very close similarities of viewpoint between them. With reference to the former, both sets of authors agree on its main theoretic framework such as exists; that the major influences on it come from the humanistic psychology movement of the 1960s, more particularly from the work of Rogers and Maslow whose psychotherapies are based on fulfilment theories of the personality. At the same time Williams and Foster identify within it a rationale couched in a sociological context characterised by two main factors: a stress on the rapidity of change in the environment calling for a new type of educated person able to cope with such change, and, an attempt to mitigate the effects of alienation on human beings living in technological environments. The thrust of humanistic psychology in response to these twin factors is toward a theory of motivation, with an emphasis on the growth of self-awareness as an ultimate good.

Williams and Foster further point out that, eventually, this emphasis, as is to be expected, is directed towards objectives that focus upon the self-realization principle in life, a principle which implies that 'the thrust of human activities in healthy persons is towards growth, fulfilment and creativity'. The principle, they say, is given its theoretical shape by Rogers, who 'Crystallizes his philosophy of the person as he works through therapy'. In accordance with the aims of this therapy:

> The client will move away from facades; he will move away from 'oughts'; he will move away from pleasing others; he will move toward self-direction, toward being process, toward being complexity, toward openness to experience, toward acceptance of others and toward trust of self.[20]

And Maslow similarly emphasises this 'auto-centred' approach, his theoretic approach being, like that of Rogers, radically subjectivist. For both, the focus is on the individual who, for good measure and consistently with naturalistic philosophies, is also regarded a *priori* as being essentially good and perfectible.

As in therapy, the central aim of the educational outlook of 'romantic' humanism, the authors continue, is to make the learner progressively more self-aware, more in touch with himself, his own uniqueness, how he differs from others. There is therefore a centring of authority within the learner himself which, taken together with the therapeutic pedagogy implied by humanistic psychology, evidently transforms the typical role of the educator away from its traditional form. So that it actually comes to resemble that of the therapist, its central task being to develop within the learner an attitude of responsibility towards his own learning.

The lifelong education literature shares all these tendencies, beginning with the sociological context. Lifelong education theory similarly locates its own rationale and justification within societies that are undergoing change at an accelerated rate pressed on directly or indirectly by the effects of a scientific and technological revolution which has assumed the proportions of a veritable 'knowledge explosion' in our times. This 'knowledge explosion', in turn, renders the traditional view of education as the transmission of a stock of knowledge from one generation to the next and as the forming of a stereotyped personality, irrelevant. [21] Thus the Faure report speaks about the need for a new education for a 'new' individual, one who both understands change in its different effects and dimensions, and is able to cope with it and turn its potential to positive outcomes.[22]

From a narrower angle than the above Power states that the common theme of 'romantic' humanism is exhibited most clearly in its criticism of traditional schooling. And this again is another clear point of similarity it shares with the lifelong education programme. One recalls among Dave's 'concept characteristics' one that refers to the lifelong education programme as providing 'an antidote to the shortcomings of the existing formal education system' (13). And the criticism goes far beyond that of historical irrelevance just referred to. In his book on Gelpi, Ireland provides a synthesized list of the objections against existent schooling recurrent in the lifelong education literature and these are, in essence, very close to the ones attributed to 'romantic' humanists by Williams and Foster, and Power.[23] Thus Power, for instance, says that the main charge 'romantic' humanists level against schools is that they are 'little more than assembly lines perpetuating a conspiracy against individuality by accepting a commission to produce a standard product', this neglect of individuality being typically described as 'dehumanizing' for the learner.[24] And the same accusation is made on the

side of lifelong education by Lengrand who similarly
complains that no consideration is allowed in
schools for individual differences of character. On
the contrary pupils who do not conform to pattern
become marginal, as do those whose rate of
development is slower than the 'average'. Moreover,
he argues, the need for selection prevails over
pedagogical considerations and failure is thus
institutionalized at the cost of senseless wastage
of intellectual and monetary investment. Education
should, Lengrand says, allow every individual to
develop in accordance with his own nature and as a
function of learning capacities that are his own,
not in terms of ready-made models suited for one
kind of personality, that of the 'gifted' pupil who
learns easily and does not question the school
order. Finally, and from a slightly different point
of view, he charges schools, as presently organized,
of resting on a truncated conception of the human
personality in that the capacity to acquire knowledge is given precedence over all other forms of
expression; emotional, social, aesthetic or physical. They therefore adopt a learning programme
which not only has the practical effect of fragment-
ing the personality but also of separating the individual from life.[25]

All these tendencies are appearing at a time when,
lifelong education theorists argue, the human personality is already constantly menaced with
'abstraction', threatened with falling victim to
elements within our contemporary civilization that
conspire to divide it, to break up its unity. Lengrand is not the only one who emphasises these
'alienating' effects of the modern situation on persons, Suchodolski and others do so also. In
addition, however, Lengrand, like the Faure report,
repeatedly accuses the school of contributing
greatly to the 'dissociation of the parts of the
personality' which is the main symptom of this
alienation. This is because, corresponding with the
priority given to knowledge acquisition, the school
arbitrarily isolates one aspect of the personality,
the intellectual aspect in its cognitive form, as
being alone educationally relevant while the other
aspects are forgotten or neglected and either
'shrink to an embryonic state' or develop in a
disordered fashion, threatening the very balance of
the personality. In this situation, Lengrand
argues, some essential elements of the human person
are actually either atrophied by schooling or else

are temporarily, and even, sometimes, permanently, paralysed.[26] While the Faure report says:

> The neglect and disdain from which some elements of educational programmes continue to suffer, the deficiencies and imbalance of curricula appear to us to be among the most serious symptoms of the disease of which education is both the symptom and the cause. The separation of its intellectual, physical, aesthetic, moral and social components is an indication of alienation, undervaluation and mutilation of the human person.[27]

And again we find this tendency to separate education from life similarly constitutes the grounds for serious complaints levelled against schooling by 'romantic' humanists. Couching their objections similarly in the language of 'relevance' they ask how schooling can be educationally relevant when in schools 'thought' is falsely divorced from 'life' which, they argue, is the crucible of real not fictional problems. And, in any case, they insist, the question of relevance is not one that can be decided by the school since, in fact, it is really a personal one and as such requires a private verdict not a statement of policy. For these reasons there is a tendency among 'romantic' humanists to conclude that traditional schooling is largely a waste of time while, at the same time and for the most part, drawing back, like the lifelong education movement, from the inference that the whole concept of school be abolished.

The Faure report, in effect, regards the deschooling thesis an an 'extreme' one based on the erroneous postulate that 'education constitutes an independent variable in each society'.[29] What is in question for lifelong education theorists is not whether school in itself is important or necessary, but whether it is a good thing in its current form. From this point of view the problem is not only that current schooling preserves the outworn formulae of the past but also that it continues to project the same dichotomies of the past, and there can be no remedy for this situation, lifelong education theorists hold, before schools recognize that, at a time when abstract knowledge is coming to be viewed more and more as part of a continual process acting on and reacting to daily life, new solutions are required. For on such recognition depends the further recognition that the common stream of education in schools should combine theory, techniques and practice, intellectual and manual labour. The dislocation of these different combinations constitutes in concrete form the much criticized separation of education from life; its consequence in psychological terms is that the child's personality is split between two worlds each discordant with the other; one in which it learns like a 'disembodied creature', and the other in which it fulfils itself through some 'anti-educational' activity. A conclusive comment on this issue is that:

> most education systems do not help their clients – whether they be youngsters or adults – to discover themselves, to understand the components of their conscious and unconscious personalities, the mechanisms of the brain, the operation of the intelligence, the laws governing their physical development, the meaning of their dreams and aspirations, the nature of their relations with one another and with the community at large. Education thus neglects its basic duty of teaching men the art of living, loving and working in a society which they must create as an embodiment of their ideal. [29]

Yet another point of agreement between the two sides relates to their criticism of the monopoly the school has always exercised on education. That monopoly, both argue, helps to conceal the insufficiency of what is on offer as against the real educational needs of contemporary individuals. Both, therefore, emphasise the educational importance of the wider society. 'Romantic' humanists, rather surprisingly, insist that 'social interaction' is the great educator'; but the explanation could be that they view such interaction as a way to 'curb the school's pretensions'.[30] Similarly, the Faure report argues that the school must be transcended by 'broadening the educational function to the dimensions of society as a whole'. It quotes Plutarch, in this connection, who said that 'the city is the best teacher', approvingly, and, of course, devotes much space to the elaboration of the principles and practices of the 'learning society'. [31]

Williams and Foster refer to the seven goals which Roberts has claimed to be the main ones for a humanistic education. These concern:

> personal development (the student becomes more
> in touch with himself and knows more about
> himself); creative behaviour (originality,
> creativity, imagination, new interpretations,
> novel meanings are valued); inter-personal
> awareness (how people influence each other);
> subject orientation (the focus is on the stud-
> ent's feelings about a whole subject); specific
> context (both affective and cognitive learning
> of a specific bit of course content); method of
> teaching (effective possibilities for teaching
> and learning); and teachers and administrators
> (the educator as a growing person and model for
> the students).[32]

Roberts' goals, they point out, are further developed by a set of 'imperatives' designed by Fairfield
to implement them in educational settings.[33] In
the context of the comparative analysis that is the
object of this section, what is especially interesting about these 'goals' and 'imperatives', because
they are so close in essence (and sometimes even in
description) to those distinguished in various places by lifelong education theorists, is their provenience. They are, Williams and Foster say, inspired:
(1) by the Social Education movement, which sought
to foster cooperative individualism through education; (2) by Progressive Education, whose common
principles were seen by Dewey as the 'expression and
cultivation of individuality, free activity, learning through experience, acquiring new skills as a
means to attaining ends, concentration on the 'here
and now', and acquaintance with a changing world';
and (3) by the Open Education movement which 'encourages an equally active role for teacher and
learner' in order to 'develop greater classroom
democracy with an emphasis on a cooperative sharing
environment'. [34]

LIFELONG EDUCATION AND EXISTENTIALISM

Evidently we could continue to cite other statements
and positions held in common in confirmation of the
fact that 'romantic' humanism as an educational
theory shares its more consistent orientations with
elements in the lifelong education literature.[35]
The identification of this convergence between the
two is made more consistent by their separate iden-

tification with existentialist thinking. This is not enough however to establish with any firmness the relationship of lifelong education theory itself with existentialism, nor to explain the nature of that relationship. This is the matter to which we must turn next in this section, and we can start by observing that within the lifelong education litera- ture there is the same pronounced awareness of the psychological pressures to which people living in an environment of accelerating change are exposed, particularly when the technology is used in a so- cially irresponsible or malicious manner and is turned to utterly materialistic purposes, as one finds in existentialist writings. There is the same sensitivity to the dehumanizing effect of a consu- meristic mass culture that is shared also by exis- tentialist writers, Jaspers most especially, and that makes a personalized and utterly individualis- tic outlook appear as the only intelligible alter- native to the threat of alienation posed by such a culture to the individual personality and, more especially, its sense of identity.

Reference has already been made to Suchodolski's brand of humanism. The central contention of Suchodolski's essay is that people today are faced with the threat of alienation from many sources in both capitalist and socialist countries (though more so in the former). Lifelong education, or indeed any positive educational action, is impossible, he argues, where these conditions of alienation exist; the first strategy of the 'learning society', therefore, must be to overcome the forces of alienation within itself by reassessing its own cultural values. The existentialist, of course, with his profound distrust of collective action, does not believe this strategy possible, and a somewhat similar doubt seems to lie at the core of the thinking within the 'pragmatist' trend in lifelong education theory, which does appear to hold out hope of internal revolutions through education, but which also pins its faith in this possibility on 'progressive' individuals rather than on any form of collective action. The existentialist will respond to the threat of the modern world by emphasising the value of the personal and subjective both in terms of educational and cultural action, and his counter- part among lifelong education theorists is to be found in such as Paul Lengrand, who similarly holds that 'Modern man is the victim of abstraction', and for whom the appropriate educational response does not focus on collective action but is similarly personalized.[36] Lengrand, in fact, affirms the value of individuality in all its forms and *per se*. He argues that before the 'challenges of this age' which a highly technologized culture provokes, there are two responses open to the individual that correspond, in turn, to the existentialist's distinction between an inauthentic and an authentic existence; either passivity, an attitude of resignation and surrender, 'watching the cauldron of doctrines and beliefs without great concern over their contradictions and changes of front', or the acceptance of responsibility, the recognition of 'the obligation to be oneself'.[37]

One thing that is clearly attractive to lifelong education theorists about existentialism is that it offers, as Lengrand's argument indicates, an ultimate justification for their programme, for it makes education the price of 'freedom' one needs to pay in a continuously challenging social milieu: 'In one sense, the modern individual is condemned to autonomy, obligated to freedom', and this obligation carries with it the price of education — 'education which never ceases, which mobilises every capacity and every resource of being, whether from the intellect or from the heart and imagination'.[38] In fact, lifelong education is made necessary for Lengrand by the fact that it is only by being in a situation where one can fight the obstacles and challenges continuously met with in a meaningful way that one is demonstrating one's humanity, and in each case the nature of the combat is a purely personal one and requires personal solutions.[39] From this point of view, he believes that the best that the educator can do for the learner is to put him in a position where he can fend for himself, where he comes to be autonomous, and the same contention is made by the Faure report. Self-directed learning is therefore made the general aim of all formal learning by both, and indeed by all lifelong education theorists besides, who revert to the concept of 'educability' which, in turn, is translated into different conditions for the achievement of learning autonomy, which include the appropriate forms of motivation and skill, to give it form.[40]

In effect, having rejected the view that education has primarily to do with the transmission of knowledge, or of a culture, or has anything to do with imposition of any kind, Lengrand concludes, employing an existentialist jargon, that:

> Education is not an addendum to life imposed
> from outside. It is no more an asset to be
> gained than is culture. To use the language of
> philosophers, it lies not in the field of
> 'having' but in that of 'being'. The being in
> a state of 'becoming' at each different stage
> and in varying circumstances is the true sub-
> ject matter of education.[41]

If the individual is always 'becoming' then his
education, which intimately concerns his 'being in a
state of 'becoming'', must always be in some sense
incomplete and ongoing because the very nature of
his existence demands it. The same conclusion derived from considering the nature of being is also
reached from the existentialist point of view, where
being is characterized by the constant need to
choose, since choice is always to some extent
demanded of the individual as a condition of life
itself. Even in the most restrictive of circumstances, existentialists tell us, we are obliged to
choose, since, however restrictive these may be, a
minimal possibility of choice is always *logically*
possible. At the same time, however, this 'formal'
autonomy is meaningless because it is merely logical, it has no human or moral value. It is only the
effective autonomy of authentic individual choice
that has such value and is therefore of worth. It
is thus that Lengrand and Suchodolski insist upon
the value of 'responsibility'. It is, they say,
absolutely incumbent upon the individual to take
over his own cultural and educational project as the
very assertion of his humanity. Thus Lengrand insists that it is vital both for the learner and for
the educator to have an authentic conception of
both. From the point of view of culture this amounts
to an understanding that:

> A man's culture is the sum total of the efforts
> and experiences through which he has become
> steadily more himself. These efforts and exper-
> iences, even if he shares them with thousand
> and millions of human beings, are his own and
> relevant only to himself. Culture only exists
> to the extent to which it has been lived and
> tested within the particular history of a man
> who is leading an existence, who is building a
> life, who is conscious of the universe and who
> takes part in its shaping by his own decisions.
> [42]

Contrasting with this conception of culture there is another 'geographical' outlook which the individual is continuously presented with and which he needs to avoid if he is to affirm himself as a person, a culture of 'bad faith'. The 'geographical' concept of culture sees culture not as a personal possession but as a 'self-contained domain comprising the sum total of knowledge accumulated over the centuries'. As a domain one has the option of entering or staying outside. Moreover, once one enters one comes to occupy more or less of this territory depending on chance and other factors. Thus, the 'geographical' concept of culture divides the world into the cultural rich and the cultural poor, the privileged and the victims, the initiates and the uninitiated.[43]

Corresponding to these different conceptions of culture, there are for Lengrand two ways in which the human phenomenon can be viewed, both of which are significant to the manner in which the educator may choose to approach education; one is the 'sociological', the other is the 'psychological' or 'philosophical' (it is significant that he brackets the two together). The first, he says, is 'monopolised by the masses, by the forces at work, by structures and institutions, and it is those they consider important'. The second, that which, he says, should impel educators, is:

> conscious primarily of human existence in its individual form. What interests them (educators) above all is the single, unique, irreplacable life-story of an individual, the awakening of a consciousness, the whole set ways of thinking, feeling, and establishing relationships with himself and with the world which are peculiar to the individual, his own particular way of tackling and solving the problems he encounters both outside and within himself, which is, and always will be, different from other people's ways.[44]

Indeed the orientation the practice of education should take once we get these perspectives right practically suggests itself of its own accord. For, Lengrand argues, the psychological/philosophical approach clearly assumes that the aim of the educator is to help form the mind, the body and the character, and where else, he asks somewhat rhetorically, do mind, body and character belong but 'within the restricted and yet limitless space of a particular individual in the context of his own being and becoming?'.[45]

This individualist and auto-centred philosophy of education comes strongly across from other quarters within the lifelong education literature also. Thus we find the Faure report declaring that 'Teaching, contrary to traditional ideas and practice, should adapt itself to the learner; the learner should not have to bow to pre-established rules for teaching',[46] and 'The new educational ethos makes the individual the master and creator of his own cultural progress',[47] and finally, '(education) is no longer focused *on* the learner, nor anyone, nor anything else. It must necessarily proceed *from* the learner'.[48] And if we return to Cropley's defining principles of lifelong education as recognised by the UIE, referred to in earlier pages, we find the same reference to the self-fulfilment of each individual as the ultimate aim of education, and to the value of having the skill and the motivation to engage in self-directed learning activities placed above all others.

CAN THE LIFELONG EDUCATION PROGRAMME BE AN EXISTENTIALIST ONE?

The question is, *can* the lifelong education programme be a straightforwardly existentialist one? One must beware not to confuse it with the different question whether existentialism can supply the basis for a lifelong education programme, which it clearly can. The issue it is meant to raise is not the latter one but whether the programme of the lifelong education movement, its operational definition in particular, as it appears in the literature, can be aligned with existentialist philosophy thus resolving the ideological ambiguities described in Chapter 2 and giving form to the programme's humanism. It needs to be understood also that the question is about the *theoretical* resolvement of the programme not the practical; in other words it is about *theoretical* possibilities. It asks whether the programme would continue to remain internally coherent and consistent if it is aligned with existentialism, and an answer to it must have two parts: first, it must involve consideration of the difficulties brought against existentialist thought with regards to its general compatibility with educational practice - in other words, it needs to see whether the credentials of existentialism as an educational theory are right; second, it must see whether there are not any *a priori* objections to the attachment of the movement's programme with existentialist thought based on some conflict of defining principles between the two.

Starting with the first, there are evidently serious difficulties involved with bringing existentialist thought in general to bear on educational practices, because such practices are typically assumed to involve institutional arrangements, namely the presence of schools and teachers; these, in turn, are considered indispensable in any sophisticated society for the transmission of its culture, on which its very continued existence depends. A consistent existentialist outlook, it would appear, must logically view schools or any form of collective learning within some form of institutionalized framework as undesirable. Power says:

> At best, existentialism's advice to education is vague. After adverting to existentialism's fundamental subjectivism and pluralism, not much remains on the level of philosophical principle for application to any theory of schooling.[49]

It would also seem that existentialist thought, with its emphasis on subjectivism as the only truth, must be totally incompatible with any formal education since the latter implies the presence of an educator acting upon the learner. The discussion of the other section, in fact, raised the point that 'romantic' humanists, who are of the same theoretic temperament of the existentialists, are typically unhappy with the very concept of school, while they embrace a conception of education as a kind of therapy involving a one-to-one relationship between learner and facilitator (the term 'teacher' seems an inappropriate one within this theoretic context). That they are nevertheless reluctant to throw over the concept completely accounts for their unwillingness to take over existentialist thought.

From another point of view one needs to recall the point made earlier that existentialism, with its psychological orientations, lacks a proper social philosophy; a proper theory of society. Thus while existentialists describe to us the kind of society we already have and furnish us with a phenomenological critique of the individual's existential condition within it, they nowhere tell us what, in effect, it ought to be in order to improve that condition; this is because they hold an aversion for prescription or theory. In fact, as we saw earlier, the lack of any social theory in existentialist thought does not so much denote a gap, a lacuna within it, as a necessary consequent of it. The question is, can an adequate educational theory be constructed in the absence of a social philosophy?

The difficulties with conceptualizing an existentialist education programme grows when education *means* schooling. For if by education we mean `school', then it is difficult to see how an existentialist philosophy can find a legitimate defence against the difficulties outlined above. For `school' is historically a social construct, a human invention of an institutional kind which presupposes the involvement of a cooperative enterprise with shared interests and beliefs, and a shared ethic; the need for all of which the existentialist denies, and the value of which he typically rejects. But if education is understood in a wider sense than `school' does a social philosophy continue to be required for an education programme?

Rousseau has furnished a theoretical account of how education can dispense with a social framework in Emile, while Illich and others have proposed a de-schooling philosophy. The stock reply to the former's naturalism is, however, that the social is re-introduced through the presence of Emile's tutor, while Illich replaces the school with learning networks that are `new educational institutions'. Within a more contemporary and practical viewpoint, an increasingly large amount of adult education is being done in the Freirian manner, outside `schools', without a formal curriculum, and with facilitators acting out therapeutic roles rather than traditional teachers — but this renders the learning situation, if anything, not less but increasingly social, and Freire's pedagogy, or andragogy, is backed by a social analysis and an alternative philosophy. Finally, not even a social doctrine of `authenticity' can replace a social philosophy proper, as Van Cleve Morris suggests it can do, for the very concept of an `authentic society' where `each individual takes *personal* responsibility for the law he obeys, the conventions he consents to, the values he appropriates for his own life',[50] is as impossible as the possibility of a General Will which will always reflect in practice the views of every single member of the society whose it is, which does not demand compromise of its members, and is not sometimes prepared to `force them to be free'.

On the other hand, societies have dispensed with schools in the past where all their specialized needs could be catered for by the training of a limited few by tutors. However, they were clearly not democratic societies, and the arrangement would most certainly fail to satisfy the increasing demands for specialized learning that characterizes all kinds of modern societies. As was pointed out earlier, Illich has suggested, theoretically, that societies can be deschooled. But again, though the suggestion is made seriously as a reaction to the effects on society which the pervasiveness of schooling engenders according to his own analysis, deschooling is not a possibility that he eventually canvasses adequately since his commendable efforts to combine individual freedom of action in learning with social cooperation must assume, in the absence of school or any formal substitute, that the ability for autonomous learning is either something one is born with or one can effectively win for oneself, or is something that can be left to peer interaction or parental guidance, and whereas the former assumption defies all evidence to the contrary, the latter leaves the child to the mercy of chance and parental good-will, which may not in itself be a bad thing in a perfect society where everybody's motives are the right ones (as in Skinner's utopia for instance), but not otherwise, in this imperfect world of ours where children often need to be protected from the intentions of grown ups, including their own parents.

At any rate we have already seen that lifelong education theorists do not accept the move towards deschooling society. On the contrary they are committed by their programme to a revised theory of schooling that fits with their reconceptualizing of education itself as a lifelong matter. Indeed, as we have seen, referring to the existent schooling system, one of Dave's `concept characteristics' speaks of the lifelong education programme as an 'antidote to (its) shortcomings' rather than as a radical substitution of it (13), and another retains the importance of 'formal institutions of education' as 'one of the agencies of lifelong education', though not the sole one (4). And existentialist philosophy, as our earlier discussion showed, can contribute nothing to these designs.

However even more fundamental than its theoretical incompatibility with the concept of school, which as we have seen, is considered indispensable by the lifelong education programme, the existentialist point of view is incompatible with the very having of an educational programme, lifelong or of any other description, since any programme, even a personal one, constitutes an attempt towards systematization and unity of outlook of some sort, and these are contrary to a subjectivist outlook. Thus, for instance, there lies a fundamental incompatibility between the kind of systematized synthesis that constitutes Dave's 'concept characteristics' and the radical individualism of existentialist thought. A response to it consistent with the latter would be to avoid such exercises as Dave's. But this is not a move open to the movement. Not that, in the eventuality, it would cease to remain a movement, for movements, as was observed earlier, can admit to different degrees of cohesion, the move is not blocked on *logical* grounds, but that systematization is essential for policy-making, and, as we have seen, if anything unifies the lifelong education movement it is agreement over the fact (as was pointed out in Chapter 2), which is also considered *the distinctive feature of the movement*, that its conceptualization of the otherwise bare idea of education as something lasting for life *includes the institutionalizing of that idea.*[51]

The fact that the lifelong education programme presupposes the need for social and political action in order to operationalize the concept also forestalls what would otherwise appear as an attractive compromise. It could be suggested that the existentialist outlook be left as a description of the *adult* component of the programme, with perhaps a type of schooling that would lead to 'authenticity', that would 'awaken awareness in the learner — existential awareness of himself as a single subjectivity present in the world'[52] (Van Cleve Morris certainly thinks it possible, though how it could be effected it is difficult to understand), as its other component.

Also, a connected objection to this form of compromise solution would be that, conceived of in this way, as a two-tier programme, one would be violating one of the programme's other fundamental principles, namely that within its perspective, the educational process should be viewed as a *unified whole*, as integrated both vertically and horizontally. In effect, a two-tier programme would simply restort to the situation current in most countries today, and to the situation in educational theory *prior* to the advent of the movement; before, that is, the lifelong education theorists took the bare idea that education should be for life and turned it into a programme. It would simply regard lifelong education as a purely personal project left to the perception of truly 'authentic' individuals without any social or institutional support. And this is a consequence none of the theorists within the movement would accept, for it would mean, effectively, the abrogation of the movement's programme. It would mean denying lifelong education the separate conceptual space its theorists have worked to give it within educational theory. Moreover, it would mean giving up the policy prescriptions with which they have filled that space and denying the very case they have made for these prescriptions.

CONCLUSIONS

In sum, it is clear that the lifelong education programme needs to look elsewhere than towards existentialism for its philosophical statement, though the attractions of existentialism are not to be denied, and its positive insights can still be creatively included. Among the former one could include the fact that existentialism avoids the problem of ideology by rejecting the need for one, and this makes it an attractive proposition for any who deliberately seek to avoid ideological commitment while asserting the value of individual freedom; both considerations that weigh heavily on UNESCO-sponsored projects or documents. But the price to be paid for these 'advantages' is an impossible one, for theoretic consistency demands that they can be won only through the effective sacrifice of the programme itself. Indeed, there exist within the lifelong education literature strong statements to

the effect that *self-education* is the only authentic
form of education, but the fact that they coexist
with further statements and with programmatic principles for the institutionalization of the concept
is an indication of the looseness of the theorizing
within it, or, at any rate, of the language in which
it is expressed - one problem with rhetoric in fact
is that it frequently contradicts itself.

On the other hand, the positive points are plenty,
though they require more than careful pruning of
their existentialist meanings.   Indeed they need to
be extracted from the whole framework of existentialism in order to bear fruit, and need to be re-
introduced within a social philosophy of some kind.
This means that the emphasis on individuality needs
to be tempered with some account of a just system of
cooperative behaviour within which the individual
needs to pursue his own life project and within
which the policy aspects of the education programme
need to be construed.   The phenomenological outlook
of existentialism gives us valuable insights into
the current state of our technological civilization,
which, in themselves, constitute a strong recommendation for continuing learning, but it cannot be
satisfactory to define an 'authentic society' simply
as one composed of authentic individuals and leave
it at that.   Existentialism merely tells us that a
truly human existence is 'authentic', and that the
'Other' poses a threat to its pursuit, it also
tells us that certain social conditions, those prevailing in modern societies, are potentially threatening to individuality. But it cannot tell us which
social conditions would make authenticity more possible, because such authenticity is, for the existentialist, by definition, pursued *against* society,
whatever its kind - the only answer is subjectivism.

A subjectivist educational philosophy, on the other
hand, renders impossible any concept of schooling
or any collective educational action - more especially the setting up of education programmes for the
purposes of policy making.   The subjectivist must
view lifelong education as a personal thing. These
are factors that render subjectivism unacceptable to
the outlook of the lifelong education movement. How
do other educational philosophies feature in this
respect? The next chapter is a critique of liberal
philosophy of education from a lifelong education
perspective - it is evidently an important one given
the very great influence of that philosophy.

NOTES AND REFERENCES

1. Giustiniani, V.R. 'Homo, Humanus, and the Meanings of 'Humanism'', p. 171, *Journal of the History of Ideas*, Vol. XLVI, NO. 2, April-June, 1985.

2. Williams, A.J., and Foster, L.E. 'The Rhetoric of Humanistic Education', p. 37, *The Journal of Educational Thought*, Vol. 13, No. 1, 1979.

3. The entry, according to the authors, defines the 'new' humanism in the following way: 'While traditional humanism views mankind in need of shaping from without because of an innate flaw, the new humanism sees the individual person containing within himself the power and pattern of his own development'. (ibid., p. 38)

4. ibid., p. 40.

5. Power, E.J. (1982) *Philosophy of Education: Studies in Philosophies, Schooling and Educational Policies*, p. 159 (New Jersey, Prentice Hall)

6. Cooper, D.E. (1983) *Authenticity and Learning*, p. 1 (London, Routledge and Kegan Paul)

7. op. cit., p. 161.

8. Richmond, K. 'The Concept of. Continuous Education', p. 75, in: Cropley, A.J. (ed.) (1979) *Lifelong Education: a stocktaking* (Hamburg, UIE Monographs, 8)

9. As is deliberately stated by Dave, and as is implied by the concept of 'vertical integration' (see Chapter 2, Note 31), which assumes as part of the individual's development his integration with the wider life.

10. *Fear and Trembling*. Also in the same work, in reply to the question, 'What is education?', Kierkegaard answers that it is 'the curriculum one has to run through in order to catch up with oneself'. (Bretall, R. *A Kierkegaard Anthology*, p. 125 (New Jersey, Princeton University Press, 1973 edition))

11. Quoted from *Schopenhaur as Educator*, in: Cooper, D.E. (1983) *Authenticity and Learning* , p. 14. op. cit.

12. Passmore, J. *A Hundred Years of Philosophy*, pp. 470-471 (Harmondsworth, Penguin, 1972 edition)

13. This formulation is Heidegger's (*Being and Time*) 'Dasein is an entity which does not just occur

among other entities. Rather it is ontically distinguished by the fact that, in its very Being, that Being is an issue for it'. (translated: Macquarrie, J., and Robinson, E. (Oxford, Blackwell, 1980 edition))

14. The concept of `bad faith' is Sartre's. In its simplest terms it means lying to oneself: avoiding making `authentic' choices and exercising self-deception in doing so. It is found explained in Part 1, Chapter 2, of *Being and Nothingness*, and in other places.

15. Macquarrie, J. *Existentialism*, pp. 16-17 (Harmondsworth, Penguin, 1985 edition)

16. Olafsen, F.A. (1967) *Principles and Persons*, p. 194 (Baltimore and London, The Johns Hopkins Press)

17. A notable exception is Sartre's in his *Critique of Dialectical Reason* where his attempt to effect a reconciliation with Marxism (with which existentialists have, more typically, contrasted their views) through a reinterpretation of the dialectical structure of human action, or *praxis*, necessitated his incursion into social psychology. Here Sartre is forced to admit that though obligations are initially (in the evolution of the community) self-imposed by individuals, and spontaneous, they eventually come to `transcend' the individual wills of the members of the formed community as an `absolute right'. Interestingly, Sartre, in this place, describes the pledge which brings the group into being, the contract, as `the beginning of humanity'. Otherwise Merleau-Ponty also admits to the existence of a social morality as `collective funded meaning' but is only prepared to recognize its importance as `facticity'.

18. Morris, V.C. (1966) *Existentialism in Education*, p. 104 (New York, Harper and Row)

19. ibid., p. 105.

20. Williams, A.J. and Foster, L.E. `The Rhetoric of Humanistic Education', p. 43, op. cit.

21. Thus, Faure, for instance, argues that as a result of accelerated change `*for the first time in history, education is now engaged in preparing men for a type of society which does not yet exist*'. This fact poses challenges for education which traditional systems concerned with reproducing the contemporary society and existing social relations, are not equipped to respond to. (op. cit., p. 13)

22. `The new man must be capable of understanding the global consequences of individual behaviour, of conceiving of priorities and shouldering his

share of the joint responsibility involved in the destiny of the human race'. (ibid., p. xxv)

23. Ireland, T.D. (1978) *Gelpi's View of Lifelong Education*, pp. 8-10 (Manchester Monographs 14, University of Manchester) The headlines are: (a) Formal education is expected to provide the basis for an individual's participation in society and the economy; (b) Education has been based upon a process in which the teacher teaches and the student learns; (c) The traditional role of school has been that of reproducing society and the existing social relations of society; (d) Because of the predominant equation of `education schooling', learning in school has become dissociated from other sources of knowledge; (e) Education has failed to achieve the measure of equality which was expected of it; (f) The failure to achieve the principle of education as a human right; (g) The expensive nature of education; (h) The unsuitability of outputs from the formal system; (i) The increasing tendency towards early specialization and the dichotomy between manual and intellectual disciplines.

24. op. cit. (1982) p. 160.

25. Lengrand, P. (1975) *An Introduction to Lifelong Education*, pp. 78-79 (London, Croom Helm)

26. op. cit., p. 95.

27. op. cit., p. 69.

28. ibid., pp. 20-21.

29. ibid., p. 66.

30. Power, E.J. (1982) p. 161, op. cit.

31. op. cit., p. 62.

32. op. cit., p. 39. The authors are quoting Roberts, T.B. `Seven Major Foci of Affective Experiences: A Typology for Education Design, Planning, Analysis and Research', in: Roberts, T.B. (ed.) (1975) *Four Psychologies Applied to Education* (New York, John Wiley)

33. ibid., p. 39. Reference is to: Fairfield, R. (1971) *Humanistic Frontiers in American Education* (New Jersey, Prentice Hall)

34. ibid., p. 40.

35. An interesting question is, where does this confluence of viewpoints between the lifelong education literature and `romantic' humanist education come from? The hypothetical answers could be different; for instance, the lifelong education theorists could simply be directly influenced by the writings of the radical `romantic' theorists, or the two viewpoints may owe their similarity to their independent derivation from similar cultural or philosophical roots. It lies outside my scope

however since it is an entirely empirical one.

36. op. cit., p. 95. Lengrand also states, with reference to lifelong education, that it is 'to remedy the destructive effects of modern civilization that the foundations of a new education are being laid'. (p. 96)

37. ibid., pp. 36-37. It is worthwhile quoting the full passage from his book in order to illustrate the point being made in this section: 'Every man is in fact faced with the same choice: either to adopt an attitude of resignation and surrender, watching the cauldron of doctrines and beliefs without great concern over their contradictions and changes of front; or on his own account to participate in research. Clearly, the second solution is alone compatible with a full and whole-hearted acceptance of the condition of man. For the right to be man is complemented by the duty to be man, and this means acceptance of responsibility: the obligation to be oneself; to be responsible for one's thoughts, judgements and emotions; to be responsible for what one accepts and what one refuses. How could it be otherwise at a time when there are a hundred ways of belonging to a spiritual, religious or philosophical community? In one sense, the modern individual is condemned to autonomy, obligated to freedom. This is a deeply uncomfortable situation, but a stirring one. It can only be sustained by one who is willing to pay the price; and the price is education — education which never ceases, which mobilises every capacity and every resource of being, whether from the intellect or from the heart and imagination'.

38. Lengrand contends, in true existentialist fashion, that 'Existence has always meant for man, for all men, a succession of challenges'. (p. 25) But, he continues, these challenges have taken new and sharper forms in this century which he deals with in a section of his book called 'Challenges that Face Modern Man'.

39. ibid., p. 47. Thus, for Lengrand, as for the Faure report, this 'new' individual who will be the product of a new education becomes 'a person in the fullest sense of the term'. This is because the new education concentrates on 'being rather than on having, and on having only to the extent that resources feed and sustain the individual in meeting the requirements and succeeding stages of his own development'.

40. Skager, drawing on the literature, synthesizes the qualities of educability as: (1) Self-

acceptance: one's positive view of oneself as a learner; (2) Planfulness: the ability to diagnose one's own learning needs and devise appropriate strategies; (3) Intrinsic motivation: persistence in learning in the absence of external controls or rewards; (4) Internalized evaluation: ability to act as one's own evaluation agent; (5) Openness to experience; (6) Flexibility: a willingness to adopt a problem solving attitude in the face of changing conditions; (7) Autonomy: the readiness to determine one's own conditions of relevance.

41. op. cit., p. 61.
42. ibid., p. 52.
43. ibid., p. 13.
44. ibid., p. 7.
45. ibid., p. 7.
46. op. cit., p. 220.
47. ibid., p. 209.
48. ibid., p. 161.
49. op. cit., p. 161.
50. op. cit., p. 103.
51. One needs to note that, in this respect, Lengrand shares all the preoccupations typical of the movement, including that the concept be explored for its policy implications and, with reference to the argument to follow, that the lifelong education programme conceptualize education as a totality.
52. op. cit., p. 110.

Chapter Five

LIFELONG EDUCATION AND LIBERAL PHILOSOPHY OF EDUCATION

BACKGROUND

`Humanism', `existentialism'! These are not philosophies that are particularly popular among the philosophers of education of the English-speaking world.
Some description of the orientations that have characterized the outlook of these philosophers was
already made in Chapter 1. There the point was made
that the overwhelming mass of contributions to Anglo-Saxon philosophy of education comes from a liberal standpoint, whether explicitly declared or
thinly disguised behind a facade of `neutrality'
supported by an analytic methodology. Where an
ideological debate is recognised, the `other side'
addressed is thinkers of a Marxist persuasion. The
point was also made, in Chapter 2 this time, that
within liberal philosophy of education the technical
definition of education used is that which includes
only formal or intentional learning, the informal
and non-formal being commonly considered as not
counting as part of people's education, although
they may be relevant and valuable for other purposes
of life. Which means that liberal philosophers
typically operate with a very restricted conception
of education; so restricted in fact as to make education simply equivalent with schooling or with the
continuation of schooling into universities and
other institutions of `higher learning'.

These twin tendencies to keep education apart from
`life' and to so conceptualize education as to eq-
uate it with schooling are perfectly exemplified in
an essay written by Michael Oakeshott called `Educa-
tion: the engagement and its frustrations', where
the major `frustration' to education, for Oakeshott,

is that of confusing it with what goes on in life,
for in so doing one deprives `School' of its most
vital characteristics.[1]

To begin from the beginning, Oakeshott defines
education as:

> a specific transaction which may go on between
> the generations of human beings in which
> newcomers to the scene are initiated into the
> world they are to inhabit.[2]

One needs to note the terms used and the positions
the statement implies. First, we are told that
education is a `specific transaction'; ie., it is
not a `transaction' of just any kind, but one of a
certain sort. Oakeshott later specifies that what
is being `negotiated' in this transaction `is not
the transfer of the products of earlier generations
to a newcomer, nor is it a newcomer acquiring an
aptitude for imitating current adult human perfor-
mances; it is learning to perform humanly'.[3] One
may well feel a bit puzzled as to what Oakeshott
could mean by `learning to perform humanly', and,
further on, by being `initiated into the world they
(newcomers) are to inhabit', since a central argument of his essay is that education implies learning
that is `detach(ed) from the immediate, local world
of the learner, its current concerns and the directions it gives to his attention'.[4] But his meaning becomes amply clear when he specifies that the
inheritance of human achievements and understandings
into which education initiates the young is one
where these are `animated, not by the inclinations
he (the learner) brings with him, but by intimations
of excellences and aspirations he has never dreamed
of ',[5] and this is something school alone can
provide, since school is the only place where the
learner `may encounter not answers to the `loaded'
questions of `life', but questions which have never
before occurred to him'.[6] Second, there are always, says Oakeshott, at least two sides involved
in any given transaction, so, education being a form
of transaction, there can be no such thing as `self-
education'.

Oakeshott, in fact, specifies that in education the
two parties to the transaction are the newcomer or
`postulant to a human condition', and the adult as
teacher. The home, the nursery and the kindergarten
may be places where learning takes place, but they

do not count, since such learning is usually ruled, he says, by inclination and is a by-product of play. Education, in fact, he continues, only begins with the appearance on the scene of a teacher with something important to impart which is *not* immediately connected with the current wants or interests of the learner:

> But education, properly speaking, begins when, upon these casual encounters provoked by the contingencies of moods, upon these fleeting wants and sudden enthusiasms tied to circumstances, there supervenes the deliberate initiation of a newcomer into a human inheritance of sentiments, beliefs, imaginings, understandings and activities. It begins when the transaction becomes `schooling' and when learning becomes learning by study, and not by chance, in conditions of direction and restraint.[7]

The `idea of School', Oakeshott contends, is essentially that of a personal transaction between a `teacher' and a `learner': `The only indispensable equipment of `School' is teachers'. `School' itself, on the other hand, is typically a `monastic' institution in respect of being `a place apart where excellences may be heard because the din of world laxities and partialities is silenced or abated'. Within the school the first lesson the newcomer learns is, therefore, that not all knowledge counts, that learning is not a `seamless robe', the possibilities are not limitless. Thus a deliberately organized curriculum circumscribes knowledge, or the context that needs to be learnt, into `disciplines' or `subjects'. Moreover, school cultivates within the learner certain indispensable habits of life related to the effective `engagement to learn by study' which becoming educated requires; habits of `attention, concentration, patience, exactness, courage and intellectual honesty'.[8]

Oakeshott's programme is a typical liberal one.[9] With this fact in mind, it becomes a wonder how many liberal philosophers of education declare that they actually subscribe to the idea of lifelong education, to the extent 'that recently Anthony O'Hear has felt that he could assert that there is no controversy among philosophers over the view that education is for life; this is in fact, he says, how it is held by philosophers as far apart on other

matters as Peters and Dewey.[10] The question
whether this is indeed so is one that has been
tackled elsewhere in some detail; succinctly, it can
be shown that O'Hear's statement conceals fundamental discrepancies relating to *how* these views are
held by the two philosophers, which, in effect,
render the education programmes with which they work
entirely different ones.[11] Peters's position on
the matter in clearly defined and succinctly stated
in a statement of his in *Ethics and Education* in
which he declares that there are at least two
'truths' contained in the 'slogan' that 'education
is for life':

> One is that if people are properly educated, so
> that they want to go on when the pressures are
> off, the conceptual schemes and forms of
> appraisal, into which they have been initiated
> in schools and universities, continue to
> develop. Another is that 'living' cannot be
> separated from the ways in which people have
> learnt to conceive and appraise what they are
> doing.[12]

In effect, when he describes the statement that
'education is for life' as a slogan, he is accurately reflecting how it is currently held in many
quarters, not the least among liberal philosophers
of education. For a slogan is a form of exhortation
to do something. Where the 'slogan' that 'education
is for life' is concerned it is a valuable one because it derives from 'conceptual truths' implied by
definition from the concept of education itself,
which further implies conceptual schemes and forms
of appraisal into which people are initiated in
schools and universities and which themselves have
intrinsic value. This being the case, it follows
logically that they are of a kind which it would be
worthwhile to continue to develop for life. But an
exhortation or recommendation, however strongly
made, is not the same thing as a policy actively
pursued. The fact that Peters regards the view that
'education is for life' as a slogan demonstrates
that after recommendation he would leave the matter
of whether to engage in lifelong education or not up
to the individual's personal initiative. *He does
not see lifelong education as a key idea to be further explored for its policy implications.*

At this stage it is important for us to get our
perspectives right. The question is not whether

Peters and other liberal philosophers of education
support the idea that education is for life or not,
for many clearly do in some form or other. The real
question is, what kind of lifelong education
programme do they support? One answer is provided
for us in the quotation from Peters; it is the
extension of school and university learning into
adult life. So, in effect, even conceived of as a
lifelong matter, there is no discontinuity in
Peters' statement with the view expressed by
Oakeshott that education is conceptually tied with
schooling; if it does not take place within the
building we call school, it still involves a
continuation and development of the kind of learning
that goes on in the school, and, one assumes,
according to definition, will continue to involve
intentional learning under the guidance of
teachers.[13]

In actual fact, it may be the case with some liberal
philosophers of education that they do, like O'Hear,
recognise that 'Not all education is formal education' or is related to schooling. O'Hear himself
explains that he is writing about formal education
because this suits the purposes of his book and in
order to 'keep things in manageable proportions',
the presupposition clearly being that formal education, or schooling is something that can be written
about separately and is therefore uninfluenced by
these other forms of education he has in mind and
that are not formal.[14] And Peters also, similarly
acknowledges another sense of education besides that
which he writes about, a sense in which it is a
'fluid concept' with a 'loose undifferentiated meaning' as compared to his own. But, like O'Hear, it
is not a sense that interests him either.[15] The
point being made is that whatever other meanings
they allow education, liberal philosophers are interested in *one* only.

Peters *defines* education as schooling, as do most
other liberal philosophers of education, - as the
initiation of the young into a form of life regarded
as desirable by teachers - and *this is how he writes
about it*. This is what really matters whatever his
other statements that appear to support the idea of
lifelong education may be. O'Hear himself is not
even interested in verbal consistency at least.
Thus he describes his intention in his book as that
of providing 'some general account of what it is we
will want our children to have learned by the time

their education is over'.[16]   Note, 'by the time
their education is *over*' — this from one who later
says, as we have seen, that the view that education
is *never* over is uncontroversial!   I assume that,
this being the case, he himself must support it!
Surely the consistent statement should therefore be:
'by the time their *schooling* is over and they are
ready to continue with their education'?!   But the
fact is that O'Hear is no more aware of any inconsistency in his position, verbal or otherwise, than
is Peters.   Like most other liberal philosophers of
education who acknowledge that education is essentially for life, both ignore this acknowledgement
completely when it comes to writing about education.[17]   O'Hear is right in one sense at least;
for philosophical purposes, as far as he and his
fellow philosophers are concerned, education *is* over
when schooling is over, or when the aims of schooling are achieved.

Do these discrepancies mean that liberal philosophers are really paying no more than lip-service to
the ideal of lifelong education?   Not necessarily
so.   The real reason could be that the meaning of
education they operate with is considered sufficient
and that they would pass on to define adult or post-
school education simply as more of the same thing.
This is what, in fact, Peters appears to assume when
he says that what is involved in continuing education is wanting to go on developing the conceptual
schemes and forms of appraisal into which one has
already been initiated in the school.   At the same
time, that same meaning imposes its own restrictions
on how they can consistently conceive of adult or
post-school education; first because within that
meaning education is something teachers do to pupils
or students, and this fact, as we have said, renders
the term 'self-education' a self-contradictory one
in their language, second because it comprehends
only a limited kind of learning and knowledge, that
described by Peters.   The liberal philosopher does
not deny that other kinds of learning are relevant
or valuable in different ways, or cannot take place
otherwise than through being taught or teacher-
directed.   What he denies is that they are
educationally valuable or significant.[18]

It goes without saying therefore that Peters does
not even reserve the neglected 'loose undifferentiated meaning' of education he refers to for adulthood.   That adult education is, for him, simply the

continuation of school learning is, as we have seen, something he practically expresses explicitly. But would he want to continue to be consistent to the extent of retaining that a teacher needs to be involved for education to take place? We cannot be sure, but what is certain is that many liberal philosophers of education hold up some conception of *autonomy* as their educational ideal. They would therefore, probably, want to answer no, because a successful schooling aimed towards autonomy will have given the individual the skills as well as the motivation to go it alone afterwards, thereby making tutelage unnecessary. At the same time such a view could consistently allow the educational relevance of non-formal learning, providing that what is being developed through its activities is the conceptual schemes and forms of appraisal appropriate to the study of the disciplines, not something else, thereby preserving continuity with the school. If we consider this programme as 'education for life', it cannot evidently be called a *lifelong* education programme since, to be properly so called, Peters and the other liberal philosophers would also have to fall in with Lengrand's condition that educational value be conceded to infant learning (see Note 7). Its proper name would be *continuing* education.

All of this, however, does considerable violence to the original liberal technical definition of education, since all it keeps constant from that definition is the knowledge condition, otherwise it drops the condition that learning must be formal and that it requires the direction of teachers, although continuity could also be claimed with the latter in an extended sense in which the learning to be continued started with a teacher. Such a programme would leave the matter of adult education entirely to individual initiative, since, on the one hand it is evidently unthinkable that education should continue to be forced on adults,[19] and, on the other, it is clear that institutions already exist to continue the work of teachers and schools as liberal philosophers identify it — these are the universities and the other formal tertiary establishments, attendance at which is voluntary.

JOHN WHITE AND LIFELONG EDUCATION

It is clear that in order to proceed to the kind of programme sketched in the last paragraph of the

previous section liberal philosophy of education
would need to effect important departures from its
present outlook. First, it would be necessary for
liberal philosophers to recognize that their initial
definition of education as it is creates problems
for an education conceived of in broader terms than
childhood. Second, they will need to concede the
relevance of non-formal learning to the practice of
education. Otherwise they can evidently continue to
insist that *only* teacher-guided learning is education and that education cannot be pursued outside
institutions or outside some form of tutorship,
which is not, if I read them rightly, what most
liberal philosophers intend, though it is a theoretical possibility. This latter position would win
them consistency but would extremely restrict the
possibilities of their education programme. On the
other hand a broader liberal programme could, as was
suggested earlier, continue to hold the knowledge
conditions that characterize the liberal outlook
and, evidently, liberal political ideology, constant.[20] It would then be possible to assume that
these conditions are consistent with other forms of
learning than the teacher-based though it could be
conceded that teacher-based learning, especially in
its characteristic form as schooling, is indispensable to set the ball rolling. The context of education, then, from the point of view of a *continuing*
education programme, would not necessarily be the
school, but any locus of individual, cooperative, or
tutor/teacher led learning which achieves for the
individual the kind of knowledge and 'mental development' in terms of which liberal education is
defined, at any time in life.

This solution appears deceptively simple; in fact it
is not. For besides the changes proposed one would
need to effect another one of an even more radical
kind; it would be necessary for liberal philosophers
to discard a number of concepts and emphases that
are current in liberal philosophy of education and
that constitute an obstacle to reconceptualizing
education in this way. And this proposal appears to
be the most difficult to pursue, in fact it does not
seem currently possible. This is because the necessary presupposition for it to happen is a prior
cognition on the part of the liberal philosophers
themselves, of the fact that a really consistent
view of education as something that continues for
life requires the reassessment of their educational
outlook in the manner described above or in other

ways. And this awareness, as was argued in the previous section, currently appears nowhere, since almost all these philosophers continue to hold their declared support for lifelong education against a theoretical outlook which restricts education to childhood and formal learning within schools, blissfully unaware of any inconsistency on their part.

I say 'almost' because in fact the point is taken by John White who devotes a whole section to lifelong education, which he correctly characterizes as a *challenge* to the liberal education programme to which he himself subscribes.[21] White recognizes the argument made above. He also recognizes that what is currently being proposed in the name of lifelong education is a much more radical reappraisal of education even than that outlined above. White recognizes that the lifelong education programme demands a total reconceptualization of the whole of education rather than these limited corrective measures. His concern in his book however is not to contribute to the discussion of how the liberal programme can be better aligned with the concept of lifelong education, but to reject the concept on behalf of liberal education. And in the process he evidently lights upon the spots where the inconsistencies between the two are most pronounced. In doing so he highlights the concepts and emphases the current liberal programme would need to discard in order to achieve compatibility with the concept of lifelong education — although, evidently, he does not advocate that it should do so, taking the inconsistencies, on the contrary, as reasons for rejecting lifelong education.

White's attack on the lifelong education concept takes different forms: (1) he argues that the concept violates and renders meaningless the central concept of liberal philosophy of education; the concept of the 'educated man' or 'person'; (2) he argues that it removes the emphasis from childhood, which no longer remains 'special' from the educational point of view; (3) he argues that it can be reduced *ad absurdum*. All of these are meant as serious objections made by a serious philosopher, and therefore need to be met; they are also objections that do not appear elsewhere in philosophy of education. White's section, in fact, constitutes the only real philosophical critique of the lifelong education concept available at the time of writing this book, and the fact that it is made from a hostile or, more accurately, sceptical position, renders it additionally important. It will therefore be considered in some detail in the pages to come, beginning with the problem he raises over the incompatibility of the lifelong education concept with that of the educated man.

With reference to it, White says:

> If education is to be reconceptualized as a 'lifelong process' and not as something belonging only to youth, then we might as well drop the concept of the educated man: there is no line to be crossed; the journey goes on for ever.[22]

And he evidently thinks the concept so crucial that it should be guarded against this eventuality.

The reasoning behind this viewpoint goes something like this: being an intentional activity guided by rational procedures, education must have an aim or a set of aims of some kind. That aim or set of aims must reflect qualities that it is desirable that people should have and that their education should give them; we call the individual who acquires these qualities an 'educated person'. The educated person, then, is one who possesses certain qualities that are deemed desirable and that are achieved through education; he can be described as the embodiment of the aims of education. The language of aims is thus an important one for the liberal philosopher of education and he is ready to pursue its logic. The language of aims is the language of deliberate action, the language of 'targets' to be aimed at; to have an aim means to have a target in focus on which one can adjust one's sights. When the language of aims is pursued further in connection with education the analogy immediately presents itself; education is a set of end results towards which teachers direct their pupils with specific criteria of achievement in mind. The latter is understood within the terms of the analogy itself since one cannot properly be said to be aiming at something without the understanding that one also knows what it means to hit it, how a successful aim shows itself. To pursue the analogy a little bit further, just as success in hitting the target closes off the action begun by aiming at it, so education is closed off when the aims of education have been achieved and one has acquired the qualities of the educated person. But this whole language game cannot be played if one introduces into it the alien concept of lifelong education; because the concept renders the conclusion we have just reached paradoxical. For if a person is *educated*, then the aim of education has been reached; as far as he is concerned his education is completed, the line has been crossed – whatever learning lies beyond cannot be his continuing *education*.

The language of liberal philosophy of education is oriented in this way; it recognizes the ultimate purpose of educating people as being that of achieving for them the characteristics of educatedness as they are identified by liberal philosophy. With particular reference to White he in fact describes his own clearly stated set of educational aims, his set of qualities of the educated man or person, and distinguishes them from those of other liberal philosophers of education by the fact that while the latter focus on the knowledge conditions, in the main, he himself focuses on virtue. His concept, therefore, he says, avoids that over-emphasis on the cognitive which has rendered liberal conceptions of educatedness the object of so much criticism. At the same time, and in conformity with our previous exposition of the liberal argument, educatedness is for him, as it must be with all the other liberal philosophers of education, a point of arrival, like stepping into a new state. It is for this reason that the need for a demarcation line which will mark it out presents itself for him. And he finds it necessary to dedicate some pages to the unenvious task of trying to sort out the question of where the line lies. His conclusion is, in fact, that it cannot be defined very specifically:

> This is partly because there are no sharp lines, only blurred areas, in anybody's case, and partly because people learn at different rates and some may be slower than others in reaching the blurred areas. Some may never reach it, although we may still want to call them partially educated, since they have travelled some way along the same road as others.

But, in any case, a person is 'more or less educated':

when he has formed something like a coherent
life plan in the light of all the considerations built into the substantive account of
educational aims presented earlier, and is
aware of the kinds of future circumstances
which might cause him to adjust his valuations
as he goes through life.[23].

So, there are no sharp demarcation lines that mark
off the point of arrival that is educatedness, only
'very blurred areas' that individuals will reach at
different times in their lives and that some people
may never reach at all since it is clear that not
everybody will be able at any stage in his life to
reach the condition where his life appears to him as
a coherent life plan fulfilling 'all the considerations built into the substantive account of educational aims' that White distinguishes. Few people,
in fact, will ever be 'something of a philosopher',
which is what, ultimately, he expects the educated
man to be, although he recognizes the merits of
those who can only ever manage *part* of the journey.
[24]

At the same time, this very indeterminacy in establishing where the demarcation line into educatedness
lies, and White's own unwillingness to close the
fruits of education off for the individual arbitrarily before these have been achieved, because of
their very value, renders him reluctant to take any
age as a 'cut-off point', though he does insist that
educatedness may be achieved, indeed ideally should
be achieved by the end of schooling, since one's
schooling should have turned one into an educated
man. But the fact that with many it will not have
done so and that some at least will arrive later
means that the possibility of educatedness must be
kept permanently open, though, as White perceives 'a
logical gap immediately opens up between aims and
terminal school objectives',[25] on this account.

The question is, how does he respond to the
perception of this gap? The logical way would seem
to be that of holding up continuing education as a
back up for those who have been unfortunate enough
to have failed to achieve educatedness at school —
this would turn it into a species of compensatory
programme for a defective schooling. In fact White
suggests something of the kind but he warns us not
to confuse it with lifelong education:

We might then envisage compulsory full-time
schooling until say 16 or later, possibly followed by compulsory part-time education for
another period, with strong official encouragement to continue one's education on a voluntary
basis beyond this point. This would not be
'lifelong' education, since the overall objective would only be to produce educated persons
and this might be achievable while people are
still young.[26]

True, this programme would not be lifelong
education, but it would not be 'upbringing' either.

This is in fact how White, like most other liberal
philosophers of education, defines education, as
'upbringing'.[27] And, evidently, the consequence
of so defining it is to tie the concept specifically
with that of childhood. Education, as upbringing,
is something that older people, notably teachers, do
to the younger. So the obvious question, with regard to the programme White outlines above, is, how
is this definition compatible with it? How does one
continue with one's education on a voluntary basis
beyond full-time schooling if education equals upbringing? Moreover, White emphasises the fact that,
as upbringing, education has nothing to do with the
will or desire of the educand.   This is because
upbringing necessarily implies compulsion: children
do not decide whether they want to be brought up or
not - their upbringing is both a non-voluntary and a
necessary thing. This is because, as O'Hear points
out, there are certain kinds of knowledge and certain dispositions that it is desirable children
should have when they grow up, and it appears that
having them cannot wait. Among these perhaps the
most important, from White's point of view, are
dispositions of a moral kind, the 'main girders' of
which need to be put in place in childhood.

From the point of view of lifelong education,
however, the problems with defining education as
upbringing are evident. On the one hand restricting
upbringing to childhood, as liberal philosophers do,
and defining education as upbringing renders it
contradictory to describe education as a lifelong
process; if education happens in childhood then it
becomes incoherent to refer to it as lifelong. If,
on the other hand, we keep the formula education
equals upbringing and propose to consider the former

as lifelong, notwithstanding, we can only be, consistently with this definition, proposing lifelong
upbringing. This latter conclusion is, in fact, the
one White would consistently be committed to if he
wishes to keep the programme described above together with his definition of education as upbringing — it is the only way in which he can consistently close the gap.

So if space is to be found for the view that
education is a lifelong process within the liberal
programme, a considerable amount more will be
involved than the philosopher's pious approval of it
as a truism and a recommendable slogan. The fact
is, as White's difficulties with the concept show,
the liberal paradigm is not so conceived as to
absorb it; it operates with a language game that
makes its inclusion paradoxical, mainly because it
is a language game focused upon the understanding
that education denotes some kind of upbringing that
leads to a state of educatedness, and bringing
somebody up is an intentional activity with finite
and well-defined results that are ascertainable. In
other words the task of adapting the liberal
education programme to absorb the principle of
lifelong education is a much more formidable one
than may appear to be the case at first glance.

THE CONCEPT OF THE EDUCATED MAN

We have seen that White is right in claiming that
the concept of lifelong education does not go with
that of the educated man. But while this means that
a liberal programme that focuses on the latter cannot accommodate the former, it is not itself a criticism of the former, it is simply the statement of a
fact, tantamount to statement that 'X is incompatible with Y', no more. The question why Y should be
retained in preference to X is a totally different
one, in our case it is the crucial one, but it is
not one that White even attempts to tackle. It is
only by showing in a decisive way the necessity of
retaining the concept of the educated man, by showing, for instance, that the language of education
itself is rendered incoherent in the absence of such
a concept, that one can object *on philosophical
grounds* to any reconceptualizing of education that
does away with it; and this is something White does
not do. He seems to assume that the concept is
required but he does not argue for it.

This, however, is clearly insufficient. All the more so since he would, in fact, be quite pressed to offer a defence of the current concept of the educated man from attack from some quarters within liberal philosophy of education itself. For instance from the kind of objections brought against it in Jane Roland Martin's essay on 'The Ideal of the Educated Person'.[28]

The specific target of Roland Martin's attack is in fact Peters' concept of the educated man, but she makes it clear that her objections are equally applicable to other similar conceptions that differ from that of Peters only in detail; Downie, Loudfoot and Telfer's, for instance, and that of Woods and Barrow, as she herself indicates. Her first objection is to the expression 'educated man' itself. What is at issue, she points out, is not a simple matter of nomenclature; the question is a much more serious and substantial one than that. For, drawing on an impressive bulk of feminist research, Roland Martin makes the startling claim that the term itself is, in fact, accurate because *Peters' model is sexist*; so the problem is not a terminological one but a conceptual one. It is 'sexist', she argues, because, for one thing, it describes the process of becoming educated as that of being initiated into the *existing* forms of knowledge or disciplines, and these, she says, clearly 'incorporate a male cognitive perspective'[29]:

> the intellectual disciplines into which a person must be initiated to become an educated person *exclude* women and their works, *construct* the female to the male image of her and *deny* the truly feminine qualities she does possess. [30]

For another, the model:

> coincides with our cultural stereotype of a male human being. According to the stereotype men are objective, analytic, rational; they are interested in ideas and things that have no interpersonal orientation; they are neither nurturant nor supportive, neither empathetic nor sensitive. According to the stereotype, nurturance and supportiveness, empathy and sensitivity are female attributes. Intuition is a female attribute too.[31]

This means, Roland Martin says, that in confrontation with Peters' conception of being educated women are put in a `double bind': `To be educated they must give up their own way of experiencing and looking at the world, thus alienating themselves from themselves'.[32]   And this fact effectively puts them in a `no-win situation', for, to begin with, it is a *priori* more difficult for women to succeed on terms that are so heavily loaded in favour of men. Moreover, even if they do succeed in acquiring the qualities of educatedness described by the model, women do so at a price which is not demanded of men and which is far from insignificant; that of de-naturalizing themselves. Furthermore, Roland Martin continues, the emotional suffering entailed by having to pay such a price is augmented by the fact that even if a woman does acquire the traits characterized by the ideal, these are appraised negatively by others, notably by men themselves (just because they appear to be de-naturalizing).   So that, in effect, a liberal curriculum that objectifies the educated man, or person, more often than not the difference is only a matter of nomenclature, as its ultimate aim puts a woman in a position where, if she `has acquired the traits of an educated person (she) will not be evaluated positively for having them, while one who has acquired those traits for which she will be positively evaluated will not have achieved the ideal'.[33]

These objections cannot themselves be dismissed lightly, and Roland Martin adds to them from an even broader and inclusive perspective. She argues that, as we have seen, not only is the current liberal ideal of the educated person damaging to women, it is also `far too narrow to guide the educational enterprise' in another significant manner, which makes it not fitting for men either.  For the model which embodies it is too heavily biased towards the cognitive, to the extent that `it presupposes a divorce of mind from body, thought from action, and reason from feeling and emotion', it therefore `provides at best an ideal of an educated *mind*, not an educated *person*'.[34]  Further, this same bias on the cognitive, Roland Martin says, makes the model an utterly individualist one which eschews any kind of social orientation for educational goals: `Concern for people, and for interpersonal relationships has no role to play: the educated person's sensitivity is to the standards immanent in activities, not to other human beings'.[35]

Finally, Roland Martin says, the model deliberately, and again to the disadvantage of women, rules out what she calls the 'reproductive' (as distinguished from the 'productive') social functions from the concept of educatedness. She argues that Peters' conception of the educated person, in fact, whatever its pretensions, is a 'functionalist' one: 'he assigns to education the function of developing the traits and qualities and to some extent the skills of one whose role is to use and produce ideas'.[36] Thus, for the model to be sufficiently broad, 'the two kinds of societal processes which Peters divorces from one another must be joined together'. [37]

White, who uses the term 'educated man' throughout his book, does, to some degree, succeed in avoiding some of this criticism. Sensitive to the over-emphasis on the cognitive which all the other models display, he makes, as we have seen, virtues more central than knowledge in his own model. Thus, the educated man, White says, 'is someone who has come to care about his own well-being in the extended sense which includes his living a morally virtuous life, this latter containing a civic dimension among others'.[38]

To *some* degree only because White's Aristotelian model of virtue is utterly rationalist; his virtuous man is one who is 'knowledgeable in all sorts of ways'. Moreover, though being knowledgeable may not be 'a self-justifying state on its own', still 'knowledge is necessary to virtue', and the forms of knowledge virtue requires 'are indeed complex and extensive', so that the virtuous man needs, as 'something of a philosopher', to be 'able and prepared to think things (ends-in-themselves, means and obstacles and an understanding of 'what personal well-being consists in, i.e., how these elements need to be integrated within an autonomous life-plan') through without falling into obscurity or blindly taking over the pronouncements of author-ity'.[39] In short, we are practically back where Peters started with regards to the traits, charac-teristics and skills of being educated, what changes with White's model is its orientation towards the civic, and while the importance of this change needs to be acknowledged it does not itself nullify the other criticism contained in Roland Martin's essay.

It is important to note that Roland Martin herself
does not recommend that the concept of educatedness
or of the educated person be abandoned. What she
demands is that it be broadened in different ways;
in the first place to include `experience and
activities that have traditionally been considered
to belong to women',[40] also to include the `hid-
den curriculum', and so on. In other words what she
wants is a redefined liberal programme which takes
in these omissions and which does not draw too sharp
a line between certain `logical and contingent rela-
tionships'; between the results of conceptual analysis and `the contingent relationships which obtain
between them and both the good life and the good
society'.[41]

Because of this proposal to broaden considerably the
concept of the educated person which Roland Martin
makes, she finds herself constrained at one point to
raise the question `whether we should adopt one or
more ideals of the educated person'.[42] But she
leaves it undiscussed. And yet it is an important
question for it seems to entitle the further
question whether it is useful, on her description,
to retain a concept of the educated person at all if
it is going to be multiplied in several different
ways. Moreover, once one advocates the having of a
multiplicity of ideals one raises complications
making it difficult to specify what the aims of
teaching should be in such a situation. The
implication is clearly that teaching should, in this
light, have different aims, but this suggestion
clearly starts a train of consequences that would
take us right out of the liberal education programme
into something quite different.

UPBRINGING

The second major problem White sees with the concept
of lifelong education is, as we have said, its conflict with our usual way of identifying education
with childhood. We have seen how he himself defines
education as upbringing, with the additional comment
that this is in fact how it is defined by the major-
ity of liberal philosophers of education. And,
White argues, this is just since `Whatever else
happens there must be some sort of preparation for
life in any society'.[43] So the first argument for
defining education as upbringing is that the bring-

ing up of the young is necessary in any kind of society, that upbringing is a necessary phase of life both for the individual and for society itself and that it is therefore something no society can possibly ignore or leave to chance and therefore needs to institutionalize in a formal matter as education. White also presents a variation to this argument. Education, he says, belongs specifically to youth because 'the main girders of the kind of education I am recommending will have to be put in place in the early years'.[44] This argument presents a somewhat different twist from the first; White is here making a case for the priority of youth because his own programme requires it.

Neither objection however appears to carry much force against conceptualizing education as lifelong. The first appears particularly fragile because there is nothing about a reconceptualized view of education as a lifelong process that *a priori* precludes a due recognition of the sort of preparation White indicates, or, more generally, denies the relevance of upbringing, indeed the more usual offenders in this respect are his fellow liberal philosophers of education who draw sharp conceptual distinctions between the sort of upbringing that counts as education and 'socialization'. The lifelong education programme itself stipulates only that there needs to be continuity between the different phases or stages of the individual's development, it does not deny the need to consider the defining characteristics of each different stage and give it due weight. On the contrary, the particular needs of each stage, and the demands made on it by society are considered within the programme to be educationally important. The programme does not, in sum, deny the fact or value of upbringing, what it refuses to do is to *define* education as upbringing, and that is a different thing.[45]

The second is similarly weak because it appears to assume that there can be no viable alternative to White's programme and that, therefore, incompatibility with it is a conclusive objection against any educational viewpoint not only the lifelong education one. In fact, this is substantially the same argument as that presented earlier, where the concept of lifelong education was rejected on the grounds of its incompatibility with the concept of the educated person. The same kind of response can therefore be made to it; White is merely making the

point that the view that education is a lifelong
process does not go with its definition as
upbringing, just as it does not go with a concept of
educatedness, any more.

At the same time his concern that conceptualizing
education as a lifelong process would cause us to
neglect placing the 'main girders' of his education
programme in youth arises from a just observation.
This is that conceptualizing it in this way means
removing education's traditional focus on youth and
thereby reducing the relation between upbringing and
adult learning to one of mere co-equivalence. This
is in fact true, the concept of lifelong education
implies this consequence. Not only that, the
advocates of lifelong education actually tend to
focus more strongly on adult education than youth.
But this is only to redress the current imbalance in
the contrary direction that White supports. The
question to be asked is whether the latter imbalance
in favour of youth is still desirable; whether it is
still a good thing to focus education on youth and
upbringing. Lifelong education theorists argue that
it is not, and they present their case accordingly.
At the same time they would agree with White that
there are certain 'girders' that need to be placed
in youth, though they would opt for a different set
of girders than his in identifying the kind of knowledge that should be focused on in upbringing. They
would, in fact, support the case for educability as
against initiation into forms of intrinsically valuable knowledge (the disciplines), as the focus of
formal learning. How, on the other hand, they would
focus their moral objectives, is a question that
admits of different answers though, as will be argued later, a particular kind of socialization *is*
implied by the normative statements in the lifelong
education literature.

The important point to be made in clarification of
White's objection is that the lifelong education
programme de-emphasizes the prominence of youth not
by downgrading its importance but by upgrading the
educational importance and value of adulthood. So
the case White needs to make is against upgrading
the educational importance and value of adulthood if
he wants to reject conceptualizing education as
lifelong.

White, however, finds still further cause for
disquiet with the lifelong education programme

besides. We have already mentioned the fact that, for him, tying education up with upbringing makes it a matter of coercion rather than voluntary will. White shows concern that thinking of education as lifelong or as 'a way of life' may 'blur the vital distinction between a person's upbringing, which for him cannot be voluntary, and his adult learning activities, whether cultural or occupational, which should be voluntary'.[46] The problem that such 'blurring' may serve to obliterate the *sine qua non* nature of upbringing has already been considered and seen to be unreal. The problem now raised returns us to the problem of the logical gap between achieving educatedness and the terminal objectives of school raised, as we have seen, by White himself. It was pointed out in fact that in accordance with his programme, the only logically consistent way to close the gap is to conceptualize the continuing learning which he proposes as continuing *upbringing*. And while he appears to be unconscious of this consequence where his own position is concerned, he seems very much aware of its critical possibilities with regards to the lifelong education programme and warns that the countervailing argument for liberty in adulthood makes it unacceptable to enforce education beyond childhood. Nevertheless he feels that he should otherwise push the principle of continuing education as far as he thinks permissible. Thus we have already seen that he envisages the possibility of 'compulsory part-time education' for a period beyond schooling, and would give 'strong official encouragement' for those who are inclined to continue voluntarily beyond. It is interesting to see what he has in mind by 'encouragement':

> This (encouragement) goes a little further than saying that post-compulsory provision should exist on a voluntary basis. It could mean, for instance, providing incentives in time or money for young workers to undertake educational courses or to pursue their own self-education. It could mean reshaping conventional social expectations via the media, for instance, so that becoming educated in a full sense becomes the done thing. It could mean not only strengthening and making more accessible those agencies - career guidance units, marriage counsellors, almoners, Gingerbread groups, Cruse, psychiatric services and so on - which help people to reflect on the shape of their lives

as a whole (sometimes after the disruption of eg. a serious illness - divorce or bereavement), but also reconceptualizing them as *educational* agencies. Looked at this way, the period of compulsory education would have the function of laying the groundwork for a coherent life-plan, with strong encouragement for the individual after this period to reconsider and revise this life-plan with help from formal and informal agencies, if necessary.[47]

But a feeling of confusion on reading this important passage is natural - White himself has apparently elaborated a perfectly coherent programme of continuing education, expanding upon the principles outlined before. But when he refers to young workers undertaking educational courses or pursuing their own self-education, how is he using the term 'education', does he still mean to refer to it as upbringing? Clearly not, for the term 'self-upbringing' is a contradictory one. On the other hand, the term 'self-education' should not even feature in White's language game. And when he refers to the possibility of reconceptualizing the various agencies he mentions as *educational* agencies does he mean that their aims are set for them by the aims of education entailed by the concept of educatedness and ideally already attained in the school? Or is he operating with a different, wider, meaning of education as something which 'help(s) people to reflect on the shape of their lives as a whole?' Naturally, the inconsistencies become more glaring once the programme is elaborated further, nor is this fact lost on White. In fact, he realizes that an education programme of this kind poses problems for him.

But, even more serious as far as he is concerned, is the fact that what appears to push him, nevertheless, in its direction, is the apparent implication of a concept which he evidently considers crucial to his own description of educatedness, to his own education programme; the concept of a 'life plan'. We have seen how having an integrated life plan of a certain kind is, for White, the sure sign of being educated. He now poses himself the following problem: if being educated means being in possession of an integrated life plan, it may still be argued that a person's life plan is always subject to change as life itself forces us to re-evaluate and change our priorities. This being the case it may be contended that a person's life plan is never fully settled and therefore 'His education, in my sense, must go on throughout his life. The only satisfactory upbringing *is* lifelong education'.[48]   In other words White seems to be conceding, as indeed he must, that logic and his own description of educatedness drive him towards a view of education as a lifelong process, and this is indeed a catastrophic suggestion as far as the coherence of his own programme is concerned.   How does he respond to it?   He simply continues to say that although there is 'a lot which is true and important' in this argument it is nevertheless an 'exaggeration' for it would, he says, for instance, imply that 'the 80-year-old man who is readjusting his priorities in the light of old age still has not completed his upbringing'.[49]

The feeling that would appear legitimate at this point is one of desperation.   For it is so evident, so patently clear that the *reductio* in this argument depends upon the illicit interchangeability of the two terms 'education' and 'upbringing' that it is a real wonder that White does not see it.[50]   Observe: His *education* etc.... (Hence) The only satisfactory *upbringing* etc.', and, there is something absurd about the view that an 80-year-old 'has not completed his *upbringing*'.   True, but there is nothing absurd about the view that an 80-year-old man has not yet completed his *education*, particularly if he still has the capability of 'readjusting his priorities', and I do not think that White would want to deny it.   Indeed, he could not consistently deny it, for did he not himself hold that there is *no cut-off point* for the achieving of educatedness?   Surely this position in itself should have demonstrated to him the nonsense of making education and upbringing one and the same thing.   But apparently it has not.   Or is it because it is only by to-ing and fro-ing in this way between the two terms that he can win his point that he continues to appear blind to it?   Surely he cannot really think that this argument about the 80-year-old man lets him off the conclusion he is so desperate to avoid!

Indeed what the argument shows up is not the absurdity of conceptualizing education as a lifelong process but the absurdity of defining education as upbringing, because so defined it clearly cannot stand for all the things we want to apply it to or say on its behalf.   It does not even suit, as he himself is in practice forced to concede, White's own account of education, and this not merely because of the

implications of including within it the concept of
a life plan, but also because that account is such
that within it he wants to hold that one's education
can, and with many people will, need to go on beyond
one's upbringing even if education is conceived of
as the achievement of educatedness.

Finally, any *a priori* uncertainty over the *moral*
implications of holding that education is lifelong
only exists *if* education is defined as upbringing.
For, if it is, then it is clearly not only absurd to
hold that an 80-year-old should continue with his
education, it is also clearly immoral, given the
logic of the term 'upbringing' as described earlier,
and the 'countervailing right to freedom' for adults
which White cites.   If we, however, refuse the
definition then there is no problem, particularly
if, by further   implication, we thereby include
'non-formal agencies' and activities within our
 alternative, broader, conception of education.
There are places in White's book, not least in the
lengthy quotation reproduced earlier, where he does
operate with a broader meaning of education because
this alone will suit his purposes.   Surely then, on
balance and all things considered it appears more
worthwhile for him to abandon his definition of
education as upbringing rather than continue to hold
on to it, especially if the price to be paid otherwise is either to live with the inconsistencies
brought to light in these pages, or the abandonment
of all that has been shown to be inconsistent *in his
own position* with the definition.

CONCLUSIONS

This chapter has considered the different problems
relative to the compatibility of the lifelong education concept and what it entails, and the liberal
education programme as it is rationalized by liberal
philosophers of education.   No need to devote a
separate chapter to a similar comparison of the
concept with the orthodox Marxian programme is felt
because there are no real fundamental differences
between Marxists and liberals over the technical
definition of education that guides their respective
programmes; both conceptualize education in formal
terms and, more narrowly, tend to identify it with
schooling.   Thus, as is well known, Marx himself
wrote very little specifically about education,
though many of the concepts he explored in his soc-

ial philosophy have been utilized in educational theory, while Gramsci who, of all the Marxist thinkers, was perhaps the most interested in the subject, while similarly contributing concepts from his broader political writings, like that of 'hegemony' for instance, to educational discourse, was extraordinarily conservative where his explicit contributions to education are made.[51] For the most part Marxist philosophers have been content to criticize the liberal education programme for the values it rationalizes through its curriculum and for its contribution towards the liberal-capitalist *status quo*, otherwise they have retained the same focus and, basically, the same emphases, in some cases substituting the concept of the class-based 'organic intellectual' perhaps for that of the 'educated person'.

With reference to the liberal philosophers of education, we have seen that they are, for the most part perhaps, ready to concede the view that education is for life in the temporal sense of the expression (otherwise the tendency is to distinguish education from life in the manner described by Oakeshott and considered unacceptable to the lifelong education programme), but that they also, at the same time, define it as something formal, involving teachers and concerning childhood and youth. In Peters' view a liberal lifelong, or more accurately, continuing, education programme would quite simply encourage people to continue to develop what has been achieved in schooling on a personal basis. White, who has taken up the question more specifically, unlike Peters' whose contribution is a mere passing comment, would agree partially and with important reservations. For, he points out, the scope of such a programme must continue to be the achievement of *educatedness*, therefore, logically, once this is achieved for any particular person, his education is completed. There will therefore be a number of people who will not need lifelong education because their 'journey' will have been completed early on in life, ideally by the end of school. The only concession to the concept of lifelong education then that White makes in his book refers to a continuing compensatory learning for those who need it. It is impossible to ascertain how far Peters would be in accord with this conclusion, but White is certainly right in insisting that this is not the proposal of a lifelong education programme since its lifelong expression is a concession to failure not an ideal for everyone.

At the same time White has shown most clearly where
the problem of achieving compatibility between the
liberal programme and the concept of lifelong education lies.   He has shown that reconceptualizing
education as a lifelong programme inevitably violates certain key concepts retained to be indispensable by liberal philosophers, notably that of educatedness or of the `educated person', it also
challenges the liberal tendency to define education
as `upbringing'.   In the chapter we have not made a
specific list of the points of contrast between the
liberal   programme   and   the   movement's   lifelong
education programme, which are evidently numerous
because they can easily be made by the reader for
himself.   What we have said is that a liberal
continuing   education   programme   which   departs
minimally from the original liberal programme could
continue to rationalize the traditional schooling
aims and activities and define its `continuing'
component   as   the   extension   of   these   aims   and
activities in time, providing it abandons the
concept of educatedness.   Some further modifications
to the original programme, though by no means minor
in themselves, may, it is suspected, also meet with
the approval of many liberal philosophers in order
to give the continuing programme more breadth and
freedom; the main ones would be the removal of the
conditions that education requires the participation
of teachers, which would allow the concept of `self-
education', and that it typically takes place in
school and similar institutions [52].

A   total   reconceptualization   of   education   as   a
lifelong programme, on the other hand, would, as
White shows, require even more radical modifications
than these; it would require a completely different
theatre of discussion, a completely new language
paradigm the bringing into operation of which would
effectively entail the very abandonment of the
current liberal education programme.   The question
to be addressed once it is accepted that the key
concepts to be abandoned are not indispensable to an
intelligible   description   of   education,   is,   how
consistent would this reconceptualized programme be
with liberal social and political philosophy — how
consistent would it be with the *ideological* core of
the liberal education programme?   The question is a
substantially different one from that which faces us
when   we   inquire   into   the   possibility   of   an

existentialist lifelong education programme, where
the problems, as we have seen, arise from the very
unwillingness of existentialist thought to present
itself as a programme, and from the fact that there
is no real ideological core to existentialism as a
philosophy.

No more than a cursory glance through the literature
is required to establish that the ideological focus
of the liberal education programme is the concept of
personal autonomy; this is considered by most
liberal philosophers to be the highest political
good. The focus on autonomy, on the other hand,
encourages an individualist educational philosophy,
and several liberal philosophers have carried the
individualist orientation so far as to draw sharp
conceptual distinctions between education as the
development of 'mind', and 'socialization' which is
the turning of individuals into 'current men'. To
this extent they have shown the same diffidence
towards the social as that shown by existentialist
thinkers. At the same time they have typically
stopped short of pitching their ideal of autonomy at
the level of 'authenticity' demanded by the existentialist while insisting that autonomy is something
people need to be educated into. They have thus
avoided holding aims that, when translated
educationally, are incompatible with schooling,
while at the same time insisting that schools should
avoid indoctrinating people. This they can do by
concentrating on *initiating* pupils into forms of
knowledge that are intrinsically valuable in morally
unobjectionable ways that eventually lead to the
liberating of the mind. This is the paradigm that
dictates how 'upbringing' is to be conceived. And
White, who shares all these views, continues to
emphasise the difference between autonomy and the
existentialist's authenticity by stressing that
being autonomous implies having a coherent life plan
not making criterionless choices; it is thus that
autonomy, unlike authenticity, can be made the
object of education.

What kind of social philosophy do liberal philosophers contextualize their concept of individuality
into? Broadly speaking liberal social/political
philosophers are in two camps; one expresses itself
in terms of a minimalist conception of the state and
of collective intervention, the other finds its mode
of expression in the concept of a welfare state. The
first extols individual enterprise and holds the

collective intervention at a regulatory minimum
where individual freedom is threatened, the second,
while similarly extolling the merits of individual
enterprise holds notions of a collective good that
should regulate that enterprise. Now it is clear,
without going into details, that a philosophy of the
first kind would be inherently antagonistic towards
anything but a minimum of collective intervention in
educational matters. It would presumably grant every
individual the right to a minimum education, enough
to get him into the `market', though it would be
clear that the basis of such a right would be an
individual not a social one, but it would grant
nothing beyond. Certainly its rationale is contrary
to the view that adult continuing education should
be institutionalized, it would hold rather that,
like all other things continuing education should be
a matter of personal private enterprise. A philosophy of the second kind, on the other hand, is clearly compatible with a policy of institutionalization;
a good model would be the one proposed by White and
subsequently rejected by his supposed *reductio ad
absurdum* — which, we have seen, is no *reductio* at
all, and which, in any case, is a puny reason for
rejecting what is otherwise deemed valuable and
true.

NOTES AND REFERENCES

1. Oakeshott, M. `Education: the engagement and
its frustrations', in: Dearden, R.F., Hirst, P.H.,
and Peters, R.S. (eds.) (1972) *Education and the
development of reason* (London, Routledge and Kegan
Paul)
     2. op. cit., p. 19.
     3. ibid., p. 22.
     4. ibid., p. 24.
     5. ibid., p. 25.
     6. ibid., p. 25.
     7. ibid., p. 23. Glenn Langford is one
prominent liberal philosopher who disagrees with
these restrictions. Langford, who believes that to
become educated is to have learnt to be a person,
also recognizes both a formal *and* informal sense of
education. In the former 'two parties may be distinguished, one of whom, the teacher, accepts responsibility for the education of the other, the pupil',
the latter is simply 'defined negatively as education in which this condition is not met'. (p. 3) He
also holds that there is 'room for the concept of

informal education in educational discourse', and continues to say; 'I do not think it is stretching language unduly to apply the term 'education' to infants'. ('The concept of education', in: Langford, G., and O'Connor, D.J. (eds.) (1973) *New Essays in the Philosophy of Education*, (London, Routledge and Kegan Paul)). This difference, however, should not be over-estimated. For one thing Langford's own comparison between his position and that of Hirst and Peters, in the same essay shows that he is in accord with them on fundamental points. For another, in a later work Langford holds that the question 'What is education?' is not an 'abstract' question but an 'empirical question about the activities of a particular group of people (teachers)', and that it therefore 'can be answered only by reference to the activities of these people'. (Langford, G. (1978) *Teaching as a Profession*, p. 78. (Manchester University Press))

8. ibid., p. 26.

9. Anthony O'Hear has described the programme in this way: 'Education, or the part of overall education which counts as liberal education, on the view being considered consists in initiating students into disciplines such as those of mathematics, science, history, literature and the arts. These disciplines exist in their own right, and there are people expert and authoritative in them. Students are to be taught by teachers who have some claim to authority in what they teach. All involved, students and teachers are to be guided by the standards of excellence inherent in the disciplines themselves, wherever these standards might lead, even to conflict with church or state. It follows from this commitment to excellence that the voice by people either inside or outside the discipline. Students are to be assessed in the light of their achievements in reaching the standards involved. Some, it is to be expected, will be able, under encouragement, to achieve high degrees of excellence in what they study. Some of them will be able eventually to make contributions of their own to the disciplines, continuing and adding to the traditions. On the whole, the disciplines are taught and engaged in for their own sake, because they are recognised to be valuable in their own right and a part of any fully civilized existence. Liberal education, then, is not primarily vocational or practical. Finally, it recognizes expertise, and works through the recognition of expertise and strives ultimately for work of exceptional quality

in the subjects concerned, which by definition is not generally attainable. ((1981) *Education, Society and Human Nature,* pp. 4-5 (London, Routledge and Kegan Paul))

10. op. cit., p. 35. O'Hear says that 'Peters, like Dewey, regards education as something life-long and essentially 'incompletable''.

11. Wain, K. 'Lifelong Education: a Dewyian challenge', *Journal of Philosophy of Education*, Vol. 18, o. 2, 1984.

12. Peters, R.S. (1966) *Ethics and Education,* p. 161 (London, Allen and Unwin)

13. Elizabeth Steiner, who otherwise considers taking education as schooling to be too narrow, defines it as a 'teaching-studenting process'. The relationship, she argues, could involve other than the professional teacher-pupil one, and could take place in 'homes, churches and corporations', besides schools. What is essential to education, she says, is that the learning it involves is guided, and studenting deliberate. Liberal philosophers who are in sympathy with this characterisation of education will evidently oppose any broadening of the concept, as will be subsequently proposed, to include non-formal learning. (Steiner, E. 'Educology of the Free: a Theory of Liberal Education', *Philosophy of Education*, 1980)

14. op. cit., Introduction.

15. Hirst, P.H., and Peters, R.S. (1970) *The Logic of Education* (London, Routledge and Kegan Paul)

16. op. cit., p. 1.

17. In Downie, R., Loudfoot, E. and Telfer, E. (1974) *Education and Personal Relationships: a Philosophical Study* (London, Methuen), for instance, we read that 'education must be a continual process' and that among the qualities of the educated man one should count this disposition to continue with one's education for life (p. 8). But, at the same time, the authors have already, on earlier pages, described education as a kind of relationship between teacher and taught which has as its object 'the cultivation of the mind, or theoretical reason, and the transmission of culture'. (p.5)

18. Thus Hirst and Peters (op. cit., 1970) describe their own definition of education as providing 'criteria by reference to which decisions taken on economic, or medical grounds, or on personal grounds' are distinguished from those taken on *educational* grounds'. (p. 20)

19. In effect, the liberal concept of adult

education must live with yet another violation of
the usual liberal definition of education if it is
not to be accused of paternalism; this is that education involves compulsion. Indeed part of the discussion of the section to follow refers to John
White's contention that education means 'upbringing', and that compulsion is a necessary part of
upbringing.

20. For a description of liberal ideology and
its educational implications see Cohen, B. (1981)
Education and the Individual (London, George Allen
and Unwin), as also O'Hear's book being referred to
in this chapter.

21. White, J. (1981) *The Aims of Education
Reconsidered* (London, Routledge and Kegan Paul)

22. op. cit., pp. 130-131.

23. ibid., p. 134.

24. ibid., p. 122.

25. ibid., p. 136.

27. We have already seen that this is how
Oakshott, Peters and O'Hear in fact define it. Other
examples could be quoted, for instance Warnock, M.
(1977) *Schools of Thought* (London, Faber and Faber).
'But education is concerned with the right raising
of children, and with the provision for them of a
good future'. (p. 11)

28. Roland Martin, J. 'The Ideal of the
Educated Person', *Philosophy of Education*, 1981.

29. op. cit., p. 6.

30. ibid., p. 7.

31. ibid., pp. 8-9.

32. ibid., p. 11.

33. ibid., p. 11.

34. ibid., p. 11.

35. ibid., p. 8.

36. ibid., p. 12.

37. ibid., p. 12.

38. op. cit., p. 121.

39. ibid., p. 122.

40. op.cit., p. 16.

41. ibid., p. 16.

42. ibid., p. 14.

43. op. cit., p. 132.

44. ibid., p. 131.

45. The importance of this distinction cannot
be over emphasized. The real question is why must a
liberal philosophy of education remain committed to
defining education as upbringing. In Chapter 1 we
saw that White gives his reason for so defining it
as convention; this is the way most people view it
and this is what interests them. Nothing further

need be added here to the comments made there in response to this explanation. One further question does however come to mind: would White be prepared to change his definition of education if people came to see it differently, say as a lifelong process?

46. ibid., p. 132.

47. ibid., p. 136.

48. ibid., p. 133.

49. ibid., p. 134.

50. It is not really a wonder, for, in continuation of his statement 'Whatever else happens there must be some sort of preparation for life in any society', he adds, 'If you prefer to call it 'upbringing' rather than 'education', I don't mind; the important thing is the concept not the word'. (p. 132) In other words he confirms that, for him, 'upbringing' and 'education' mean the same thing.

51.   Entwistle, H.(1979) *Antonio Gramsci: conservative schooling for radical politics* (London, Routledge and Kegan Paul).

52. Paterson would appear to be an exception to the arguments made against liberal philosophers of education in this chapter. Against Peters, in fact, he argues that adult education is a positive (or welfare) *right* — 'adults have a moral right to continuing lifelong education' (p. 233). But his definition of *education* falls squarely within the description of liberal education we have made — 'liberal adult education', as he calls it is simply the extension of the liberal curriculum into later life. Although he consistently describes education as the development of the *person* rather than the child he continues to be bound by the strictures of that definition, even to the extent of tying education with the activity of teachers. (Paterson, R.W.K. (1979) *Values, education and the adult* (London, Routledge and Kegan Paul)).

Chapter Six

LIFELONG EDUCATION AND JOHN DEWEY

BACKGROUND

In the previous chapter the point was made that
though both Peters and Dewey could with some truth
be said to have supported the view that education is
for life, the two are fundamentally at odds about
how it should be held, the former describing it as a
conceptual truth and recommending it as a slogan,
the latter as his definition of education. Consequently, for Peters it means no more than that adults should be encouraged to continue to develop
further 'conceptual schemes and forms of appraisal'
already cultivated in the school, while for Dewey it
is the name of a programme operating with a rather
wider definition of education than schooling.
Dewey's philosophy, this chapter will argue, unlike
Peters', has all the right elements to render it
compatible with the movement's lifelong education
programme, for it similarly strives to conceptualize
education as a lifelong matter and therefore adopts
a language relative to this intention. There are, in
fact, several well-known passages in *Democracy and
Education* and elsewhere that bear this fact out. Of
these, perhaps the most comprehensive being that
which states that:

> It is a commonplace to say that education
> should not cease when one leaves school. The
> point of this commonplace is that the purpose
> of school education is to insure the contin-
> uance of education by organising the powers
> that insure growth. The inclination to learn
> from life itself and to make the conditions of
> life such that all will learn in the process of
> living is the finest product of schooling....
>
> Since life means growth, a living creature

lives as truly and positively at one stage as
at another, with the same intrinsic fullness
and the same absolute claims. Hence education
means the enterprise of supplying the conditions which insure growth or adequacy of life,
irrespective of age.[1]

For in it Dewey reproduces the basic rationale and
principles of the lifelong education programme in
synthesized form: (1) education is a process, a
process of growth; (2) growth itself is a function
of life and vice-versa; there can be no growth
without life, on the other hand there can be no real
life without growth either - it is growth or the
ability to grow that renders human life valuable;
(3) human beings potentially live 'as truly and
positively at one stage as at another', hence their
right to grow cannot be restricted to any one stage
or age in life; (4) therefore education, being
itself a process of growth, is a lifelong matter,
while being also a *right*, it demands the supplying
of conditions that ensure it irrespective of age;
the individual has the same right to it as he has to
life itself; (5) finally, schooling, as itself one
of the stages in life has, within this perspective,
one overriding responsibility over all else: 'to
insure the continuance of education by organizing
the powers that insure growth', this by fostering
the inclination to learn from life itself, and by
rendering the conditions of life such that 'all will
learn in the process of living'. Can the contrast
with Peters and the other liberal philosophers of
education referred to in the previous chapter be
more stark?

What we see in Dewey's educational philosophy is how
facile it is to arrive at the rationale of lifelong
education from a different point of departure than
that assumed by liberal philosophers of education;
how facile it is to accommodate the lifelong education programme within a different theoretic context
or language paradigm from that espoused by liberal
philosophers of education; how easily education can
be reconceptualised in a manner that avoids completely the several theoretical obstacles White sets up
in its way, if we adopt the concept of *growth* rather
than that of educatedness as our theoretic focus.

That Dewey did consider the concept of growth in
this way is unequivocal. Besides its centrality in
the passage just quoted, it is a well-known fact

that Dewey explicitly *defined* education as growth
(it is in fact presupposed by the first statement of
the programme synthesized subsequently to the
quotation). Moreover, he explicitly stated how the
concept is related to that of lifelong education in
the following way:

> When it is said that education is development,
> everything depends upon *how* development is
> conceived. Our net conclusion is that life is
> development and that developing, growing, is
> life. Translated into its educational equival-
> ents, this means (1) that the educational pro-
> cess has no end beyond itself, (2) the educa-
> tional process is one of continual reorganiz-
> ing, reconstructing, transforming.[2]

The problem is that Dewey's metaphor has come under
repeated attacks from philosophers of education who
have complained about its 'permissiveness'. This
permissiveness, they say, would render the concept
of education itself an empty one . From another
perspective, as educational criterion, it would be
open to abuse, they say, in the sense that growth
can itself be of different kinds, some morally and
intellectually undesirable, unless it is guided into
the right channels; i.e., unless it is restrained
and controlled by definite *aims* that constitute the
real criteria for educational activities.[3] And
this criticism raises once more the question whether
any education programme can do without some concept
of educatedness, the question implicity raised but
inadequately tackled by White.

It is notorious that Dewey himself was incapable of
adequately defending his principle against these
objections, or, at least, of providing a defence
that was satisfactory to his critics. In *Experience
and Education*, his specific reply to the criticism
was that the principle of growth contains its own
intrinsic value criterion, it needs no further regu-
lation.All we need ask, he says, is 'Does this form
of growth create conditions for further growth, or
does it set up conditions that shut off the person
who has grown in this particular direction from the
occasions, stimuli and opportunities for continuing
growth in new directions?'[4]'

But it is clear that this reply merely postpones the
issue, it does not really answer the criticism. For
becoming a burglar, the example Dewey himself cites

of growth in the wrong direction, could very well provide the burglar with the time and resources that would, in turn, create opportunities for further and different forms of growth in all sorts of other ways, many of which may actually be desirable in themselves. The criterion he sets in his question will therefore be adequately met in this case. What would continue to render the practice that leads one to grow into a highly expert burglar objectionable nonetheless is the very immorality of stealing; the fact that we still consider burglary to be wrong in itself no matter what the otherwise positive effects on the burglar may be. The point is made against Dewey with particular insistence by liberal philosophers of education who insist that education is a normative enterprise, and the normative considerations it involves are partly moral. Thus Peters states that education implies that 'something worthwhile is being or has been intentionally transmitted in a morally acceptable manner'.[5] He further states that talk about 'growth', 'self-realization' and gearing the curriculum to the interests of children glosses over this fundamentally normative aspect of education'.[6] Or, as White would put it, its upbringing aspect wherein moral principles like 'Thou shalt not steal', are cultivated in the young.

One way of reinterpreting the principle in a manner that avoids these difficulties has, however, recently been proposed by Beckett, who argues that 'Growth theory, (however), is an account, not of a moral enterprise, but a non-moral phenomenon. It is,.... primarily concerned with what happens to the educand, and only secondarily in what the educator might do'.[7] In other words, it could be part of the *technical* definition of education which defines how the concept will be approached not what its content will be, though the second will evidently depend heavily on the first. In this sense it would fit in with that class of decisions concerned with questions about whether we are going to define education as a formal, or intentional enterprise, or whether we are going to broaden the approach to include the informal and non-formal, rather than substantive decisions, among which those related to the kind of upbringing it is desirable people should have feature prominently. In fact, the point has already been made that it is the decision to approach education as a process within the individual rather than an activity of teachers that renders it consistent to include the informal and non-formal

aspects of learning within one's technical definition of education. Once this point is made, although
Dewey himself does not make it, it becomes possible
to reinterpret the concept of growth in a manner
that is both useful and free from moral objection of
the kind usually raised against it.

As to the first criticism, it is not even accurate
to say that Dewey's own conception of growth is that
of a process that is directionless, even if his
statements do appear to justify this interpretation.
In effect, it is a fact that Dewey himself honed
down considerably the concept of growth which he
would make educationally significant in different
ways. It is not, therefore, accurate to say that by
identifying education with growth he denied the
former any conceptual space and rendered it meaningless. Thus, he specifically contrasted *his* sense of
growth with mere 'maturation' and also ruled out
certain other conceptions of growth with which he
declared himself to be out of sympathy. These are,
to begin with, those according to which growth is
directed towards 'an ideal and standard a static
end'. [8] All conceptions of this kind, Dewey says,
in tacit criticism of the view that educators should
aim at achieving the educatedness of their pupils,
regard education as a *process of preparation*, of
getting ready, where what is prepared for is 'the
responsibilities and privileges of adult life'.[9]
And those conceptions of growth where 'The goal is
conceived of as completion, perfection', to be reached through an 'unfolding of latent powers', which
is the other form taken by education as 'preparation'.[10]

It is very clear what education programmes Dewey is
attacking as departing from the wrong conception of
development.[11] There is first that philosophical
outlook that looks to some conception of educatedness as a final point of arrival and which belongs,
quite clearly, to the liberal educational tradition.
With the second, on the other hand, Dewey has in
mind those conceptions of human development that
belong to a philosophical outlook which starts from
a theory of a whole, an absolute, which is 'immanent' in human life, and which regards education as
'the gradual making explicit and outward of what is
thus wrapped up'.[12] The main proponents of this
view Dewey identifies as Froebel and Hegel who, in
different ways, both viewed development as the unfolding of a ready made latent principle; the diff-

erence between them lying in their accounts of the actuating force behind this development, the former locating it in the presentation of symbols corresponding to the essential traits of the absolute, the latter in 'a series of historical institutions' that similarly embody the absolute's essential traits. [13]

Dewey's main objection is to the 'static understanding of life' which these conceptions represent, and he gives reasons for it. In the first place, human nature itself, he says, rebels against it; no person will ever willingly accept at any stage of his life that his potentiality for growth has come to a close - that he will now cease to grow. As Dewey puts it:

> every adult resents the imputation of having no
> further possibilities of growth; and so far as
> he finds that they are closed to him mourns the
> fact as evidence of loss, instead of falling
> back on the achieved as adequate manifestation
> of power.[14]

In the second place, where a universal end is postulated to regulate education programmes it is always the case that 'an abstract future is in command',[15] while the present interests of the learner and current relevances are attributed little or no worth. Not only, where the end identified is perfection 'it is so beyond us that, strictly speaking, it is unattainable'.[16] We are therefore constrained either to translate it into something else, something that stands for it, and therefore, like Froebel 'substitute(d) for development as arbitrary and externally imposed a system of dictation as the history of instruction has ever seen',[17] or else fall in with romantic conceptions of education which view 'every manifestation of the child as an unfolding from within; and hence sacred',[18] in which case development becomes 'a vague sentimental aspiration rather than anything which can be intelligently grasped and stated'.[19] Finally, the political translation of a conception of development regulated by a universal end can, as in Hegelian philosophy, lead to the reification of the current institutions as necessary manifestations of the absolute against which individuals can have no rights or competing interests and within which, accordingly, 'personal development and nurture, consist in obedient assimilation of the (existent) spirit'.[20]

In sum, what Dewey had against programmes regulated by `static' conceptions of education; i.e. by conceptions that translate themselves into fixed ends, whether identified by some agency external to the learner or, supposedly, lying within, is that while they claim to read off the meaning of education either into the concept itself (which is the alibi of the analytic philosopher), or into the `nature' of the educand, or into history, they really amount to no more than arbitrary imposition on the individual whose personal interests and needs are sacrificed or considered irrelevant in the process. His own contention was that `aims' are things that people have, `education' itself has no aims, and can therefore only be read into the purposes and activities of the people whose they are; teachers, philosophers, administrators, or whatever. There is, however, a more fundamental way of viewing education, and the growth metaphor brings it out. For what it implies, as Beckett points out, is that the educator can only intervene in, and try to modify, development which is already occurring.[21] Therefore there is a more primary factor, with respect to education, which we can come to understand not by examining concepts or by inquiring into the aims or reasons people have for teaching particular things, but by considering it as a process and trying to understand its nature as a typically human enterprise.

This is the significance of the account of education with which Dewey begins *Democracy and Education*, an account which is not usually credited with the importance required if the intention is to understand his educational philosophy accurately, perhaps because of its Darwinian language. Here Dewey specifically identifies education with human survival. Human beings, he says, like all other living beings survive only if they are able to interact successfully with their environment. With lower living beings that environment is nature, with living beings of the highest order, including humans, it is both nature and society. Moreover, with human beings specifically, the environment has become less and less natural with time and more social, so that `survival' has, correspondingly, become more of a social concern than anything else. This is the case, at least, with industrialized societies. Dewey refers to this process of adaptation as education in its most fundamental sense, and he makes it clear that, as such, education refers not only to an individual but also to a social need; if no individual

can survive within society without being educated to
it, no society can itself survive without education
which also, at the same time, guarantees the transmission of its culture, which is what the individual
is educated into. This mutual relationship just
described makes it unrealistic, Dewey contends, to
separate the individual from the social where educational matters are concerned. We shall need to return to this contention later. To continue with the
present point, Dewey also specifies that human beings differ from other species in *how* they can interact with their environment, and it is this additional difference that gives education its particular quality as a distinctive human enterprise. Thus
beings are not merely able to adjust to the conditions in which they find themselves, they are also
capable of *changing* the conditions themselves by
acting on them: 'Adaptation, in fine, is quite as
much adaptation *of* the environment to our activities
as of our activities *to* the environment'.[22]

This way of viewing human interaction with its environment has, in turn, important consequences for
how that environment itself needs to be conceptualized. 'The things with which a man varies', says
Dewey, 'are his genuine environment ... the environment consists of those conditions that promote or
hinder, stimulate or inhibit, the *characteristic*
activities of a living being',[23] and the 'characteristic activities' of living human beings are of
course, for Dewey, *social*. But, apart from that,
what he is saying is that education implies considerably *more* than can be calculated for by specifying instructional aims, since its fundamental relationship is not with instruction but with life itself. More, with regards to this relationship with
life, Dewey claims that the symmetrical interactive
association with the environment which it implies,
and which he calls *intelligence* accounts for our
ability for 'experimental selection' with which he
contrasts the having of 'an ideal and standard a
static end'. Finally, translated into socio-political terms, this human capability for 'experimental
selection', becomes the very basis of democracy as
Dewey undertood it.[24]

In conclusion, the metaphor of growth itself can be
rendered intelligible in the manner indicated earlier, as a non-moral phenomenon. The process it
denotes receives its normative content and is deliberately modified in different ways within specula-

tion about the ideal *quality* of human life itself,
or within actual lived conditions. Then, moral,
social, vocational and other conditions are brought
to bear upon how it is defined as education. There
are, then, *two* aspects to education; as *process* and
as a deliberate act defined in terms of the *aims* of
people. Neither can do without the recognition of
the other but, ideally, from Dewey's point of view,
the latter should be an *aid* to the former, not a
frustration of it. This is an exceedingly important
point with vital implications, and it gives further
sense to Cooper's observation, that Dewey sees the
relationship between education and society as one in
which the latter should ideally adapt to the former,
and not the other way around.[25]

On the other hand Callan is right when he insists
that *Dewey's* conception of growth is a normative one
and gives rise to a type of education designed for a
certain kind of society.[26] For it is clear that
in its most fundamental aspect Dewey regards education, and therefore the kind of growth that characterizes it, as a form of 'democratic socialization'
rather than a mere directionless process. Confirmation of this is, furthermore, explicitly provided
by Dewey himself who brings the criterion of growth
even more under harness when he specifies a 'control' or 'direction' aspect of education to which,
in due recognition of the point I made in the previous paragraph, he argues, growth must itself be
made subject. It is, in fact, here that Dewey gets
himself into even more troubled waters than he does
with his growth metaphor, as we shall see later.

COMPATIBILITIES WITH THE LIFELONG
EDUCATION PROGRAMME

This chapter began with a quotation from *Democracy
and Education* which, straightaway, suggested a very
evident coincidence between Dewey's educational
philosophy and the lifelong education programme.
One single quote followed by a list of implications
drawn from it and that are coordinate with the principles of the programme may not be enough however to
prove the point and, in fact, it was further claimed
that there are numerous passages in Dewey that could
be cited in its support. A further exercise similar
to that engaged in in Chapter 4 establishing a certain coordination between elements in the lifelong
education literature and 'romantic' humanist educa-

tional theory, could therefore be made with respect
to Dewey also.   It will not, however, be attempted
here because something of the kind has already been
made by Cross-Durant whose article has already been
referred to in earlier pages of this book for other
purposes.[27]   Many of the statements and passages
in Dewey's work that are directly or indirectly
related to the idea of lifelong education are cited
there and compared with pieces selected from the
lifelong education literature, taken mostly from the
articles in Dave's book *Foundations of Lifelong
Education*, which is also, of course, an important
source of reference for lifelong education theory in
this book.   The reader can therefore be referred to
Cross-Durant's article for the purpose of drawing up
the convergences required.   Here they will be taken
as established or at least establishable, and some
of the major ones can be enumerated briefly in point
form as follows:

1.   Both agree that education is to be viewed
primarily as a process of growth in the individual
that is ideally ongoing and lifelong.
2.   Both agree that, in view of this fact, all
learning that influences growth in positive ways is
educationally relevant, whether it is intentional
(formal or non-formal), or non-intentional (non-
formal and informal).
3.   The inclusion of informal learning within
either programme's definition of education means
that both consider the learning environment to be
crucial.   Both share the broad conception of
'environment' described by Dewey.   In fact, Dewey's
contention that 'the very process of living together
educates',[28] could be considered the very basis of
the concept of the 'learning society' which is
crucial to the lifelong education programme.
4.   As far as school is concerned, it is
considered by both as being *one* among any number of
educational agencies available in any society at any
time since both conceptualize *every* social institu-
tion as potentially educative.   As such its educational role is redimensionalized away from the customary traditional one; and its own value is measured in terms of its ability to coordinate its own
efforts and interests with those of the wider society.   In short, it loses its priority and becomes
part of the 'learning society'.
5.   Both agree, accordingly, that the
fundamental concern of the school should be not the
reception and storage of information but the organi-

zing of the powers that ensure continuing growth for each individual.[29]

These points, in a way, constitute a clarification and broadening of the synthesized programme drawn from the quote from Dewey made at the beginning of the chapter and referred to earlier. They refer, more or less, to the technical definition of education which Dewey and the lifelong education theorists share. There are, however, other interesting points of convergence between the two sides that could easily be ignored. One that interests us in particular relates not to the technical definition of education in the two programmes but to their respective ideological components. That there is this ideological point of convergence will have occurred to the reader earlier, when reference was made to the fact that Dewey was one of the signatories of the *Humanist Manifesto*, though this, in itself means little in view of the variety of different forms 'humanism' takes. The other ideological point of contact between the two evidently relates to the presence of the 'pragmatic' trend within the lifelong education movement.

That Dewey's pragmatism gives rise to a humanist outlook is not surprising. The connection between pragmatism and humanism is, in fact, an historical one. It was claimed by all the American pragmatists, though it was F.C.S. Schiller who devoted most attention to it. Schiller described pragmatism itself as the application of humanism to the theory of knowledge, or as the epistemic arm of humanism. For pragmatists, in accordance with humanist beliefs, 'take Man for granted as he stands, and the world of man's experience as it has come to him',[30] as their point of departure. Schiller continues to define pragmatism as:

> the philosophic attitude which, without wasting thought upon attempts to construct experience *a priori* is content to take human experience as the clue to the world of human experience, content to take Man on his own merits, just as he is to start with, without insisting that he must first be disembowelled of his interests and have his individuality evaporated and translated into technical jargon, before he can be deemed deserving of scientific notice.[31]

For Schiller, then, humanism *is* a readily definable

'philosophic attitude' when it is disciplined by a
pragmatic epistemology. The holding of this common
pragmatic epistemology, in turn, also establishes a
further link with humanism that is of interest to
us, the link with philosophical hermeneutics which,
like the pragmatic humanist understanding, is also
'hospitable to the view that the universe is ultimately a 'joint-stock' affair'.[32] It is not surprising either, then, that Dewey is linked with the
hermeneutic outlook also, as we saw in Chapter 1.

Schiller himself, like Dewey, makes no specific use
of the term 'hermeneutic', but the hermeneutic understanding clearly underlies his account of the
pragmatist epistemology which, he claims, is ultimately derived from William James. James it was, in
fact, who first advanced the relevant pragmatist
doctrine in connection with what he called the
'will-to-believe'. This he described as an
intellectual right to decide (in certain cases)
between alternative views each of which seems to
make a legitimate appeal to our nature by *other than
purely intellectual considerations*, i.e., by means
of their emotional interest and practical value, the
limiting condition to its applicability being,
mainly, the willingness to take the risks involved
and to abide by the consequences. James' theory of
the 'will-to-believe', Schiller notes, frequently
brought upon him the charge of 'irrationalism'.
But, Schiller argues, common sense has always felt
that there are 'reasons of the heart of which the
head knows nothing', postulates of faith that sur-
pass mere understanding, and that these possess a
'higher rationality' which a bigoted intellectualism
has failed to comprehend. Pragmatism, he says,
indicates the rationality of 'irrationalism', without itself becoming irrational, it thus restrains
the extravagance of intellectualism without itself
losing faith in the intellect. It effects 'a reconciliation between a reason which is humanised and a
faith which is rationalised, in the very process
which shows their antithesis to be an error'.[33]

Dewey's own appeal to humanism in *Democracy and
Education* is an aid towards resolving yet one more
dichotomy within the educational world, that between
humanism itself and 'naturalism', by trying to show
that naturalistic studies (meaning the study of the
physical sciences) have a place in integration with
the 'humanities' in a humanistic curriculum, his
presuppositional premise being that a humanist phil-

osophy can first resolve the deeper philosophical
dichotomy between `mind` and the world proposed by
the Platonic tradition. The basis of Dewey's nexus
of `naturalism` with humanism therefore takes the
following shape:

> Human life does not occur in a vacuum, nor is
> nature mere stage setting for the enactment of
> its drama. Man's life is bound up in the pro-
> cesses of nature; his career, for success or
> defeat, depends upon the way in which nature
> enters it. Man's power of deliberate control
> of his own affairs depends upon ability to
> direct natural energies to use: an ability
> which is in turn dependent upon insight into
> nature's processes. Whatever natural science
> may be for the specialist, for educational
> purposes it is knowledge of the conditions of
> human action. To be aware of the medium in
> which social intercourse goes on, and of the
> means and obstacles to its progressive develop-
> ment is to be in command of a knowledge which
> is thoroughly humanistic in quality.[34]

In other words, the successful management of human
affairs, not the least *social* human affairs, depends, in the first instance, on an understanding
and management of `nature`. This is the value the
pragmatist assigns to the physical sciences, a humanistic value. At the same time his refusal to
acknowledge final solutions, absolute, or dogmatic
of any kind enables him to hold his belief in the
possibilities of science at a level far-removed from
`arrogance`. The other side of the picture, of
course, as far as Dewey is concerned, where science
comes in, concerns the other value of scientific
research as a methodology which could and should be
readily applied to human affairs in the wider sense,
since science is the typical method of `experimental
selection` referred to earlier as the best means of
conducting such affairs. From this point of view,
as is well known, Dewey's `ideal` society is envisaged on the model of a scientific community where
knowledge is communicated openly, held up to public
scrutiny, and accepted or rejected on the basis of
criteria held in common. If this combination of
these twin insights is what the Faure report means
by a `scientific humanism`, then it is well in accord with the spirit of pragmatism, if, on the other
hand, it denotes a species of positivism and is
envisaged as a passage to utopia then it clearly is

not.

The other thing that is important about pragmatism, Dewey's in particular, is the 'here-and-now' of its concern, or what Santayana calls the 'foreground' — 'A foreground is by definition relative to some chosen point of view, to the station assumed in the midst of nature by some creature tethered by fortune to a particular time and place'.[35] In other words its *historicity* with regards both the questions that regard the world and human being itself, which it shares with existentialists like Heidegger whose existential being is 'thrown', and wherever he is thrown happens to be the foreground that becomes the focal point of philosophical concern; with Dewey, as we have seen that foreground is given another name, 'environment'. 'Pragmatism', says Santayana, 'may be regarded as a synthesis of all those ways of making the foreground dominant: the most close-reefed of philosophical craft, most tightly hugging appearance, use, and relevance of practice today and here, least drawn by the hire of speculative distances'.[36] So described, Dewey calls it *instrumentalism*, and the dominant foreground for him, as we have said, as for Heidegger, is the social world, though Dewey's instrumentalism is unencumbered by conceptions of authenticity, and his faith in scientific method gives him a problem-solving edge over the existentialists whose concern with the 'here-and-now' is purely analytic or phenomenological, while his is practical or functional.

This instrumentalist emphasis on the 'here-and-now' results in two things that are of interest to us. For one thing it denies, in an *a priori* manner, the value of futuristic speculations or utopic blueprints for the purposes of planning or policy in the educational or any other field of human action, for all our current knowledge can give us is the 'warrented assertibility' which makes it rational to act in particular ways according to the evidence and experience available, and no more. Dewey's own rejection of 'static' conceptions of development discussed earlier owes itself to this epistemology. For another it explains Dewey's conception of education as a lifelong process in an even more fundamental, though connected, way than is implied by recourse to his theory that it is a process of growth. The reader is again asked to recall the quotation from *Democracy and Education* with which this chapter opened. Part of the quotation stated that 'Since life means growth, a living creature lives as truly and positively at one stage as at another, with the same intrinsic fullness and the same absolute claims'. This bold assertion can in fact only be made if the 'here-and-now' of every moment of life is conceived of as intrinsically valuable, or valuable in its own right - it becomes *practically* valuable to Dewey if it leads to further growth. He puts the point in the following way:

> the ideal of growth results in the conception that education is a constant reorganizing or restructuring of experience. It has all the time an immediate end, and so far as activity is educative, it reaches that end - the direct transformation of the quality of experience. Infancy, youth, adult life, - all stand on the same educative level in the sense that what is really *learned* at any and every stage of experience constitutes the value of that experience.[37]

Again, here we have at the same time an explanation of the value that Dewey attributes to change in the scheme of things, because there can be no growth without change - the problematic nature of human existence generated by continually changing social and other conditions is thus, for Dewey, as for all the pragmatists, not a cause for 'anguish' or 'anxiety', but one of perpetual stimulation towards a more efficient and creative reorganizing and restructuring of the conditions of life which is the sure sign of growth and of the experimental spirit at work. Accelerating change, therefore, is, yes, a source of challenge, of continuous challenge at different levels, but it is also a positive sign of an active humanity. The real problem does not lie with change itself but with the lack of supportive systems that would make change a positive rather than a negative feature of life; most especially the lack of educational systems that can respond in the required manner. Thus we find Dewey complaining, like the lifelong education theorists, about formal teaching in the school that it tends to be 'remote and dead - abstract and bookish', detached from 'urgent daily interests', or 'isolated from the subject matter of life-experience,' and so on,[38] though this may not be due so much to a defective understanding of the situation by the policy-makers as to a conscious political plan, since it is evident that education for a fixed and static order

accomodates the *status quo* better than one that
encourages an experimental outlook, that concentrates on the dynamic aspects of life, and that
encourages the view that the *status quo* itself is
merely a temporary solution which needs to be re-
viewed critically and continuously in order to identify features of it that need reorganizing and restructuring.

One major problem with pragmatism is that refusing,
as it does, blueprints or models or static conceptions to work on it falls back on the principle of
utility as the only criterion of value; thus, from
the pragmatist's point of view an improved arrangement of any kind is simply one that `works better'
in the here-and-now.   But this criterion is not
really enough, not even in the physical sciences
where it appears to work best, because even the
physical sciences work with theories of what it is
to `work better' or to `progress' scientifically.
Anyway, theories that are appropriate to a description of the physical world are not necessarily
transferable to social and political life, where the
evaluations sought are frequently normative.   That
is unless you are prepared to conflate the normative
into the descriptive, which is, in fact, what Dewey
tends to do.

Dewey's general position, as regards value judgements, is, in fact, behaviourist.   It is that they
are really, like judgements of fact, propositional;
they make truth-claims and are reducible to psychological judgements that can be verified empirically
in action:

> Valuations are empirically observable patterns
> of behaviour and may be studied as such. The
> propositions that result are about valuations
> but are not of themselves value-propositions in
> any sense marking them off from other matter-
> of-fact propositions.[39]

Thus a typical value statement like X is good',
translated in the functional terms of the pragmatist, is rendered incomplete. From the pragmatist's
point of view in order to say that something is
`good' intelligibly we need to answer the further
question `good for what?'; or, better, when we des-
cribe something as good we must have in mind something else in respect of which we are describing it
as good. Thus even our valuations arise in response

to some identified problem; 'when there is something
the matter; when there is some trouble to be done
away with, some need, lack, or privation to be made
good, some conflict of tendencies to be resolved by
means of changing existent conditions'.[40] Otherwise the conventional criteria will do.

This background helps us understand both Dewey's
conception of democracy and his attitude toward the
individual and the social in general. We can recall
to mind his famous twin-criteria for the former; for
Dewey there is democracy to the extent that there
are 'many interests consciously communicated and
shared', and there are 'varied and free points of
contact with other modes of association',[41] and
the criticism that is generally levelled against the
side of his book where he deals with the democratic
ideal; that there is no discussion at all of 'the
institutional arrangements necessary to support
it... no proper discussion of liberty, equality and
rule of law, no probing of the problems of representation, participation, and the control of the execu-
tive'.[42] What these criteria indicate, in fact,
as Flew points out, are merely 'formal' characteristics which Dewey believes any democracy should have,
rather than concrete material conditions.[43] And
this is clear also from his later expansion of the
criteria themselves:

> The first signifies not only more numerous and
> more varied points of shared common interest,
> but greater reliance upon the recognition of
> mutual interests as a factor of social control.
> The second means not only freer interaction
> between social groups (once isolated so far as
> intention could keep up separation) but change
> in social habit — its continuous readjustment
> through meeting the new situations produced by
> varied intercourse. And these two traits are
> precisely what characterize the democratically
> constituted society.[44]

For, citing this background, it is possible to respond to it that *this is as far as Dewey's pragmatism
could consistently allow him to go*. He could not, in
fact, without contradicting the basic premises of
his philosophical position, describe how things
'ought' to be in the sense of ought that involves
making prescriptions that are universally applicable
for any society, any more than he could fix aims for
education. His analysis of democracy, in effect,

parallels that of education in that both are treated
as processes with open-ended futures rather than as
institutions bound by their own logic. As with education so with politics all we can do, from Dewey's
point of view, is stipulate certain conditions within which, consistently with the pragmatic world-
view, decisions should be made, not what they should
be. These conditions are, as we have seen, again
from his point of view, those that are typical of a
scientific community and that include the permanent
possibility of experiment against a stable background of values and criteria respected by all. Thus
what the socio-political situation in any given
society 'ought' to be in theory is what it *would* be
in practice were the conditions being fully realized
- were the opportunities, mechanisms, and environ-
mental factors that satisfy his twin criteria fully
in place, were society really a *community*. What
therefore constitutes the defining democratic features of any democratic society, within Dewey's
conception of the word, is not its set of institutions but the presence of these conditions, the same
as what is constant in the educational process is
the presence of growth, otherwise different societies, with regards to their socio-political options,
like different individuals, with regards to their
learning options, will choose for themselves how the
process should be concretized.

The reply to Peter's point that Dewey failed to
discuss the institutional arrangements of 'democracy' is that, for Dewey 'The problem is to extract
the desirable traits of forms of community life
which actually exist, and employ them to criticize
undesirable features and suggest improvements',[45]
not to work with democratic models.

CONTROL AND CONFORMISM

Once Dewey's conception of democracy and of the role
of the social in the lives of individuals is understood, there appears to be no grounds for the criticism, frequently levelled at him, that his educational philosophy is a defence of conformism and
conspires to bury the individual beneath the collective. Nor does there seem to be any justice in the
contention made recently that Dewey's philosophy,
taken as a whole, embraces a contradiction in this
respect, in that he is, at one and the same time, 'a
champion of permissiveness in the classroom' and 'an

apostle of social conformity'.[46] Both evaluations
can in fact be challenged. The charge of permissiveness evidently arises from Dewey's belief that education should be regarded as growth. We have already
seen that his meaning of growth, however, actually
falls far short of romantic theories of growth that
can be described as permissive, and even of Rousseau's naturalism.[47] We need therefore spend no
more time on this question and can turn instead to
the accusation of conformism.

At the end of the first section of this chapter it
was noted that Dewey sets nearly as much store on
the `control' aspect of education as he does on its
function as growth. In point of fact, at the start
of the relevant chapter on the subject in *Democracy
and Education*, he specifies that control `denotes
the process by which (the individual) is brought to
subordinate his natural impulses to public or common
ends'.[48] And the popular reaction to this thesis
has, predictably, been most unfavourable. Nor does
his case appear to be helped by the fact that he
indicates `habit' as the most democratic form of
control, although he takes care to specify more than
once that the control of `habit' is not achieved by
naked external coercion. For `habit' is not, Dewey
says, in its relevant sense, personal either. On the
contrary it is `intellectual', by which he means
social: `It consists in the habits of *understanding*,
which are set up in using objects in correspondence
with others'. At the same time Dewey rejects all
abstract conceptions of mind and insists that it is
`a concrete thing', an instrument which is fundamen-
tally social. Dewey also argues that the object of
formal education is to develop a `socialized mind',
a mind that has `the power to understand (things) in
terms of the use to which they are turned in joint
or shared situations'.[49] And it is the possession
of such a mind, Dewey argues, that constitutes the
best form of social control; a conclusion that sends
shudders down the frame of liberal philosophers of
education — for does it not amount to the champion-
ing of social control in the name of *education*, a
social control of the most perverse kind?

The question has been the subject of a recent exchange of arguments between Callen and Essiet, the
latter arguing against the former that there is no
actual discontinuity between Dewey's `pedagogy of
freedom' and his democratic ideal.[50] The substance
of Callan's argument is, in fact, that the latter is

completely 'illiberal', unlike the former, while
Essiet insists that both are equally free and cites
a string of statements from Dewey's writing to prove
his point. To which Callan responds by continuing to
argue that Dewey's allegiance to freedom is merely
verbal, and this shows, he says, in the fact that
Dewey expresses no strong concern anywhere for 'individual rights (that) would be necessary to give
some security to the range of personal liberty'.[51]
Moreover, Callan argues, another reason why Dewey's
democratic ideal is of itself 'repugnant to individuality' is because it is permeated by a 'fraternal' ethic.[52]

Thus Callan does concede that 'there are occasional
affirmations of the value of individuality' in
Dewey's writings.[53] He cites perhaps the most
famous of these where, in *Democracy and Education*,
Dewey criticizes Plato's philosophy for failing to
recognize the uniqueness of individuals, and, ultimately, presenting itself in such a manner as to
amount 'in net effect to the idea of the subordin-
ation of individuality',[54] as an example. Moreover, he also admits that these can be supplemented
by Dewey's evident and frequently expressed distaste
for social stratification by classes. Nevertheless,
he continues to insist that Dewey's respect for
individuality is only skin-deep, the main emphasis
of his work, Callan says, being on a certain kind
of personal uniformity, though he is again forced to
refer to Dewey's expressed objections to social
adaptation understood as conformity, because, he
says, these objections to conformity were limited to
external constraint at the same time as Dewey was
concerned to advocate an internalized conformity,
and this is also 'patently inimical to individual
uniqueness'.[55]

It is clear that this criticism is not to be answered, as Essiet does, by drawing up a list of
quotes from Dewey's work, impressive as this may
appear, in favour of the individual, thereby con-
cluding that the case for his support for personal
freedom is made. Because a, perhaps, equally long
list could be made up to 'prove' Dewey's apparent
tendency to subjugate the individual to the social
and to show his distaste for the individual. We must
revert instead to a close examination of what Dewey
was attacking or supporting in the name of the individual. If citing a list of quotations does not
make the case for the pro-Dewey argument, nobody

accusing him of advocating conformism can honestly
do so either without first considering seriously
what he could have meant by stating, for instance,
that `Democracy is an absurdity where faith in the
individual is impossible',[56] and by making other
statements in a similar vein. But before we move on
to such an examination, a comment about Callan's
statement that Dewey made `occasional affirmations'
in favour of the individual is required. Quite simply, this is not true. As Essiet shows, Dewey did
not make `occasional affirmations' on this score, he
made several declarations, and not just in *Democracy
and Education* but elsewhere also.

What was it, then, that Dewey was attacking or
supporting in the name of the individual? The first
crucial point to make in answering this question
refers to Dewey's sense of history; the fact that
his statements with respect to the individual are
conditioned by what he took to be a moral crisis in
American and other Western industrialized societies
in modern times. This crisis, as he saw it, is a
direct outcome not so much of changed historical
conditions as of the failure of liberalism to respond to them adequately. There was, he insisted,
nothing wrong with the original liberal values themselves, `those that mark off one person from another
and that are expressed in initiative, invention, and
energetic enterprise', indeed he actually described
them as `something that should be permanently em-
bodied in any future social order';[57] their value
lying in the conception of freedom which underpinned
them. What was objectionable to him was the corruption of these values that had turned them from a
positive into a negative force in human life. The
cause of this corruption Dewey attributed to the old
liberalism's own lack of a historical sense which:

> blinded the eyes of liberals to the fact that
> their own special interpretations of liberty,
> individuality and intelligence were themselves
> historically conditioned, and were relevant
> only to their own time. They put forward their
> ideas as immutable truths good at all times and
> in all places; they had no idea of historic
> relativity, either in general or in application
> to themselves.[58]

This lack of a sense of history had, in fact,
according to Dewey, caused liberalism to betray
itself by becoming the orthodoxy of capitalism,

which had instinctively seized upon this weakness and turned it to its advantage. By unconsciously elevating the critical insights of the old liberalism about a specific time and situation to the status of universal truths capitalism could in fact, Dewey says, effectively reinforce its own conservatism, its own resistance to all further social change and basic criticism.

These points are forcefully made in 'Toward a New Individualism', where Dewey traces the historical evolution which gave rise to modern individualism through 'a fusion of individual capitalism, of natural rights and of morals founded in strictly individual traits and values (which) remained, under the influence of Protestantism, the dominant intellectual synthesis'.[59] This evolution, Dewey says, was accompanied by the optimism that sheer 'individual energy and savings would be serving the needs of others and thus promoting the general welfare and effecting a general harmony of interests'.That optimism has today been shelved by even the most stalwart supporters of this type of individualism, says Dewey, but they have simply turned instead to 'proclaiming its consistency with unchanging human nature – which is said to be moved to effort only by the hope of personal gain – and to paint dire pictures of the inevitable consequences of any change to another regime'.[60]

One can easily see why this position is wholly unacceptable to Dewey. For one thing there is much here that is in conflict with his pragmatism, which, for instance, recognizes no 'unchanging human nature' and which, on the contrary encourages the value of changing human conditions through social experimentation. For another Dewey's humanistic outlook could not accept that human nature is motivated solely by the hope of personal gain. But, even more fundamentally, Dewey insists that the old individualism is bankrupt historically. Its net result in our times, under the prevailing conditions, is that it has instilled in people 'a confusion that is an expression of the' inability to find a secure and morally rewarding place in a troubled and tangled economic scene'.[61] This bankruptcy of the old individualism, in turn, Dewey argues, plays into the hands of collectivists, into the hands of those who 'would keep it alive in order to serve their own ends, and they slur over the real problem – that of remaking the individual'. Even socialists are held captive by

the old ideal; discontented by the injustices lying
within the present scheme of things, they think that
redress requires collective social control, but the
object of this control is to mend inequalities by
'the extension of the earlier individualism to the
many'.[62] What they want therefore is the widest
distribution of the old individual in society,
whereas, for Dewey, what is needed is quite simply a
rejection of the old individual *in favour of a new
one.*

In sum, it should be amply clear from the above what
kind of individualism it is that Dewey is against;
it is the kind which 'has now shrunk to a pecuniary
scale and measure'.[63] He is similarly opposed to
the society to which it gives rise where the virtues
of individuality are vocally proclaimed but otherwise either suppressed in thought and speech, or
reserved for a small number. Thus, in a comment
reminiscent of Marx, he says:

> One cannot imagine a bitterer comment on any
> professed individualism than that it subordi-
> nates the only creative individuality — that of
> mind — to the maintenance of a regime which
> gives a few an opportunity for being shrewd in
> the management of monetary business.

At the same time Dewey also makes it clear that:

> Just as the new individualism cannot be achiev-
> ed by extending the benefits of the older econ-
> omic individualism to more persons, so it can-
> not be obtained by a further development of
> generosity, good will and altruism.[64]

Of these, he says, there is already plenty, but he
wants something more. Thus 'fraternalism' is indeed,
as Callan says, the moral basis of Dewey's new
social order. Dewey assumes, like Hume and the old
liberals, that benevolence is a 'more or less constant expression of human nature', and notices
approvingly its increase, considering this 'prophet-
ic of a type of mind already in a process of formation', but there is still lacking what Dewey describes as 'the organic character that will enable it
to manifest itself in ordinary human relationships
outside of relief and assistance'.[65] Social relationships, for Dewey, need to be imbued throughout
by the fraternal ethic, to the extent that they
become naturally fraternal. They therefore cannot

be left to the mere expression of human nature,
though it is clearly of crucial importance that
human beings possess, all things being equal, a
benevolent disposition. They also require a system
of social arrangements that are compatible with
fraternalism and encourage it; in other words society needs to be a `community'. And it also re-
quires the support of an individual mind socialized
accordingly.

Is an ethic of fraternalism necessarily `inimical to
individual uniqueness'? It depends on what one
means by `individual uniqueness'. If it means a
personal philosophy of subjectivism that denies the
value of the `Other', viewing him necessarily as
`hell', or if it means, not necessarily from the
same point of view, encouraging a dichotomy between
authenticity and the meaningless, valueless `herd',
or if, from another point of view, a politico-econo-
mic one, it denies any `social contract' that gives
the many the right to regulate social and economic
affairs, and therefore considers legitimate those
contracts only that are entered into individually by
knowing and `willing' parties, then Dewey was cert-
ainly against it. For Dewey certainly believed in
the right of the state to intervene in favour of the
common good and, furthermore, he was against everything that cannot be communicated or shared with
others.[66]

Callan describes Dewey's fraternalism `illiberal',
what justice is there in this charge? If by `illib-
eral' he really means `non-liberal', then he is
perhaps right in the sense that fraternalism is a
socialist rather than a liberal value. But he is
not right if by `illiberal' he means, as the context
suggests he does, threatening to freedom. For it
is not a necessary fact that an ethic of fraternalism is a *priori* antagonistic to freedom, unless
freedom is conceptualized in one of the ways described above as a form of subjective voluntarism, or
in similar ways. Moreover, most liberal theorists
today readily declare themselves in favour of some
form of welfarism and against minimalist or `night
watchman' conceptions of the state, as being more
just. And justice is, as Rawls has pointed out, of
prior value to freedom where social relations are
concerned, and should therefore be considered super-
venient.[67] Furthermore, a redistributive conception of justice is not a *priori* anti-liberal, as
Rawls has also shown, indeed it is the essence of a

just social contract which should give prior consideration to the disadvantaged. The ethic of fraternalism, in short does not even offend the liberal outlook as such, it only offends that 'old' liberalism which Dewey condemns, as the rationale of capitalism, and which Callan must be taken to support.

In summary, then, Dewey is against the 'old' individualism because the original ideals that promoted it, valuable in themselves, have been corrupted by capitalism, because it encourages the assertion of a few at the expence of the many, and because it is historically superceded or bankrupt. We have now seen what he was against, the question that remains is, what was he for? Who is this *new* individual who would replace the old? Dewey repeats the Aristotelian warning that human individuals conceived of outside some society are monstrosities, he therefore emphatically rejects any theory of individuality that views the individual and the social as dichotomous or even exclusive entities. At the same time he admits that such a theory lies at the heart of the individualism with which, for reasons explained earlier, the Western intellectual tradition is tragically saddled. But, he argues, a proper evaluation of that individualism reveals not the assertion but the 'loss of individuality', since what has happened in fact is that 'while individuals are now caught up into a vast complex on associations there is no harmonious and coherent reflection of the import of these connections into their imaginative and emotional outlook of life'. [68] This is because the capitalistic social order has created a moral and intellectual vacuum between the individual and the collective into which forces hostile to the individual have stepped. This vacuum is the missing intermediary which the dichotomous social ethic of the 'old' liberalism has so effectively dissolved; the *community* - Dewey's 'new' individual is a 'refound' individual; the communal being.

It turns out then that Dewey's attack on the individual is really an attack on what he considered to be the loss of *real individuality* to the Western world. If we reassess the criticism made against him made by Callan and others on this score it becomes clear that the opposition to Dewey is actually based on a conflict of theories of freedom old in philosophy. The deeper problem is how to resolve the tension between the claims of individual liberty

and the rights of government.   One side to the conflict has consistently defended a theory of 'possessive individualism', while the other has, just as
consistently defended a theory of 'communal individuality'.   Possessive individualists 'tend to subsume
dignity under the ideal of autonomy and to conceive
of the latter in terms of liberty.... in their conception we can best realize our humanity by protec-
ting as large an area as possible within which the
individual is not directly coerced by others'.[69]
Their forefather is Locke, who invented the political theory that societies exist to protect the
fundamental 'natural rights' of individuals, which
they should therefore not interfere with in any way,
against older conceptions that valued society as
community.   His most direct philosophical opponent
is Rousseau who rejected the Lockean thesis that the
community is fiction and, while pushing the thesis
of individual freedom as far as it will go (the
individual is only free to the extent that he is
subject to laws he makes for himself) concluded
that, at the same time, the individual needs to be
socialized into a communal viewpoint.   It is clear
that Dewey is on Rousseau's side in the conflict and
that his grounds for so being are as much moral as
historical, to the extent that he ultimately sees
the problem as being 'the formation of a new individuality integrated within itself and with a liber-
ated function in the society wherein it exists'.[70]

CONCLUSIONS

A great deal of the discussion in this chapter has
centred around two subjects; Dewey's pragmatism, and
the attitude towards the individual reflected in his
philosophy.   This is because the exercise to establish the points of convergence between his education
programme and the concept of lifelong education as
it is represented in the movement's programme
through a comparison of statements in his writings
with others found in the lifelong education literature has already been made elsewhere.[71]   Repeating
it here would therefore have been superfluous.   What
the chapter sought then was the *reason* for these
points of convergence, while their existence was
taken as given.   Nevertheless, a long statement from
Democracy and Education quoted at its beginning will
have given the reader a clear sample of the
correspondence of ideas and principles between the
two sides, which was rendered even more specific by

the short discussion of it that followed.

There was also a considerable discussion of Dewey's conception of education as 'growth'. The standard criticism brought against it was examined and two things emerged as a result: first, the point was made that Dewey presents the concept of growth in a much more sophisticated and qualified form than is, albeit not without justification, usually imagined; second, that most of the criticism itself can be avoided if the growth principle is used as a *formal* rather than a normative principle when brought to bear on education. As a formal principle it refers to no more than what we have been calling the technical definition of education in his programme; his decision to consider education as a process in motion from the beginning of life onto which formal teaching enters and to which it should contribute in an interactive way with other aspects of learning that similarly contribute to the process, informal and non-formal. Dewey further argues that, conceived in the appropriate way, educational growth has no fixed or static end to mark it off. And these theses also belong, implicitly, to the concept of lifelong education, and furnish the deeper, if unexpressed, rationale of the programme.

One of Dewey's contentions quoted in the first page of the chapter was that one consequence of viewing education as growth or as a lifelong process is the implicit recognition of a standing right to education at any time in a person's life. But though he was thus theoretically committed towards granting equal value and consideration to adult learning as to childhood learning and schooling, he actually focused practically all his attention on the latter and did not explore any of the many valuable insights that bear on the issue of adult education in his work. To this extent the programme of the movement, which shares the same insights, could be viewed not only as continuing but, in a sense, completing Dewey's work by extending the range of its application into the area of adult learning. Not that it has neglected the earlier stages; sophistication has been lent to the Deweyian thesis that the first stage in formal learning should be given to 'learning-to-learn' through the development of the concept of 'educability', which gives due importance, as Dewey did, to motivation, and expands considerably on the skills and dispositions required for self-directed learning. But there has been an

even stronger concern with the area of adult or
later learning reflected in advances in andragogy
and the psychology of adult learning in the past two
decades or so, although this increasing sensitiza-
tion to the learning needs of adults, even of the
old, has not as yet been matched by a deeper philosophical investigation into the related social,
moral and epistemological issues.

At the same time, if the growth metaphor is a useful
one for collecting together the elements of the
lifelong education programme's technical definition
of education into a common formal description,
things become more problematic if it is taken
further to include Dewey's further elaborations of
it. For Dewey's central thesis that all growth that
is valuable must be directed towards social or
shared outcomes, and that strictly 'private' growth
has no educational value, appears to come into
immediate conflict with that tendency within the
lifelong education literature, described in Chapter
4, to describe growth in existentialist terms. As
soon, in fact, as we move away from the meaning of
growth as a technical or formal description of
education we move straight into the ideological core
of Dewey's programme.

The fact that it conflicts with the existentialist
trait in the literature is not of itself a problem,
because the net outcome of our discussion in Chapter
4 regarding the compatibility of the lifelong education programme with existentialist thought was a
negative one. We saw there that the existentialist
account of individuality, which is radically subjective, poses formidable problems with relation to the
existence of schooling and to the very having of an
education programme which, because they are problems
of theoretic consistency, seem insurmountable.
Dewey, on the other hand, like liberal philosophers
of education who otherwise define education as the
pursuit of autonomy, avoids the difficulties of the
existentialist by emphasizing the need to give
growth *direction*. What still needs to be asked
however is whether the direction he indicates, and
the *method* of direction (or 'control') he advocates
can be taken over by the lifelong education
programme for the required reorientation of its own
theory of individuality away from its present
existentialist leanings.

It is the consideration of this question that makes

our discussion of the accusation that Dewey's is a philosophy of conformism in this chapter an important one. For that accusation raises once more the spectre of the `dual potential` of a lifelong education programme to act as an agent of repression as much as freedom. If the charges brought against Dewey were in fact true, then we would certainly have to restrict the use of the growth metaphor to that of a formal principle. We could not follow Dewey further along the line if his intention were to suppress individuality. At the same time it seems crucially important for the coherence of the lifelong education programme of the movement that we can so follow Dewey. This is because it appears that the only way that the concept of a `learning society`, which is crucial to the programme, can be brought to terms theoretically with the principle of individuality is by describing the individual in Dewey's terms, as communal, and by conceptualizing society itself as a community, again in Dewey's sense of the word. But this important claim will be taken up exhaustively in the next chapter, this one having done the important groundwork for it.

From another point of view it should be amply clear from this chapter where Dewey lies in relation to the different trends within the lifelong education movement described in Chapter 2. It is self-evident that his pragmatic outlook renders him opposed in principle to the `utopic` trend within the movement as it was described. It is also evident, by comparison between the two, that his agreement with the other trend marks a coincidence of viewpoints actually consistent with the common description of their outlooks as pragmatic. Among the most prominent of these one finds the common concern to contextualize educational debate within the particular socio-historical contexts of specific societies, the emphasis therefore on the dialectical and dialogical nature of educational practice, and all that this implies. What Dewey adds to the pragmatist position is what we have seen it to lack, a social philosophy. And this contribution is crucial, for not any kind of social philosophy is compatible with pragmatism. On the contrary, as we have seen, a pragmatic metaphysics, like other kinds of metaphysics, dictates its own logic also on social arrangements, to which pragmatists must consistently be committed. In other words Dewey can help the pragmatist lifelong education programme of the movement make up its mind about its normative commitments.

At the same time, our account of pragmatism shows why the ideological commitments of a lifelong education programme that is pragmatic cannot achieve the firmness of commitment probably expected of it by Elvin. For we have seen that in its conception change is a vital and salutory thing; it is the sign that social conditions are held in an experimental or falsifiable fashion, in the true scientific spirit. The ideological core of a pragmatic educational programme can *only* therefore be made up of *formal* principles that are open to different forms of resolution in different socio-historical conditions, and this gives it a flexibility that others lack, since all it holds constant is the formal principles themselves, all else is thrown into the lap of 'history'.

These reflections evidently bear upon that other coincidence of viewpoints between Dewey and the lifelong education theorists; their common self-declared humanism. We have seen how pragmatism is naturally related to humanism through its epistemology and metaphysics. At the same time, the value Dewey places on the community continues with an expression of humanism which, as we saw in Chapter 3, has its roots in the revitalization of Stoicism in ancient times, a tradition which was given its most coherent theoretical form by Grotius before the advent of the Enlightenment and the birth of modern individualism thrust it into the background. Those lifelong education theorists, however, who have elaborated on their humanistic position have preferred to place their emphasis, as we have seen, on individual responsibility and freedom, on conflict, on viewing education as a fight for authenticity in an alien world, and there is much to be said for this emphasis because it is true that in most modern societies life is a struggle for individuality against all the threats to it that the existentialists name. But Dewey would say that the response of the existentialists is an incorrect and unrealistic one — the solution is not to live in rebellion by making criterionless choices but to work for collective action in order to·overcome alienation. At the same time creating community is the way to make collective action compatible with individual freedom; this is the scope and purpose of the 'learning society'.

Even with the choice of a humanist ideology then, it

is the Deweyian outlook that is actually consistent
with the movement's lifelong education programme,
because it alone is compatible with the conceptualizing of a 'learning society' within it. A humanism
which emphasises a tradition of 'tragic guilt', as
Suchodolski's does, or radical individual responsibility, as Lengrand's does, or a universal human
'community', as Kirpal's and others do, cannot be
the focus of such a society.

NOTES AND REFERENCES

1.   Dewey, J. (1916) *Democracy and Education*,
p. 51 (New York, Macmillan, 1966 edition).
2.   ibid., pp. 49-50.
3.   See Hook, S. (1959) 'John Dewey —
Philosopher of 'Growth'', in: Morgenbesser, S.
(1977) *Dewey and His Critics* (New York, The Journal
of Philosophy Inc.)
4.   Dewey, J. (1938) *Experience and Education*,
p. 231, in: Cahn, S.M. (1970) *Philosophical Foundations of Education* (New York, Harper Row).
5.   Peters, R.S. (1966) *Ethics and Education*,
p. 25 (London, Allen and Unwin)
6.   ibid., p. 36.
7.   Beckett, K. 'Growth Theory Reconsidered',
p. 52, *Journal of Philosophy of Education*. Vol. 19.
No. 1, 1985.
8.   op. cit., p. 42.
9.   ibid., p. 54.
10.   ibid., p. 56.
11.   Dewey uses the two words 'growth' and
'development' interchangeably, assuming that both
mean one and the same thing.
12.   ibid., p. 58.
13.   ibid., p. 58.
14.   ibid., p. 42.
15.   ibid., p. 57.
16.   ibid., p. 57.
17.   ibid., p. 59.
18.   ibid., p. 57.
19.   ibid., p. 58.
20.   ibid., p. 60.
21.   op. cit., p. 52.
22.   op. cit., p. 47.   With respect to the
argument preceding this quote, Dewey says, 'Education is not infrequently defined as consisting in
the acquisition of those habits that effect an ad-
justment of an individual and his environment'.
(p.46)

23.   ibid., p. 11.
24.   Dewey's main objection against idealism, from the socio-political viewpoint, was that it conceived of social progress as `organic growth'. His own alternative was `experimental selection' (p. 60), generated by the twin mechanisms of `continuity' and `interaction' with the environment.
25.   Cooper, D.E. (1983) *Authenticity and Learning*, p. 112 (London, Routledge and Kegan Paul)
26.   Callan, E. `Dewey's Conception of Education as Growth', p. 19, *Educational Theory*, Winter 1982, Vol. 32, No. 1.
27.   Cross-Durant, A. `Lifelong Education in the Writings of John Dewey', *International Journal of Lifelong Education*, Vol. 3, No. 2, 1984. Cross-Durant's main argument, like mine, is that `Dewey's theory of growth could have been written for lifelong education'. (p. 123) She also points out that Dewey is in complete harmony with the underlying view of lifelong education theory in `that the continuous development of man forms an integral part of his existence'. (p.118) Another similarity she focuses on is the common belief by Dewey and the lifelong education theorists that `learning from life' is of vital educational relevance, and that therefore its influence needs to fall within the calculation of educators.
28.   *Democracy and Education*, op. cit., p. 6.
29.   These points are my own, they are not taken from Cross-Durant's article.
30.   Schiller, F.C.S. (1912) *Humanism*, p. xxi (Connecticut, Greenwood Press, enlarged second edition, 1970)
31.   ibid., p. xxiii.
32.   ibid., p. xxiv.
33.   ibid., pp. 6-7.
34.   op. cit., p. 228.
35.   Santayana, G. `Dewey's Naturalistic Metaphysics', p. 349, in Morgenbesser, S. op. cit.
36.   op. cit., p. 349.
37.   *Democracy and Education*, op. cit., p. 76.
38.   ibid., p. 8.
39.   Quoted in Self, D.J. `Inconsistent Presuppositions of Dewey's Pragmatism', p. 102, *The Journal of Educational Thought*. Vol. 10, No. 2, 1976.
40.   ibid., p. 107.
41.   *Democracy and Education*, op. cit., p. 83.
42.   Peters, R. S. `John Dewey's Philosophy of Education', p. 103, in: Peters, R. S. (ed.) (1977) *John Dewey reconsidered* (London, Routledge and Kegan Paul)

43. Flew, A. 'Democracy and Education', in *John Dewey reconsidered*, op. cit.

45. ibid., p. 83.

46. Callan, E. op. cit. Scheffler (*Four Pragmatists*, 1974) had argued that the two judgements constitute *contradictory* directions which criticism of Dewey had hitherto taken. Callan's article tries to show that they are both, in fact, correct.

47. With reference to Rousseau, an interesting fact is that he makes several statements in the early pages of *Emile* that even predate Dewey's arguments for lifelong education. For instance: 'true education consists less in precept than in practice. We begin to learn when we begin to live, our education begins with ourselves, our first teacher is our nurse'. (Dent edition, London, 1957)

48. op. cit., p. 23.

49. ibid., p. 33.

50. Essiet, F.S. 'Callan and Dewey's Conception of Education as Growth', *Educational Theory*, Spring, 1985, Vol. 35, No. 2.

51. 'A Rejoinder to Essiet', p. 169.

52. op. cit., p. 200. This point is argued by Callan in an earlier article, 'Education for Democracy: Dewey's Illiberal Philosophy of Education', *Educational Theory*, Spring, 1981, Vol. 31, No. 2.

53. op. cit., 1982, p. 169.

54. Dewey's conclusion is that Plato's philosophy lacked 'the perception of the uniqueness of every individual, his incommensurability with others'. op. cit., p. 90.

55. op. cit., p. 170.

56. Quoted in Pyong Gap Min. 'The Place of the Individual in John Dewey's Democratic Liberal Philosophy' p. 171, *Philosophy of Education*, 1979.

57. Quoted in, Wirth, A. 'John Dewey on the Relations between Industrial Democracy and Education'. p. 278, *Philosophy of Education*, 1979.

58. Quoted in Pyong Gap Min, op. cit., p. 168.

59. 'Toward a New Individualism', p. 13, *The New Republic*, Feb. 19, 1930.

60. ibid., p. 14.

61. ibid., p. 14.

62. ibid., p. 14.

63. ibid., p. 15.

64. ibid., p. 15.

65. ibid., p. 15.

66. Thus Dewey is often criticized for his attack on the cultivation of the 'inner' personality in *Democracy and Education* (p. 122), where he also refers to a 'spirtual culture' as having 'something

rotten about it'. But this rejection of the private could also be interpreted, as Flew suggests (in Peters R. S. 1977, op. cit.), as a 'Wittgensteinian onslaught upon the (logically) private as such'. (p. 89)

67. Rawls, J. (1972) *A Theory of Justice* (Oxford University Press, 1973)

68. 'Toward a New Individualism', op. cit., p. 14.

69. Tucker, D.F.B. (1980) *Marxism and Individualism*, pp. 61-62 (Oxford, Blackwell)

70. 'Toward a New Individualism, op. cit., p. 15.

71. In Cross-Durant's article, op. cit.

Chapter Seven

THE LEARNING SOCIETY

> It is vain to claim to be `fighting' for a
> learning society which will spring up one fine
> day, fully formed and equipped, shiny as a new
> toy, under the effect of ringing phrases. At
> the most, it may be one of the slogans on the
> banners in a rough political social and
> cultural battle, leading to the creation of
> objective conditions, a call for effort, imag-
> ination, daring ideas and actions.[1]

The concept of a `learning society' or an `educa-
tion-centred society' as it is more infrequently
called, is, the Faure report declares, its `central
theme'.[2]   It is referred to repeatedly in the
literature on lifelong education where its structures and policies are discussed, but it is in the
report that it is most extensively described as a
concept.   There its advent, though considered to be
currently `utopian', is confidently predicted on the
basis of certain `trends' discernible in the world,
certain movements and changes in educational practices shared by societies everywhere, developed and
non-developed.   In fact, the report declares, the
prospect of such a society seems not only to conform
to what it describes as `the present-day world's
fundamental needs and major evolutionary direction',
it also fits a number of phenomena, including educational, emerging almost everywhere and in countries
whose socio-economic structures and economic development levels are very different.[3]

The `learning society' will adopt the changed
conception of education which is lifelong education

as its cornerstone, and will be 'democratic' in a
meaningful way. Its educational programme will
accordingly be distinguished not merely by its new
policy and educational strategy, it will also adopt
different ideological goals since it will refuse, as
has been the case in the past, to 'be confined....
to training the leaders of tomorrow's society'.
This is because in a meaningful democracy, i.e., one
that is not simply 'democratic' in a formal way
because it has a constitution and certain institutions, education cannot be 'the privilege of an
elite or the concomitant of a particular age'. Nor
can it be viewed 'as if it were a gift or a social
service handed out to him (the individual) by his
guardians, the powers-that-be'.[4] It has to be a
right of citizenship, available to all at all times.

The quality of its intervention in the lives of
people will be two-fold: it will organize itself
deliberately, institutionally, as a complex of
educational agencies of a formal kind, to be
interacted with by its members, and will promote the
greatest number and variety of opportunities for
non-formal learning possible to it. It will hold
its environment in a manner that is informally
enriching and stimulative of learning. Thus the
'learning society' provides both the resources and
the context for the effective self-realization
through active learning of its members. Within it,
Faure says,

> Each person should be able to choose his path
> more freely, in a more flexible framework,
> without being compelled to give up using
> educational services for life if he leaves the
> system.[5]

The 'learning society', in short, is a society designed to be supportive of individual lifelong education. It is the logical outcome of the 'total'
understanding of education referred to in the movement's education programme and specified by the
programme's operational definition. As a concept it
pushes the premise that context is educationally
relevant to the conclusion that it should therefore
be made educationally valuable. As an actuality it
is a society that has carried this inference into
its structures. The 'learning society' is therefore
one that is exceedingly self-conscious about education in its total sense; that is conscious of the
educational relevance and potential of its own ins-

titutions and of the general environment that is its
own way of life, and is determined to maximize its
resources in these respects, to the utmost. It is a
society which follows Dewey's advice to look to all
its institutions not merely for their efficiency and
productivity but also, and more especially, for
their educative potential, one that shares Dewey's
conception of `democracy', and one that believes in
the Deweyian dictum that `living together educates'.
[6] From a more formal point of view, it is a
society that, in Illich's terms, is mobilized for
learning.

It is evident that the structure of such a society
depends on the appropriate forms of legislation and
upon the appropriate machinery to make it effective
and coherent. Evidently we are not going to go into
these factors here, although they are of immense
practical interest and importance, for several reasons. Most importantly because it is not the function of a philosophical work to go into details of
organization and planning, and, even more fundamentally, because 'conceptual models' of a single such
society are compatible with the `utopic' approach
reflected in the Faure report and described in the
first paragraph of this chapter, but discordant with
a pragmatic philosophy. Besides, Gelpi has recently
painted an utterly different picture of the world's
situation to that of the report.[7] The concept of
a single universal model of a `learning society'
only makes sense if it is pursued,as in the report,
from the premise of an evolutionary standpoint which
views different societies at different stages of
socio-economic development and with different political systems as advancing historically towards a
unitary synthesis. Gelpi, who rejects this view, on
the other hand, represents the pragmatic view that
the basic lifelong education programme needs to be
held in a dialogical relationship with both progressive and conservative forces in different societies,
and will emerge under different forms in action.

Suchodolski also has much to say about the `learning
society', this is because for him, as for the pragmatists, the concept of lifelong education itself is
'deeply rooted in the social circumstances which
determine the motives of human action and thereby
influence the evaluation of different principles and
different objectives in human life'.[8] Suchodolski
is also very much in accord with the Deweyian view
that social institutions should be structured around

individual educational needs, this is why for him, as for Dewey, though 'lifelong education is deeply rooted in social reality, its immediate foundation is the individual'.[9] And again, in even further accord with Dewey, he argues that 'the development of modern civilization has destroyed the traditional bond which used to hold people together'. Industrialization, he says, and the concomitant process of urbanization it has set into motion, 'have demolished the structures of 'neighbourly solidarity', led to the disintegration of traditional family ties and social links, and produced the restlessness and superficiality characteristic of mass civilization'.[10]

These outcomes, Suchodolski claims, have tended towards the isolation of the individual who, contemporaneously, became victim to a Calvinist and Puritan ideology which imposed its 'virtues' as the cultural model for all men. These 'virtues', of dedication, thrift, competitiveness, obedience to duty, and so on, 'became the decisive factor in the development of bourgeois society which helped to 'build up' the capitalist system',[11] whose first mode of social expression was the 'production society' but which later evolved into a 'consumer society'. 'The need to find a way out of the labyrinth of production and consumption', Suchodolski says, 'is one of the justifications for advocating a 'learning society''.[12]

In short Suchodolski's 'learning society' not only disowns the 'production society' of early capitalism, it also disowns the 'classic attitude of the consumer society', *welfare*, since the mentality of welfare 'rapidly leads to a degree of satisfaction beyond which lie boredom and satiated indifference towards all those activities of life that require a certain effort';[13] i.e., it leads to passivity, the symptoms of which are the varying forms of alienation with which we are familiar, and the cultural expression of which is a mass culture.[14] · The way to overcome these limits, Suchodolski says, is by renewing, extending and deepening one's contacts with other people, and by profound commitment to social tasks. Moreover, Suchodolski, like MacIntyre, more recently (see below), and like Gelpi (though Gelpi speaks about individuals rather than groups), believes that 'the initiatives of certain groups are of great importance for the realization of lifelong education' - if the initiatives of these groups are synthesized and disseminated 'it will be possible to show the real essence and value of life-long education'.[15]

Finally, for Suchodolski, the greatest tension a 'learning society' will need to face is that between freedom and efficiency; a truly humanistic culture will need to resolve it in some way, just as it will need to resolve the other great cultural tensions which the contemporary consumeristic ideologies contain. Thus for him, as for the Faure report, the proper solution is to harness science and technology towards properly human ends. These ends, however, he insists, can never be met for as long as a utilitarian outlook continues to dominate science and as long as the past is treated with contempt. The term 'humanistic culture' is therefore to be taken to describe:

> a kind of existence which is complete in itself and free from the influence of utilitarianism (and which) implies that we do not build up a separate, exclusive 'kingdom', but on the contrary treat with due respect all that has been the foundation of human life through the centuries, everything that has enabled man to take risks connected with harnessing nature and creating civilization.[16]

If one examines the concept of a 'learning society' against historical conceptions of the role of educa-tion within the political unit it becomes evident which tradition it belongs to. Fundamentally, it is on the side of the Athenian democracy and against Plato. What makes its re-emergence radical in our times is the fact that, notwithstanding small pock-ets of resistance on the way,[17] it was Plato who eventually won, and it is Platonic solutions that we now find operational in the Western world (and in most places outside it too), where the central func-tion of educational systems is still to produce a leadership rather than to disseminate learning demo-cratically. The difference today is that the philo-sopher king model has been replaced by that of the 'educated man', who is also 'something of a philoso-pher', who has similarly completed the journey to the pinnacle of 'the curriculum' which has success-fully initiated him into 'forms of knowledge', who is motivated towards higher 'mental development' which will consist not in his interaction with 'life' but with the endless complexities and sophistications of the disciplines; his primary object will be his self-improvement, this is why he will consider what he learns mainly from the angle of its intrinsic worth.

Alisdair MacIntyre, who recently delivered the first of the Peters lectures entitled `The Idea of an Educated Public', argues that the apparent dichotomy between the two goals modern educational systems typically set themselves that of socializing people and contemporaneously getting them to think for themselves can be resolved; it is not some permanent condition of human life.[18]   To resolve it requires, he says, the restoration of those conditions that make an `educated public' possible, and he goes back in history to see what these could be.   He argues that in order to find the embodiment of the concept of an `educated public' we need not return to as remote a time as Ancient Greece, but to 18th century Scotland. Its primary condition, he points out, was the structure of the Scottish life-style itself, which resolved itself into small local communities, and the challenges which it was forced to meet at every level, cultural, political and economic because of changing historical conditions.   Its spearhead was its universities, but its success resulted mainly from a number of factors that are inherent in the concept of community; the possession of a common body of knowledge which is accorded `canonical status' by its members, where what is meant is not that they provide`a final court of appeal' but that `appeal to them has to be treated with a special seriousness, that to controvert them requires a special weight of argument'; and the facile communication and exchange of opinion at different social levels.

It is not difficult to establish continuity between this characterization and Dewey's; first, both believe that it is vital to the interest of the individual himself to seek an active synthesis between the apparently contrary claims' of socialization and free thinking; second, both agree that the individualistic inheritance of the Enlightenment has damaged man's real interests by setting him adrift in a world where conditions have become progressively more alienating and abstract; third, both agree that the reversal of this psychological harm requires the restoration of community and a morality that accords with it (MacIntyre argues that a consistent communal morality restores the virtues to the central place in human life); fourth, both agree on the requirement for a body of knowledge to be given 'canonical status' in the manner described above. MacIntyre refers to the 'common-sense philosophy' of Reid and Stewart and describes its momentary success in providing such a body of knowledge for early 18th century Scotland, Dewey pins his beliefs on 'science' and on the regulatory function of a pragmatic outlook on life.

Finally, it is also clear that both Suchodolski's characterization of an optimal way of life in a 'learning society' from the individual's point of view, and MacIntyre's characterization of an 'educated public' itself, could be considered elaborations of the basic Deweyian contention that a *learning society*', for this is what his 'democracy' is, is a place where the twin criteria he describes are at work; where there are a number of interests which are consciously shared by its members, and where there is full and free interplay through different forms of association between them.

THE 'LEARNING SOCIETY' AS COMMUNITY

It is not an accidental fact that thinkers who have theorized about and advocated a 'learning society', like those mentioned above, have also thought of it as community, because it cannot be thought of in any other way that is morally acceptable. For the notion of community alone, as will be shown later in the chapter satisfies the tension between the ideal of 'self-realization' and the demands of socialization without subsiding either into a radical individualism or its opposite, a radical collectivism. What, then, are the basic characteristics of community, that will also therefore be the basic social characteristics of a 'learning society'? For an answer we can again turn to Dewey, who gives the question some space in the early pages of *Democracy and Education*. Dewey's primary concern there was to link the concept of community with that of communication and with the having of things in common: 'There is more than a verbal tie between the words common, community, and communication. Men live in a community in virtue of the things which they have in common; and communication is the way in which they come to possess things in common'.[19] From this premise he was subsequently able to conclude that

'Not only is social life identical with communication, but all communication (and hence all genuine
social life) is educative'.[20]

'Living together educates' is therefore true for
Dewey if 'living together' has the character of a
communal life with its emphasis on shared meanings
and interests, with its having of common beliefs and
values that are accorded 'canonical status' in the
manner described by MacIntyre, with its emphasis on
the primacy of the 'virtues', with its different and
shared routes of communication.   The similarity of
the epistemic principles of this characterization to
those represented by the Wittgensteinian concept of
a 'form of life', and indeed to those represented by
an 'education programme' as described in this book
will certainly have struck the reader.   The reasons
are evident; all three, for instance, hold a coherence theory of 'truth' and critical value, and the
beliefs and values held as 'canonical' by the community correspond to having an 'ideological core'.

The logic of community also imposes certain other
implications of its own.   Thus, conceptualized in
the sense stated above, a community necessarily
measures its own success according to the level of
individual and collective *participation* in its form
of life that it succeeds in encouraging among its
members.   It follows that no community can, as a
matter of principle, willingly permit conditions to
exist in its midst that alienate or emarginate any
of its members; this is the principle of 'fraternalism' cited against Dewey.   The extent to which a
collectivity, in fact, deserves the name of community depends on its success in drawing increasing
numbers of its members in different ways into the
ongoing 'conversation' which is its 'form of life',
and in widening in ever-increasing degrees the areas
of its life where active dialogue is possible.   On
the other hand, concomitant with this heightened
degree of participation, the logic of community
demands of its members a heightened sense of responsibility towards self and others.   The logic of
community also implies a decentralization of power
without which there can be no realistic exercise of
responsible participation.   It also carries implications with regards to size and geography, as Rousseau pointed out and as is implied by the defining
characteristics of community as described by
Dewey.[21]   In sum, it is clear that the political
embodiment of community as we have described it is

that of a participatory democracy, which is also *sui generis* a `learning society'.

Pateman has described the characteristics of a participatory democracy well, and contrasted them with
those of the contemporary theory of democracy func-
tioning in liberal democracies in the Western world.
[22] She makes the central point that the theory
of participatory democracy is built around the assertion that individuals and their institutions cannot be considered in isolation of each other, and
that therefore the *mere* existence of representative
institutions at the national level is insufficient.
She also points out that maximum participation by
all requires an active socialization into democratic
skills and dispositions that must take place in
different spheres of life in order that the necessary individual attitudes and psychological qualities
are developed. This development, in turn, takes
place through the process of active participation
itself. The major function of participation in the
theory of participatory democracy is therefore an
educative one.

Pateman argues that there is no special problem with
regards to the political stability of a participatory society, as is sometimes asserted, this is because it is self-sustaining through the very educative impact of the participatory process. Participation, she contends, develops and fosters the very
qualities necessary for it; it feeds upon itself and
gathers strength in the process of so doing, since
the more individuals participate the better able
they are to do so, and the more favourably disposed
they become towards procedures of negotiated agreement that are implied by a participatory decision-
making. There is here understood, of course, that
tacit and mutual acceptance of a body of procedures
for participation which define the accepted norms of
practice within the particular society, and of the
core of beliefs, values, and common interests definatory of a community, together with the means for
their effective and open exchange and communication,
that underlies the participatory system itself.

Pateman also contends that the evolution towards a
participatory society should ideally begin at its
industrial base, for most individuals spend a great
deal of their lifetime at work, and because the
business of the workplace provides an education in
the management of collective affairs that it is

difficult to parallel anywhere else. Spheres such as industry, she says, should be seen as political systems in their own right, offering areas of participation additional to those at the national level. A further reason for the central place of industry in the theory relates to the substantial measure of economic equality required to give the individual the independence and security necessary for equal participation.

The contention that participation in social and political life is necessary for a positive conception of individual happiness and psychological well-being as well as being a valuable form of education is an important one. For it is these factors that make a participatory democracy desirable in itself, according to Patemen, who also presents another two 'subsidiary hypotheses' besides in support; namely that participation has an integrative effect on the group and that it aids the acceptance of collective decisions.[23] But it is, of course, not an uncontroversial one because we do not currently have at our disposal research to establish whether this is true in fact, as Pedersen has shown in his review of the question. This is because the conditions for assessing a participatory democracy do not exist, because 'even if large numbers of citizens could be persuaded to make political participation part of their daily life, the political educational effect of this remains uncertain in the absence of systematic evidence', and this evidence it is almost impossible to obtain since the variables involved are too many and too uncertain.[24]

It is similarly not certain that participation need have a positive psychological effect on the individual or need lead to his happiness. Reynolds, for instance notes, with specific reference to evidence from participatory organizations in industry, which, it will be recalled, Patemen indicated as having a leading role to play in the evolution towards a participatory society, that:

> often, when participation has been put to the test, it is reported that people have seemed unwilling or incapable of assuming greater responsibility. It is a sadly commonplace experience that where the opportunity for taking part in decision making, planning, or problem-solving is extended, the process can prove frustrating and the results trivial.[25]

But something more than intuition suggests that the
cause of this situation, where it exists, needs to
be sought within the antecedent circumstances of the
lives of the people involved with regards to their
education.   It is, in fact, more than likely that
they were unwilling or unable to participate signif-
icantly or effectively at the workplace because
participation was something novel to them, it did
not feature in their earlier formal education, and
probably did not feature either within the culture
of their family upbringing or peer relationships.
In brief, if it is true, as intuition suggests that
an *effective* participation is a form of education,
it is also true that an effective participation is
something that itself needs *educating into* before it
bcomes a self-reinforcing practice as Pateman says.
It is useless, as the Faure report argues, to expect
a participatory democracy to occur in the wider
institutions if it is not first apparent within the
formal education system.

There are still other difficulties with the concept
of a participatory democracy at a more theoretical
level.   One is an old one brought against the Athenian democracy by Plato.   The whole basis of democratic decision making, said Plato, is ludicrous,
since it confuses wisdom with weight of numbers.
Furthermore, not only is it unscientific in principle, it is also, he argues, incompetent and open to
abuse in practice since it inevitably degenerates
into mob rule; this is because democratic societies
are permanently open to the threat of demagoguery.
It can in fact be argued that current Western democracies reflect a concession to the force of this
argument, particularly that aspect of it that contends that a participatory democracy sacrifices
efficiency for the doubtful value of participation
by the masses.   Again, connected with this argument
is the further contention that in a participatory
society little or no attention is given to training
in the qualities of leadership.

Another argument is that participation is not in
itself an unqualified good.   Opponents of a participatory society point to the Weimar Republic and the
use it made of mass participation as a form of political control and in order to direct the energies of
people towards the persecution of a minority in
their midst.   This is the same argument as is fetched against Dewey's criterion of `growth', as we saw

in the previous chapter, and, more relevantly,
against the primacy he attributes to community.
Thus Flew, making the point that an increasing sense
of community will not necessarily create a better
society against Dewey argues that the fact that 'a
smoked salmon is by definition smoked', does not
mean that 'it must be a better salmon the more
smoked it is'.[26] The general point being that the
existence of the conditions of communality of the
most heightened and efficient kind can go together
with the holding of thoroughly evil motives for
association and interests — we do not value a
community of murderers because, whatever else may be
the case, it is a community.

In response to the first set of these arguments, we
need to concede that belief in the value of a participatory democracy is currently, in fact, an act
of faith rather than a rigorously argued out and
empirically backed scientific hypothesis. But then,
an act of faith is required on behalf of any but a
perfect society; only that requires no faith for its
success since it is otherwise constructed, on a
'scientific' basis. Few people today however would
accept the credibility of 'scientifically' constructed states, or the desirability of deciding social
and political affairs or the public well-being
'scientifically' — the collective experience of
generations has turned out to be a much safer
criterion for making such decisions than 'science',
as Aristotle predicted. Advocates of the current
representative forms of democracy will turn to this
conclusion and point out that experience has in fact
shown representative democracy to work, it is
therefore less an act of faith than the
participative democracy which is unknown in the
modern Western world, though it has been experi-
mented with outside it, in some of the newer states,
not with very encouraging results. And there is
some truth in this, but only some, otherwise there
would be *no* truth in the analysis of philosophers,
sociologists and social psychologists, who describe
the current conditions of life in Western societies
on the psychological and cultural plane, in negative
terms with which we are all familiar. And in fact
today's revival of the ideal of a participatory
society can be viewed, over and above everything
else, as a response to these conditions, since the
claim that a positively conceived society of this
kind is psychologically and culturally beneficial
has at least an initial sound of credibility about

it and appeals to our logic.[27]

With regards to the second argument, one has to
agree that not all participation need be a good
thing, just as not all kinds of growth are desirable
or all kinds of community commendable — in short,
the point must be taken that what makes
participation a good thing, or community a good
thing, is not the fact of participation or community
itself but the ends to which it serves. But, having
said this, one needs to add that, besides the fact
that there is no reason to assume a *priori* that a
participatory democracy need be any more or any less
repressive than other kinds, the whole way of
putting the argument above is misleading. For what
really counts is whether, all things being equal,
i.e., granted that the ends for which either society
exists are good ones, it is more desirable to have a
society which is participatory or not.

In true fact every democratic society concedes the
right of its members to participate to some extent
in its affairs, popular participation being of the
very essence of democracy. And this implies that
participation is itself valued in all societies that
refer to themselves as democratic. The real difference, with regards to a participatory democracy,
is that it *emphasises* the value of participation and
strives to make it possible at all its institutional
levels. Moreover it tries to make participation
real by ensuring that the individual is given the
opportunity to act in as many areas of his life as
possible instead of always having others act on his
behalf. It thus reverses the current situation
within many societies where, to paraphrase Freire,
people have the illusion of acting through the action of their leaders.

SELF-REALIZATION

One of the main contentions made on behalf of community which is also, as we have seen, necessarily a
participatory society, is that participation is
itself conducive towards individual self-realization. Another major contention was that participation is also the community's primary method of
socializing its members. Thus we seem to have tied
up the problem of tension between the ideal of self-
realization and the demands of socialization, referred to earlier, quite neatly. But, in effect, we

have not really examined the problem adequately to see whether this is in fact so. So we need to return to the beginning to see where its roots lie.

The tension between individual freedom and socialization appears with particular sharpness in liberal and existentialist philosophy, and its origin lies in a deep distrust of collective judgements, which are largely misinformed, and of collective intentions, which are commonly repressive. In short, the collective has, from the individualist point of view, the wrong credentials for giving people enlightened guidance even when it is not being deliberately repressive in their regard. Plato gave this tension metaphysical form; in his deep distrust of the collective he sought to liberate the individual by conjuring up a world of universal 'Forms' which would constitute a different, superior point of reference. Thus the programme of 'self-realization' for the Platonic philosopher is described for him in the parable of the cave, which sums up Plato's contempt and distrust of the common stock of knowledge which the man-in-the-street shares with his neighbours, and where Plato holds forth the hope that 'philosophy', as the turning of the eye *inward* into the soul, will achieve for him better things. In the process it will enable him to win his freedom. For Plato then, the search for truth is inextricably tied with the pursuit of 'autonomy'.

It is not difficult to read the same project both into liberal and into existentialist thought. Plato's primary thesis is that the individual owes his first allegiance to the 'truth' not to his fellows. Existentialist philosophy renders the same thesis central to its viewpoint by placing its premium on *authenticity* or 'good faith'. At the same time however, in rejecting the possibility of universal truths, or the 'truth', it also rejects the Platonic hope in the liberating power of 'philosophy'. Liberal philosophy locates the truth in a more mundane sphere than Plato, the sphere of academic knowledge, the intrinsic value of which is set up by liberal philosophers of education against the 'abridgements of life', as that which is alone 'education'. It should therefore be distanced from the latter which is mere 'socialization'. At the same time liberal philosophers share the same faith in the power of 'philosophy' as Plato. Thus, although individual or social wants and needs cannot,

in their view, guide the education programme, philosophy can. For this reason, the autonomous person,
who is the end product of the programme, is a 'philosopher', if with a different point of reference to
Plato's. He is not simply one who makes 'choices',
still less is he one who makes the 'criterionless
choices' demanded by the existentialist, in fact his
life follows a consistent life-plan rationally
thought out. Or to put it in another way, the
liberal conception of autonomy is not subjectivist
in the way of the existentialist. For the existentialist 'Choose thyself!' is the unwritten command
that lies at the heart of all true autonomy projects, for the liberal, in contrast, there are objective criteria for living the good life and for
understanding the truth about things, with which
individual autonomy must coincide and which can be
recognized rationally.

These conclusions make it evident why liberal
philosophers of education are uncomfortable with the
educational aim of self-realization, while the
concept is in fact at home within existentialist
philosophy. In effect, as soon as one declares
self-realization to be the aim of education the
question arises; which 'self' do we have in mind,
which is the 'self' to be realized through
education? And two kinds of general answers present
themselves for consideration in response to it:
either the 'self' to be realized is a non-
predetermined individual self, so that the general
aim of self-realization can have, and ideally will
have, as many idiosyncratic outcomes as there are
individuals, or the 'self' to be realized is a model
self, one which is predetermined and serves as what
Dewey calls a fixed or 'static' goal for self-
realization. Liberal philosophers of education
explicitly reject the former so, if they are to use
the concept, they have to fall back on the latter.

This is the case, for instance, with Elizabeth
Telfer, whose essay on 'Education and Self-
Realization' roughly distinguishes the following
salient points with regard to the concept:[28]

1. 'unlike most words beginning with the
prefix 'self', it (the concept of self-realization)
does not seem to imply that the person who undergoes
it must be the same as he who produces it'.[29] She
notes that the prefix 'self' is not, in the case of
'self-realization', reflexive, referring back to the

agent, but rather conveys the view that what is
`realized' is *selves* or *persons*.
   2.   The relevant sense of `realization' in the
context of the term is not that of `awareness';
`self-realization' does not mean `self-awareness',
however valuable this quality independently.   The
relevant sense is rather that of `becoming real' or
`actualization'.
   3.   What is realized, then, must be certain
potentialities of which two kinds are especially
relevant: capacities and inclinations.   The first
refers to the realization of skills, the second
refers to tendencies.   Realization takes place in
two ways, either by *exercising* skills, by putting
inclinations to effect, or by developing skills and
inclinations: `If we see self-realization in terms
of the development of potentialities, we are depicting it as *becoming* a certain kind of person, whereas if we see it in terms of the exercise of potentialities, we are depicting it as *acting* in certain
ways'.[30] The distinction, she says, is conceptual
rather than practical, but it is important because
it is reflected in the ways in which various educational processes are conceived.
   4.   The notion of self-realization involves an
evaluative notion of self.   There are four forms
that this can take, four accounts of the potentialities to be developed.   Two are related to conceptions of a *generic* self, and they refer either to an
ideal or higher self, or to a balanced self or
`whole man', two are related to conceptions of an
individual self, and they refer either to an
idiosyncratic self or to an autonomous self.
   5.   There is a strong compatibility between
the activities of the *higher* self and those of the
autonomous self: `all the activities which are
naturally regarded as activities of the *higher* self
are at the same time activities which particularly
employ the *autonomous* self'.[31]
   6.   Making self-realization the aim of education means depicting education as aiming at the
individual's good in some way, it therefore rules
out the idea that the purpose of education is to
further the good of society.   It also rules out the
notion that the purpose of education is to increase
the individual's happiness since there is no necessary connection between the ideas of self-realization
and happiness.
   7.   Education is a good in itself; it is
tempting to tie the state of educatedness with that
of self-realization.   Telfer rules out the realiza-

tion of the 'balanced self' as necessary to educatedness, also the realization of a higher self
unless very narrowly conceived in intellectual
terms. She in fact finally connects educatedness
with 'intellectual self-realization', which is in
turn connected with the having of a certain range of
knowledge familiar in liberal literature.

The argument which establishes the first move in the
development of this thesis is a crucial one: Telfer
interprets the meaning of self-realization in a
manner such that it becomes intelligible to say that
I have *realized myself* when others have decided for
me what 'self' I was to realize. For from it she
can move on to legitimise the right of the teacher
to make all the educational decisions on the grounds
that the teacher knows, while the pupil does not,
which 'self' it is desirable that the pupil should
realize. This is why philosophy is important for
teachers; because the having of philosophical insights on their part ensures that the decisions
themselves are not arbitrary or taken as a mere
matter of opinion or personal interest. But, in any
case, philosophy of education offers a model ready-
made which, if they are rational and well-intention-
ed, they ought to pursue; the model of educatedness,
of the 'educated person'. So, in actual fact, it
turns out that it is the philosophers who set the
aims of education which the teacher is expected to
pursue, although not uncritically of course. And to
do this the philosopher will examine theoretically
what it is to be a 'self' or a 'person', and what
kind of knowledge and attitudes are proper to the
aim of becoming an *educated* person or self. Self-
realization, from the side of pupils, will consist
in their realizing the aim of educatedness under the
direction of their teachers. If this begins to
sound uncomfortably like an argument for their socialization, Telfer makes it clear that making self-
realization the aim of education implies viewing it
as aiming at the *individual's* good in some way, it
therefore, she says, 'rules out the idea that the
purpose of education is to further the good of society'. At the same time she hastens to add that
there is no *necessary* connection between self-realization and being happy either, which is perfectly
true, but there *is*, on the other hand, a necessary
connection between educatedness and intellectual
development, so that if self-realization is the
achievement of educatedness then it must be 'intellectual self-realization' that is meant.

This all sounds very neat and is, in fact, an ingen-
ious attempt on Telfer's part to render the concept
of self-realization a coherent part of the liberal
education programme.   But it is fatally flawed in
many ways, starting with the premise which interprets self-realization to mean the realization of a
'self' rather than the realization of *oneself*.[32]
The COED defines the term as 'the full development
of one's faculties', so that her interpretation does
not square with what one can take to be its conventional meaning, nor does it square with ordinary
usage where self-realization is normally regarded as
a *personal* thing.   Moreover, it does not sound right
when you say it; when you translate it into a statement of educational aims, where it renders itself as
'p should decide for q the mode of q's self-realization'.   Furthermore, the moment you accept that
self-realization has a non-reflexive meaning and
implies the realization of a 'self' you are opening
the door theoretically to different kinds of proposals of what that 'self' should be, not all acceptable ones. You will therefore, from a liberal point
of view, be constrained to make an additional case
for the superiority of 'philosophical' reasons over
others, which further means negotiating the hidden
reef that is the theory-ladenness thesis.   From a
different point of view, if self-realization is made
the aim of education, and it is further claimed that
what is implied by self-realization is that 'what is
'realized' is *selves* or *persons*', it sounds rather
odd to qualify it with the condition that the 'self'
implied is the *intellectual* self - one cannot say
that it is meaningless, but the combination of terms
'intellectual   self-realization'   does   not   sound
right.   The reason why Telfer fixes on *intellectual*
self-realization is of course obvious, 'happiness'
or 'the good of society' being the wrong motives,
from a liberal point of view, for making educational
decisions, since neither is sufficiently 'neutral'.
The development of 'mind', or 'intellectual development', on the other hand, fits the bill perfectly.

Liberal philosophers of education, on the whole,
have rightly preferred to avoid the concept of self-
realization and the complications it creates for
them; many have fixed upon 'autonomy' as the central
quality of educatedness, which can be a different
thing.   Peters, as the reader may remember, in a
passage quoted in an earlier chapter (pg. 170) actually *distinguished* self-realization from education

thus classifying it as something different, which probably means that he tacitly recognized its truly reflexive nature. The concept of autonomy, on the other hand, enables the liberal philosopher of education to escape a form of individualism which is utterly subjectivist, like that of the existentialists for instance, and therefore not to his taste, while avoiding the equally distasteful quicksands of `socialization', since he adopts it mainly in the Kantian form in which the individual's action is free if the rules it follows are not externally imposed, nor capricious, but imposed on the individual from within, by his own reason. From this point of view education for autonomy becomes a matter of teaching *how* to make rational choices (not what choices to make), and since the seat of rationality lies in the academic disciplines, then the development of autonomy will coincide with their study. In other words, the aim of autonomy in the Kantian sense fits in very nicely with the rest of the liberal education programme in a way that the aim of self-realization does not.

The social dimension is introduced into his picture of autonomy by Kant when he imposes a regulative condition on reason itself in its moral sphere of action by stipulating a *universalizability* criterion to which it needs to be subjected, according to which the individual can test the motives of his actions to be right or not according to whether they accord with the formal maxim that they can be willed universally for everyone in the same conditions — for this, as Kant specifies, assumes that humanity can be viewed as a single `moral community'. In this way Kant turns Rousseau's principle of the General Will on its head, translating it into a formal maxim. He thereby locates the seat of moral authority not in the collective will but within the individual himself. At the same time his theory that the individual is also member of a single moral community which is the human race contradicts Rousseau's contentions about community, at least in the moral sphere, and latches onto the old humanism of the Stoics which likewise hypothesized the existence of a human moral community. Kant continued to add, again like the Stoics, that membership of this community not only imposes duties on the individual but also gives him a `dignity' which others are obliged to respect by always treating him as an `end'.[33]

Liberal philosophers, on the other hand, have preferred to set the limits of freedom at the level of respect for reciprocal rights. They have tended therefore to follow Mill in distinguishing two classes of actions; the self-regarding or strictly private, which are sacred to the individual to the extent that interference with them by others is never justified, and the other-regarding where the limits of individual freedom are set by the like rights of others to the same freedoms. They have therefore tacitly rejected the Kantian notion of society as a moral community with its accompanying thesis that the perception of *duty* is the proper regulator of individual freedom. In its place they have proposed the thesis that the individual's interest in others derives from an enlightened self-interest. Their conception of autonomy therefore lacks Kant's social dimension completely, and it is not thus surprising that they should place it in opposition to socialization.[34]

SOCIALIZATION

Socialization is logically inimical to the pursuit of 'authenticity', and is often defined in opposition to an education focused on autonomy; it is therefore deemed contrary to at least two conceptions of self-realization. On the other hand, Dewey, as we have seen, prized it, and it was considered a valuable feature of the 'learning society' as we have described it. In either case it is assumed that socialization is not inimical to self-realization but an integral part of it, indeed the kind of socialization implied by that form of life that is a participatory society has been claimed to be psychologically beneficial for the individual. Also, in a sense, it is not as if we could really dispense with socialization. Sociologists and social psychologists affirm the all-pervasiveness of socialization. They tell us that it begins the moment we are born with our first personal contacts. Personal identity, they say, 'does not result from autonomous creations of meaning by isolated individuals, but begins with the individual 'taking over' the world in which others already live'.[35] Existentialist ontology, as we have seen, refers to this fact as our 'thrownness' in the world. Pat White declares that only a barbarian or philistine would deny its importance.[36] What do philosophers mean then by opposing socialization to self-realization, or to education?

It is evident that they would want to distinguish socialization from upbringing of the kind which counts as education and which, as White points out, itself involves compulsion. So it is not the fact that socialization is a form of control that seems to matter, for education conceptualized as upbringing also involves control. Liberal philosophers are opposed to educational philosophies of a romantic or naturalistic tendency that, like lifelong education, emphasise the importance of self-directed learning and, as we have seen, insist that there is no education without the direction of teachers. In other words they agree with Dewey's response to the criticism of his educational theory mentioned in the previous chapter that the real question to consider is not that of control or no control, but of *what kind of control*, for the former is not a realistic one to ask. So what is the kind of control they would approve of and what not?

Much of the earlier work in philosophy of education was involved with the question of how education can be distinguished conceptually from other kinds of learning that we are inclined to consider unfavourably because of the associations they have come to have. The objections to activities like brain washing, conditioning and propaganda were considered evident enough, the concept of indoctrination turned out to be rather more problematic (is it always unacceptable, what is its distinguishing feature?), but generally regarded suspiciously and also opposed to education. Peters, again, furnished the general criteria against which, he claimed, activities could be measured to decide the issues. In general, he argued, educating someone involves the 'wittingness', understanding and consent of the learner, and the teacher's intention to develop the learner's 'cognitive perspective'. The whole complex process he called *initiation*, and Peters makes it clear that the whole intention is not to get pupils to *internalize* information and habits, as with socialization, but to get them *on the inside of things* in order to understand their principles and their criteria of evidence. Moreover, the kind of knowledge with which it is to become involved is to be suitably neutral in content (should one teach religion, or political history, or civics, or morals, or not?), and superior to the mundane in quality (not bingo and push-pin for example) - the academic disciplines satisfy both these conditions.

Frankena, in a general effort to render the distinctions even more clearcut, has suggested that all understandings of education can be reduced to a single matrix.[37] In it X is fostering or seeking to foster in Y some disposition D by method M, what changes where different conceptions of education are concerned is the way the variables are translated. Thus, in socialization, X is society or its representatives, Y its younger generations, D are the dispositions regarded as desirable by society, and M are the methods that society regards as more or less acceptable. While according to what Frankena calls the 'normative' concept of education, X refers to those doing the educating, whoever they are, Y are those being educated, D are those dispositions it *is* desirable Y should have (not simply those *deemed* to be so by society, the teacher or the individual), and M are the methods that *are* acceptable or satisfactory (not on conventional but on 'moral' grounds). He thus renders clearer the view that education is to be distinguished from socialization on the basis of the kind of justification either offers for the kind of activities it denotes; that of the latter being social or conventional, while that of the former is normative or philosophical.

As the conclusion of the paragraph before the last indicates, the story however does not end here, with moral distinctions and criteria of justification. Our discussion, in an earlier chapter (Chapter 5), of Oakeshott's characterization of education, made reference to a different meaning of socialization where the conventions the term denotes are not moral but epistemic ones. For Oakeshott, as we have seen, living together *does not* educate, there is no educational value in everyday experience. It is only the school, a place set apart for the purpose, that educates, because it is here that *excellence* is pursued and *worthwhile* knowledge is to be had, as distinct from the world outside in which people are socialized, which is concerned only with knowledge that is mundane, that suffers the abridgements of life, and finally only produces 'current' men.

Mill's essay 'On Liberty' has a large part to play in the liberal's distaste for socialization in both these aspects of the word. There Mill's primary concern is to protect the individual from the 'despotism of custom', and in order to do so he sets out

to depreciate and ultimately discredit the value of
'public opinion' and to restrict its collective
jurisdiction to that area of individual action that
infringes directly on its well-being.   In other
words the value of collective action, for Mill, lies
solely in its role as corrective of individual behaviour that is vicious, he sees no potential in it
for developing what is positive in human beings,
hence his emphasis, like that of Nietzche, is on the
cultivation of originality or of 'genius', and he
contemporaneously depreciates all that is conventional. But the crucial point that is usually miss-
ed about Mill's defence of individuality is its
frank historicity.   Mill makes it clear everywhere
in his essay that he is over-stating his thesis in
order to *correct* a balance that was currently
against the individual, he is not, by implication,
proposing a theory for all times.   For Mill, the
power of the public in his time and society appeared
to be approaching overwhelming proportions. 'In our
times', he says, 'from the highest class of society
down to the lowest, everyone lives as under the eye
of a hostile and dreaded censorship'.   He further
adds, in judgement of his centemporaries and with
reference to what he judged to be their enslaved
mentalities: 'I do not mean that they choose what is
customary in preference to what suits their own
inclination. It does not occur to them to have any
inclination except for what is customary'.[38]

In this state of affairs, he continues, it is
imperative that genius and originality be given its
head and deliberately encouraged, since what is
required is the redressing of the current despotism
of custom.   In this sense Mill is ready to recognize
the value of creativity for its own sake, even if it
is eccentric or if it amounts to no more than a
negative gesture of rebellion. But it is clear that
what he is actually hoping for is the creation of a
creative elite, since this alone would be able to
ensure a wider change of attitude in society at
large.   This is because the average man cannot, of
course, be expected to aspire to genius, his virtue
can only lie in being a discriminative follower, in
making the right choice between custom and the
possibilities offered him by the creative leaders in
his society.   Thus, 'The honour and glory of the
average man is that he is capable of following that
initiative; that he can respond internally to wise
and noble things, and be led to them with eyes
open'.[39]   So, in other words, in Mill's eyes, the

average man is only ever able to realize himself by
proxy, he can never hope to be `original' since Mill
has set the standards of originality beyond him, in
the realms of `genius'. His opinions are either to
be determined by custom, or, if he is enlightened,
he will deliberately avoid custom and model them on
those of the elite, the best men around, even, and
especially, with regards moral matters. The genius
alone is truly autonomous.

Genius cannot, of course, be made the aim of
education in our democratic times, but this apart
what is notable about this account is Mill's
contention that the stranglehold of custom can be
broken if a vanguard is created to set up models
which the average man can pursue and make the object
of his life (this is probably what would be called
his education). At the same time the implication to
be derived from his reference to the current state
of affairs in his society, as a background to this
account, seems, if we are reading it rightly, that
things could conceivably be different *in a different
society*. But could it be so different that custom
becomes a valuable thing? Contemporary liberal
philosophers of education, as much as they may admit
to the desirability of having a creative elite in
society, would not go so far as to make the creation
of such an elite *the* aim of education, though they
would go so far as to make it *one* of education's
aims. Their concept of educatedness is therefore
pitched a good deal lower than that of genius, but
it remains something outside the ken of the average
man. At the same time it continues to retain the
same negative evaluation of socially derived
learning as Mill's although social and educational
conditions have changed enormously in Britain since
Mill's time. Could it be that they are guilty of
Dewey's accusation against contemporary liberals
that, unlike Mill himself, they lack a sense of
history?

Mill's proposals about how to defeat custom are, of
course, utterly different from those presented by
existentialists who propose authenticity for all,
not merely for the genius, and who would not therefore accept that anyone should pursue a model of
life set for him by another or others. The existentialist command is stern: `Choose thyself!' Setting
up a model self is therefore, for them, as repressive of individuality, as custom. The difference,
of course, lies in the fact that besides doubt about

the practicality of subjectivism, Mill is worried about the *quality* of self-realization, while the existentialists are more concerned with the *fact* of self-realization. Mill's statement that it is better to be a Socrates dissatisfied rather than a fool satisfied is evidence of this fact, as is his playing down of the original pleasure criterion of utilitarianism, and his replacement of its 'calculus' with considerations of quality. And the truth is that liberal philosophers of education have followed him in this; autonomy for them does not mean the same as authenticity for the existentialist, the autonomous self has to be a *particular kind of self* (as Telfer contends), not merely a 'self', one whose opinions are his own. Thus they have taken care to specify that 'self-determination is not equivalent to autonomy, for autonomy must be construed as *rational* self-determination'.[40] Autonomy is something people need to be educated *into*, while authenticity implies an education *out of* something that already exists.

It is therefore clear that if one approves, in general, of the kind of society that one has, then one will propose autonomy as the best way of opposing custom, and one can at the same time effect a compromise with the need that society, like any other one, experiences to socialize its young, by adopting, as many do, a position similar to Young's. Young, who otherwise regards autonomy as something of intrinsic value, says: 'my response to the argument for socialization stresses the strategic significance of awareness of our particular socialization'.[41] If, on the other hand, one disapproves completely of one's society, like Marxists living in a liberal-democratic state or liberals living in a socialist state, or disapproves of society in general, as the Rousseau of *Emile* or the existentialists do, then neither freedom nor self-realization can mean the same thing; then socialization is something to be resisted, and the liberal conception of rational autonomy to be opposed, as is the actual schooling or system of formal education of that society. Then education becomes either a matter of organized revolutionary activity for a different social order, or a matter of personal rebellion which is permanently irresolvable.

None of these solutions, evidently, conceptualizes individual self-realization *within* the context of a 'learning society', because all depart from the wrong, in this sense at least, perspective. To escape this perspective one needs first to deny, as Dewey does, the need for opposition between the individual and the social that it assumes, and the view that self-realization means the resolution of this opposition in favour of the former. For this view tends either to favour some individuals (an elite) or to render itself impossible in practice if intelligible in theory since not being subject to the will of others is only possible 'if one happened to live in a society in which all the legislative wills of the society coincided'.[42] Second, one needs to alter the excessive focus on the individual as one who needs to be *protected* from society, and this shift of focus, in fact, lies implicit within the concept of a 'learning society' or within an education programme which conceptualizes such a society, where it is implied that the first focus is on the quality of society itself.

The alternative to individualism is, in fact, *to start with the kind of society we want people to live in* rather than what individuals one wants for a particular kind of society, for then one can argue for a view of self-realization that is compatible with a desirable form of social organization rather than the other way round. If this sounds too strong on the side of socialization it is because it has not been placed within the conception of society as participatory, communitarian and self-conscious of its educative role described in the first two sections of this chapter. The question we need to ask ourselves, as Dewey points out, is how we can organize the social 'environment' itself (in the widest sense of the term that he uses) in order to make self-realization possible; how the self is realized is then up to each individual. From this point of view one does not educate against the evil of custom, one encourages the kind of custom that educates, and this is the custom of a participatory democracy conceptualized along the pragmatic lines described by Dewey, as being in a permanently open condition and holding its current solutions falsifiable in the light of changed conditions and opinions.

Finally, the ambition of self-realization itself needs to be re-dimensionalized. It must come to be understood as truly *personal* growth, rather than the pursuit of autonomy, or authenticity or some higher or inner self. Where personal growth becomes as

much as anything else, compatible with having opinions that one shares with others, that may be totally unoriginal or customary, its defining feature
being *its acceptibility to the person whose it is*,
not its measurement to some standard set by philosophers. Anthony Storr, who postulates an inner drive
towards self-realization in every individual says,
in opposition to Telfer:

> I believe that the development of the individ-
> ual and the maturity of his personal relation-
> ships proceed hand-in-hand, and that one cannot
> take place without the other. Self-realization
> is not an anti-social principle; it is firmly
> based on the fact that men need each other in
> order to be themselves, and that those people
> who succeed in achieving the greatest degree
> of independence and maturity are also those who
> have the most satisfactory relationships with
> others.[43]

In other words, not only is socialization a fact of
life, it is, as Storr argues, also an inescapable
element in personal growth. A healthy socialization
is therefore not only, from this point of view compatible with self-realization, it is, as Dewey argues, an indispensable condition for it. Moreover,
there needs to be a different assessment of the kind
of knowledge that makes for self-realization. The
pursuit of academic excellence may be satisfying for
a certain kind of personality, but it cannot be
imposed as a standard of measurement for all without
making self-realization unattainable by many, as the
liberal philosopher does. The desirability of imposing a common curriculum on all to achieve common
aims for all characterized as the qualities of an
'educated person' is, in fact, called into question
by criticism such as that of Roland Martin in Chapter 5, and that of Marxist thinkers in general who
agrue that the same qualities represent no more than
a particular cultural stereotype, that of the male
liberal. In other words the knowledge criterion
itself needs to be more *personalized* in the sense in
which the personal is also largely social, which
amounts to a re-conditioned restatement of Lengrand's contention that we need to replace the 'geographical' concept of culture with one that locates
it, in a sense, in the individual. Reconditioned
because it must be stripped of the subjectivist
connotations of Lengrand's description according to
our socialized conception of self-realization which

includes the conditions described by Dewey and Mac-
Intyre.

From this point of view the question, what constitutes a healthy socialization? becomes a vital
one, and some answer to it has already been given;
one manner in which it takes place is by exposure to
a social environment that is healthy in the manner
described earlier in the chapter. It is evident
that a necessary condition for such an environment
to materialize is the possession by its individual
members of the skills required for participation,
which can be divided into two general categories;
social skills, and the skills of self-direction. So
a second answer to the question is that the *deliberate* socialization that takes place should consist in
the teaching of social skills and in the inculcation
in the learner of his self-perception as a communal
being – this is what Dewey meant by having a 'social' mind. At the same time a mode of socializing
people by getting them actively involved in a participatory manner in cooperative activities seems to
be the best answer to the question of how they can
be socialized without recourse to morally objectionable means, for through it one avoids both the use
of naked external compulsion, and that of the more
subtle methods of conditioning, indoctrinating and
so on. One becomes socialized by developing one's
skills as a social being while putting them in practice, at the same time one's individual identity is
preserved by the fact that one's opinion counts and
is seen to count, and therefore by one's self-perception as an active participant in life. In this
way Dewey's contention that what needs to be developed is a 'social' mind avoids all the sinister
implications attributed to him by his opponents.

Dewey argued in his time that the time to encourage
the 'rugged' individualism of the past, proposed
also, though in a different sense to that criticized
by Dewey, by Mill in his essay, is past and that a
different historical context demands a different
kind of personality. More recently, Hargreaves has
similarly attacked current educational theory for
its 'cult of individualism' towards which liberal
philosophers have contributed greatly with their
over-emphasis on the value of autonomy. Hargreaves
contests the assumption that underlies this emphasis, that 'if the school can generate autonomous,
self-reliant and self-realized individuals, then
society can be left with confidence to take care of

itself',[44] and continues to say that its evident
consequence is that individuals are being 'progressively socialized into a severely defective capacity
to co-operate with one another'.[45]   Moreover,
Hargreaves also argues that through this emphasis on
autonomy, they are being denied educational opportunities essential for a successful life in a democratic society:

> The first is that of learning how individual
> identity has a social and corporate component;
> the second is that of discovering how
> individual rights can be threatened by the
> group and so discovering how and why these
> rights must be protected to give the group its
> moral base; the third is that of learning how
> personal *interests* must sometimes be
> subordinated to group needs.[46]

The point of these arguments is succinctly that
giving socialization a secondary role, or pretending
not to be interested in it, or, worse still,
claiming that 'education' can avoid it by producing
'autonomous' people, simply means that people are
socialized defectively, since the choice is not one
between socialization and no socialization but one
between a healthy socialization and a defective one.

Finally, reading Hargreaves further, it is not
surprising that the alternative education programme
he proposes against the liberal one, is one
described in terms that capture the essence and
rationale of the 'learning society' as we have been
describing it.   The conclusion to his criticism is,
in fact, that what our times require of us is a
willingness to take up 'The challenge of providing
an education to create a society which is both
solidary and just, which generates collective
identities and powers whilst nevertheless exhibiting
a respect for the dignity and rights of the
individual'.[47]

CONCLUSIONS

The concept of the 'learning society' features
prominently in the lifelong education programme of
the movement, but equal prominence is given to the
idea that education should be one with self-
realization and with self-directedness.   Earlier
chapters have shown how the concept of a 'learning

society' can be turned into a search for utopic
futuristic models generated by the optimistic
assumption that humanity is or can be made a single
community with a common historical destiny to
realize. The criticism made against this approach,
which captured the imagination of the early lifelong
education theorists, was that it was too abstract
and that it rested on assumptions that are both
theoretically and empirically dubious. Moreover, an
even more specific argument, from the point of view
of lifelong education theory, is that it tends to
lump all societies together and to assume a single
lifelong education model for them, usually that of
the developed countries, with the result that it
raises suspicions of hegemony.

The alternative approach is that proposed by the
pragmatists, who are ready to reverse all these
tendencies, to take different societies as they are
and to adopt a pragmatic approach toward the concept
of a 'learning society'. They are thus ready to
argue that there is not any one model of such a
society that can be universally imposed, and that
the shape any 'learning society' will take depends
upon an ongoing dialectical relationship between the
ideological, economic, cultural, educational features *that it already has*, and the lifelong education
programme, embodied by 'progressive' individuals or
groups within that society who are prepared to take
the 'long march through the institutions' that it
requires.

There is, however, at the same time, among the
pragmatists themselves, this 'fear of the 'dual
potential' of the 'learning society' to render
itself as easily an instrument of oppression as of
liberation — what makes the difference is not the
theoretical programme itself, which provides the
formal conditions for lifelong education from its
perspective, but the characteristics of the society
in which it is *actualized* as an education programme
in the full sense, i.e., in the sense in which it is
put into practice with all its components including
the lived ideology of that society, interacting, for
these may be repressive. So although the *content* of
a 'learning society' cannot be specified universally
for the reasons stated by the pragmatists, the
formal conditions that would avoid making it repressive can. And they have, in fact, been the subject
of this chapter which fills a serious lacuna left
open by the pragmatists, as we saw in Chapter 2.

With reference to the aim of self-realization and self-direction, this chapter has also shown that there are different ways of describing the former, making it not always compatible with the latter. For instance, what the liberal philosopher means by self-realization, when he uses the term, is certainly not self-direction *tout court*, but something that is compatible with being *rationally* autonomous, where the conditions for the achievement of this state can be pre-set — thus self-realization becomes the realization of a pre-defined 'self'. The ideal of self-realization is, in effect, more at home in existentialist and allied philosophies where it is interpreted subjectively. And, as we saw in Chapter 4, there *is* a trend in the lifelong education literature towards this interpretation. Our response to it, however, was that, apart from other problems intrinsic to the very proposal of an existentialist philosophy of education, a subjectivist interpretation of self-realization is not compatible with an education programme which features the concept of a 'learning society'. So our search for a philosophical position with which to tie the lifelong education programme turned instead to John Dewey, whose general philosophy of education was seen to incorporate precisely the same basic principles as those of the lifelong education programme, and whose ideological perspective is similarly claimed to be humanist.

Dewey described education as growth, making it clear that an abstract notion of mind that isolates it from the social world is unintelligible, so that growth is of a mind that is in some sense 'social'. He dismissed those conceptions of growth that either, like the naturalistic or romantic, fail to take this fact into account, or else conceive of growth in static terms. Both are objectionable, also, for a common reason; because they imply a 'closed' conception of education as the attainment of some end which is either the fruit of innate capacities that have matured, or the realization of some pre-set model. In either case the 'self' to be realized is a *fixed* self; both are therefore tainted for the pragmatist for different reasons, not the least being the fact that they imply imposition either by an external agent or by a deterministic 'nature'. For Dewey, therefore, neither could provide the proper basis for a theory of self-realization which requires due recognition of the essentially social nature of self and, at the same time, avoids a kind of control or socialization that is externally or dogmatically imposed. In order to effect this balance he turned instead to a theory of self-realization through *participation* in social life with all the implications mentioned in the chapter. In other words, we find in Dewey a solution also to the question of how self-realization and self-directedness can be made intelligible individual goals in a `learning society' — by conceptualizing it as community and by defining self-realization within the context of this understanding.

NOTES AND REFERENCES

1.   Faure, E., et al. (1972) *Learning to be*, p. 104 (London, Harrap)
2.   ibid., p. 5.
3.   ibid., p. 164.
4.   ibid., p. 160, ff.
5.   ibid., p. 186.
6.   It is not surprising that this should be the case, for Faure says about democracy: `the concept of democracy itself must be developed, for it can no longer be limited to a minimum of juridical guarantees protecting citizens from the arbitrary exercise of power in a subsistence society'. (p. xxvi)
7.   Gelpi, like Faure, speaks of the demand for a `new international education order' in response to the changing world, but he complains that the established order shows `a lack of consciousness of the need for innovative approaches, the attitude being, on the contrary, an obstructive one which censures or distorts the new and adventurous by reinforcing the conventionalities of the *status quo'*. (`Lifelong Education and International Relations', p. 16, in: Wain, K. (ed.) (1985) *Lifelong Education and Participation* (University of Malta Press)
8.   Suchodolski, B. `Lifelong Education — Some Philosophical Aspects', p. 71, in: Dave, R.H. (1976) *Foundations of Lifelong Education* (Oxford, Pergamon Press)  Suchodolski uses the term `education-centred society' in place of `learning society'.
9.   ibid., p. 80.
10.   ibid., p. 83.
11.   ibid., p. 80.
12.   ibid., p. 83.
13.   ibid., p. 81.

14. One is reminded here of the distinctions drawn between different conceptions of culture by Lengrand, and discussed on p. 120.

15. ibid., p. 79.

16. ibid., p. 94.

17. For instance in the case of the Florentine 'civic humanists' of the 14th century, who attacked the metaphysical underpinnings of Platonism, rejected his model of the 'philosopher', and turned instead to his second-best ideal of 'civic goodness' as one accessible to all. They therefore returned to the populist understanding of education contrary to Plato's. Furthermore, they extolled the 'active' as against the 'contemplative' life, recognizing the anti-humanist implications of the latter described in Chapter 3, and projected the ideal of free, enterprising, community minded citizens against that of self-sufficiency and withdrawal from life. At its best this ideal could find expression in the vigorous, inquiring life of the scholar, philosopher, artist, scientist, rolled into one typified by Leonardo da Vinci.

18. The lecture, along with the others, is expected shortly as a ULIE publication (*Education and Values: The Richard Peters Lectures 1985*, Haydon, G. (ed.)). I am indebted to John White for passing to me a copy of the typescript shortly after the lecture.

19. op. cit., p. 4.

20. ibid., p. 5.

21. Though Dewey made it clear that 'We cannot set up, out of our heads, something we regard as an ideal society. We must base our conception upon societies which actually exist, in order to have any assurance that our ideal is a practicable one' (Democracy and Education, op. cit., p. 83), he was prepared to think of humanity as a community in a metaphorical sense. In different places he repeats the old humanist ideal that education should break down the barriers between people, social and national. It is in fact the basis of his second criterion for democracy.

22. Pateman, C. (1970) *Participation and Democratic Theory* (Cambridge University Press)

23. The political basis of all communitarian theories of society, including Dewey's and Marx's, is evidently participatory rather than representational. The lifelong education theorists whose work is considered in this book are all of a similar persuasion. In the Faure report, where several statements on the value of participation are made,

we read: `Participation of the greatest numbers,
exercising the highest responsibilities is not merely a guarantee of collective efficiency, it is also
a pre-condition of individual happiness, a daily
assumption of power in society and over things a way
of truly influencing fate.   The citizen's job is no
longer to delegate power but to wield it, at all
levels of society and stages of life'.   (p. 10)

24.   Pedersen, J.T.   `On the Educational Func-
tion of Political Participation: A Comparative
Analysis of John Stuart Mill's Theory and Contemporary Survey Research Findings', p. 567, *Political
Studies*, Vol. xxx, No. 4, 1982.

25.   Reynolds, M.   `The Learning Environment
and the Ideal of Participation', p. 60, *Journal for
Higher Education*, 5 (1), Spring, 1981.

26.   op. cit., p. 90.

27.   There may not be any empirical evidence to
this effect, but there is much in Entwistle's claim
that, `Part of the democratic citizen's well-being
comes from the perception (however illusory) of
being a participant in political decision-making to
a larger extent than is possible in alternative
regimes, even at the expense of efficiency, and
possibly at some cost in terms of the quality of the
product of political activity'.   (Entwistle, H.
`Toward an Educational Theory of Political
Socialization', p. 17, *Philosophy of Education*,
1973).

28.   Telfer, E.   `Education and Self-Realiza-
tion', *Proceedings of the Philosophy of Education
Society of Great Britain*, 1972.

29.   ibid., p. 216.

30.   ibid., p. 218.

31.   ibid., p. 223.

32.   Norton has shown that `self-realization'
and `self-actualization' are terms with *different*
implications, contrary to what Telfer says.   `Self-
actualization' implies the existence of a pre-exist-
ing self waiting to be made real, while `To say that
a possibility that assumes a working place in the
existing world is thereby `realized' is to imply
that it was unreal before'.   It is clear that what
Telfer calls `self-realization' is more accurately
characterized as `self-actualization' of a kind.
(Norton, D.L. (1976) *Personal Destinies: A Philosophy of Ethical Individualism* (Princeton University
Press))

33.   Kant, in fact, provides the vital connections between a theory of humanity viewed as a single *moral* community, and the concept of human dig-

nity, which is logically the basis of any account of humanistic ethics and which must lie at the very core of any humanist programme. Our conception of human rights is in fact the political expression of the moral imperative to respect the dignity of every individual for the reason indicated by Kant, because he belongs to a humanity conceived as a single moral community.

34. It is usually assumed that autonomy has intrinsic worth, and that, therefore, the pursuit of autonomy as an educational aim requires no justification. But, as O'Hear has argued, the example of people who willingly put themselves under the authority of others, soldiers, members of religious orders and political parties etc., shows that it is not of ultimate value but is simply a question of individual preference. (*Education, Society and Human Nature* (1981) p. 57 (London, Routledge and Kegan Paul)) Self-realization, on the other hand is more basic, since autonomy itself is a form of self-realization.

35. Berger, P., and Luckmann, T. (1976) *The Social Construction of Reality* p. 151 (Harmondsworth, Penguin)

36. White, P.A. 'Socialization and Education', in: Dearden, R.F., Hirst, P.H., and Peters, R.S. (eds.) (1972) *Education and the development of reason* (London, Routledge and Kegan Paul)

37. Frankena, W.K. 'The Concept of Education Today', in: Doyle, J.F. (ed.) (1973) *Educational Judgements* (Routledge and Kegan Paul)

38. (Harmondsworth, Penguin) edition, 1974, p. 125.

39. ibid., p. 131.

40. Wall, G. 'Moral Autonomy and the Liberal Theory of Moral Education', p. 223, *Proceedings of the Philosophy of Education Society of Great Britain*, 1974.

41. op. cit., p. 576.

42. Baier, K. 'Moral autonomy as an aim of moral education', p. 103, in: Langford, G. and O'Connor, D.J. (eds.) (1973) *New Essays in the Philosophy of Education* (London, Routledge and Kegan Paul)

43. Storr, A. (1960) *The Integrity of the Personality*, p. 32 (Harmondsworth, Penguin, 1983 edition)

44. Hargreaves, D.H. 'A Sociological Critique of Individualism in Education', p. 194, *British Journal of Educational Studies*, Vol. xxviii, No. 3, June, 1980.

45. ibid., p. 195.
46. ibid., p. 195.
47. ibid., p. 197.

POSTSCRIPT

At the beginning of the book it was claimed that the
worth of education programmes should be measured
against two standards: that of internal consistency,
the coherence together of the different elements of
the programme, and that of relevance, the
justification of the programme against the
empirical, or historical, context within which it
must be made to work. What we have concentrated on
most in these pages is the matter or internal
consistency, and this for clear reasons. The
word`lifelong education', strictly speaking, refers
simply to a strategy, a way of looking at education
which is not new in itself and which can be rendered
programmatically in many different ways. But it is
also the name adopted for a theory, presented
through a consistent body of literature and very
loosely structured on a number of principles and
concepts; a particular working, or technical,
difinition of education itself, a `loosely
humanistic', and therefore ill-defined, ideology
embracing concepts like `self-realization' and the
`learning society', and so on. What was needed was
the coherent structuring of these principles and
concepts into a programme that is tight and
internally consistent, and this book has responded
to this need; it has given the programme the form to
compete with other educational philosophies.

The question of justification has been left in
abeyance until this point because it is felt that it
will have emerged clearly from the pragmatic
premises of the paradigm with which we have worked,
even without Dewey whose philosophy effects a
natural nexus between pragmatism and the idea of
lifelong education, and a hermeneutic culture which,
translated into political terms, takes on the formal

characteristics of a participatory democracy whose criteria and form of life Dewey outlines. The pragmatic justification of the lifelong education programme is in fact no more than a refined version of the customary justificatory arguments fetched for it by the lifelong education theorists. These ask the historicist question, what are the educational needs of a human being living a truly human life in today's world? Their reply is that they are certainly different from those that justified the traditional education programme. This is because the historical conditions have changed radically; people today encounter a way of life that is very dissimilar from that faced by their predecessors at any time in human history. The old solutions then, as Dewey argued, will not do.

The central phenomenon of today's 'environment' is accelerating change impelled by the scientific and technological revolution. The point is not, as the theorists point out, that people's lives are changing, change has always been a factor of human life. The difference today lies in the *rate* and *range* of change, as it permeates into people's lives at all levels (this is why education must be of the *whole* person) and creates severe and continuous problems of adaptation for them. The reality of this problem is reflected in the popularity of the idea of lifelong education with the man in the street who can see its empirical justification everywhere about him. In this situation, it is rightly argued, an education which is itself continuous, like change, is the only one that makes sense. We cannot any more envisage education as a finite thing, a 'preparation' for life, it needs to be conceptualized as part of life itself.

This is the central justificatory argument for lifelong education, and its force is such that it makes the policy implications, or strategy, of lifelong education the only realistic one for any political regime. Hence the feeling among lifelong education theorists that the normative part of the programme, which has been the subject of this book, is a vital one. There are other arguments of a more sophisticated nature that appear in the literature, besides that which makes lifelong education the natural consequent of a 'learning society' as described in the previous chapter, but this is the most popular and crucial. One is that lifelong education is required by human nature itself. The

Faure report, in a manner reminiscent of Dewey, refers to the 'permanent incompleteness of man', the fact that he is 'biologically unfinished', and that therefore his life must be 'an unending process of completion and learning'. The report refers to a statement of Fromm's that 'The individual's entire life is nothing but a process of giving birth to himself; in truth we are only fully born when we die', and refers to this argument from human nature as 'the major argument in favour of lifelong education'.[1] And, in similar vein, Suchodolski refers to lifelong education as a response to the essentially human need to be over-reaching oneself continually, to move beyond one's immediate horizons, beyond the boundaries of what has already been achieved. One also recalls Dewey's argument that human beings instinctively find the idea that they can grow no more repugnant if it is proposed to them at any time in their lives, even in old age. But the argument that is really regarded as the most crucial one is the pragmatic argument above .

With reference to the technical discussion of the nature of an education programme in Chapter 1, this means that what justifies the *principle* of lifelong education is that it is 'empirically progressive'; it supercedes traditional education in relevance since it is a better response to the current state of affairs in the world in which we live. But while this may be a decisive argument for the *principle* of lifelong education, it is not in itself a sufficient justification of the *movement's* lifelong education programme which includes considerably more than the principle. How is the *programme* justified? It is to be remembered that, from a pragmatic point of view, it can be no more than a *formal* programme. For a pragmatic programme concrete practices will be the result of its formal principles' dialogical interaction with the state of affairs in different societies, and there will thus be as many lifelong education programmes as there are situations where the dialogue obtains. How, then, is the *formal* programme justified? As formal, it cannot be measured empirically but against other extant or theoretic programmes, and this is where touchstone comes in. From the point of view of touchstone it is claimed that the lifelong education programme proposed is this book, with its pragmatic underpinning and its appeal to Deweyian philosophy for the clarification of its concepts is 'theoretically progressive' over the 'trends' already existent in lifelong education literature.

It is understood, of course, that we are referring
to a programme with the same conceptual structure or
language game as the movement's; one within which
the aim is the individual's fullest self-realisation
within a `learning society' that has accepted Dave's
`concept characteristics' as its operational strat-
egy, and that is democratically participatory. Other
philosophical underpinnings like liberalism and
existentialism could give rise to different programmes, as we have seen, while idealism, or some
form of scientific utopianism, offers a different
account of how we should conceptualize the `learning
society', going for a single abstract model in place
of a plurality. But the pragmatic programme has the
additional advantage of being a consistent empirical
response to the state of affairs in today's world,
and of being theoretically coherent, in its Deweyian
form, with a hermeneutic culture as described in the
first chapter of the book.

NOTES AND REFERENCES

1.   Faure, E., et al. (1972) *Learning to be*,
pp. 157-158 (London, Harrap). On the other hand,
against this thesis of lifelong education, and
against the very view that education *can* be a
lifelong process, one finds the psychological theory
that, intellectually and cognitively at least, human
beings stop growing at quite an early stage in life
at which their mental powers become stable for a
while then start to decline and degenerate.
Cropley, Allman, and others have, however, while
drawing on recent research in the psychology of
adulthood, rejected this theory. Allman, in
particular, has questioned the models of adult
development on which these conclusions rest, arguing
that they were in fact derived from the study of
children and adolescents and were therefore, in
general, made to conform to the model of formal or
propositional logic, a form of operational thought
not very prevalent among adults. The change of
perspective, she says, has come about with the
recognition of the importance of experience to adult
thinking, which led psychologists to ask whether
there are not other types of thinking structure that
change the nature of formal logic so as to render it
qualitatively more adaptive to adult needs. This
led to the discovery that formal operational thought

gives way with age to dialectical operational thought – the mind does not stop growing, it simply starts to grow predominantly in another direction. The conclusion is not that learning stops with age but that adult learning and teaching must conform to different kinds of thinking structure. (Allman, P. 'New Perspectives on the Adult: An Argument for Lifelong Education', *International Journal of Lifelong Education*, Vol. 1, No. 1, 1982).

Allman, P. 'New Perspectives on the Adult: An Argument for Lifelong Education', *International Journal of Lifelong Education*, Vol. 1, 1982.

Aristotle, *Ethics*, Thomson, J.A.K. (ed.) (1979) (Harmondsworth, Penguin)

Baier, K.E. 'Freedom Obligation and Responsibility', in: Storer (1980)

Baier, K.E. 'Moral Autonomy as an Aim of Moral Education', in: Langford, G. and O'Connor, D.J. (1973)

Beckett, K. 'Growth Theory Reconsidered', *Journal of Philosophy of Education*, Vol. 19, No. 1, 1985.

Berger, P.L., and Luckmann, T. (1976) *The Social Construction of Reality* (Harmondsworth, Penguin)

Bleicher, J. (1982) *The Hermeneutic Imagination* (London, Routledge and Kegan Paul)

Boyle, C. 'Reflections on Recurrent Education', *International Journal of Lifelong Education*, Vol. 1, No. 2, 1982.

Callan, E. 'Education for Democracy: Dewey's Illiberal Philosophy of Education', *Educational Theory*, Vol. 13, No. 2, Spring, 1981.

Callan, E. 'Dewey's Conception of Education as Growth', *Educational Theory* Vol. 32, No. 1, Winter 1982.

Callan, E. 'Rejoinder to Essiet', *Educational Theory*, Vol. 35, No. 2, Spring, 1985.

Carr, W. 'Philosophy, Fantasy and Common Sense', *Journal for Higher Education*, Vol. 4, No. 2, Summer, 1980.

Chazan, B. 'What is Informal Education?', *Philosophy of Education*, 1981.

Cohen, B. (1981) *Education and the Individual* (London, Allen and Unwin)

Cohen, B. 'Return to the Cave: New Directions for Philosophy of Education', *Educational Analysis*, Vol. 4, No. 1. 1982.

Cooper, D.E. (1983) *Authenticity and Learning* (London, Routledge and Kegan Paul)

Cotgrove, S. (1968) *The Science of Society* (London, Allen and Unwin)

Cropley, A.J. (1977) *Lifelong Education... a psychological analysis* (Oxford, Pergamon Press)

Cropley, A.J. (ed.) (1979) *Lifelong Education: a stocktaking* (Hamburg, UIE Monographs, 8)

Cross-Durant, A. 'Lifelong Education in the Writings of John Dewey', *International Journal of Lifelong Education*, Vol. 3. No. 2, 1984.

Dave, R.H. (1975) *Reflections on Lifelong Education and the School* (Hamburg, UIE Monograph)

Dave, R.H. (ed.) (1976) *Foundations of Lifelong Education* (Oxford, Pergamon Press)

Dearden, R.F. 'Philosophy of Education, 1952-1982', *British Journal of Educational Studies*, Vol. xxx, No. 1, February, 1982.

Dewey, J. (1966) *Democracy and Education* (New York, Macmillan)

Dewey, J. *Experience and Education*, in: Cahn, S.M. (1970) *Philosophical Foundations of Education* (New York, Harper Row)

Dewey, J. 'Toward a New Individualism', *The New Republic*, Feb. 19th, 1930.

Downie, R., Loudfoot, E., and Telfer, E. (1974) *Education and Personal Relationships* (London, Methuen)

Edel, A. 'Analytic Philosophy of Education at the Crossroads', in: Doyle, J.F. (1973) *Educational Judgements* (London, Routledge and Kegan Paul)

Ehrenfeld, D. (1981) *The Arrogance of Humanism* (Oxford University Press)

Elvin, L. 'Learning to be...', *Education News*, 15, 1975.

Entwistle, H. 'Towards an Educational Theory of Political Socialisation', *Philosophy of Education*, 1973.

Entwistle, H. (1979) *Antonio Gramsci: conservative schooling for radical politics* (London, Routledge and Kegan Paul)

Essiet, F.S. 'Callan and Dewey's Conception of Education as Growth', *Educational Theory*, Spring, 1985, Vol. 35, No. 2.

Faure, E. et. al. (1972) *Learning to Be* (London, Harrap)

Feyerabend, P. (1978) *Science in a Free Society* (London, NLB)

Flew, A. `Democracy and Education', in: Peters, R.S. (1977)

Frankena, W.K. `The Concept of Education Today', in: Doyle, J.F. (ed.) (1973) *Educational Judgements* (London, Routledge and Kegan Paul)

Furter, P. (1977) *The Planner and Lifelong Education* (Hamburg, UNESCO)

Gadamer, H.G. (1976) *Philosophical Hermeneutics* (University of California Press)

Gelpi, E. (1985) *Lifelong Education and International Relations* (London, Croom Helm)

Gelpi, E. `Lifelong Education and International Relations', in: Wain, K. (ed.) (1985) *Lifelong Education and Participation* (The University of Malta Press)

Gestrelius, K. `Lifelong Education — a New Challenge', *European Journal of Science Education*, Vol. 1, No. 3, 1979.

Gilroy, D.P. (1982) `The Revolution in English Philosophy and Philosophy of Education', *Educational Analysis*, Vol. 4, No. 1, 1982.

Giustiniani, V.R. `Homo, Humanus, and the Meanings of Humanism', *Journal of the History of Ideas*, Vol. XLVI, No. 2, April — June, 1985.

Graubard, A. Review Article, *Harvard Educational Journal*, Vol. 15, No. 3, August 1981.

Griffin, C. (1983) *Curriculum Theory in Adult and Lifelong Education* (London, Croom Helm)

Hamlyn, D.W. (1978) *Experience and the growth of understanding* (London, Routledge and Kegan Paul)

Hannay, A. `Towards a Humanist Consensus in Ethics of International Development', in: Storer, M.B. (1980)

Hargreaves, D.H. `A Sociological Critique of Individualism in Education', *British Journal of Educational Studies*, Vol. xxviii, No. 3, June, 1980.

Harris, K. (1979) *Education and Knowledge* (London, Routledge and Kegan Paul)

Hawes, H.W.R. (1974) *Lifelong Education, Schools and Curricula in Developing Countries* (Hamburg, UIE Monograph, 4)

Heidegger, M. (1980) *Being and Time* (Oxford, Blackwell)

Hirst, P.H. and Peters, R.S. (1970) *The Logic of Education* (London, Routledge and Kegan Paul)

Hook, S. `John Dewey — Philosopher of Growth', in: Morgenbesser, S. (ed.) (1977) *Dewey and His Critics* (New York, The Journal of Philosophy Inc.)

Huxley, J. (1969) *Essays of a Humanist* (Harmondsworth, Penguin)

Illich, I., and Verne, E. (1976) *Imprisoned in the Global Classroom* (Montreal, Writers and Readers Publishing Coop.)

Ireland, T.D. (1978) *Gelpi's View of Lifelong Education* (Manchester University Press)

Jessup, F.W. (ed.) *Lifelong Learning* (Oxford, Pergamon Press)

Kallen, D. 'Recurrent Education and Lifelong Learning: definitions and distinctions', in: Schuller, T. and Megarry, J. (eds.) *World Yearbook of Education, 1979* (London, Kogan Page)

Kierkegaard, S. 'Fear and Trembling', in: Bretall, R. (1973) *A Kierkegaard Anthology* (New Jersey, Princeton University Press)

Kirpal, P.N. 'Historical Studies and the Foundations of Lifelong Education', in: Dave, R.H. (1976)

Kolenda, K. 'Globalism vs Consensual Pluralism' in: Storer, M.B. (1980)

Kurtz, P. (1969) *American Philosophy of the Twentieth Century* (London, Collier-Macmillan)

Kurtz, P. 'Does Humanism Have an Ethic of Responsibility?', in: Storer, M.B. (1980)

Lakatos, I., and Musgrave, A. (eds.) (1970) *Criticism and the Growth of Knowledge* (Cambridge University Press)

Langford, G. (1978) *Teaching as a Profession* (Manchester University Press)

Langford, G., and O'Connor, D.J. (eds.) (1973) *New Essays in the Philosophy of Education* (London, Routledge and Kegan Paul)

Lawson, K. 'Lifelong Education: Concept or Policy?' *International Journal of Lifelong Education*, Vol. 1, No. 2, 1982.

Lear, J. 'Ethics, Mathematics and Relativism', *Mind* Vol. XCII, 1983.

Lengrand, P. (1975) *An Introduction to Lifelong Education* (London, Croom Helm)

MacIntyre, A. (1981) *After Virtue* (London, Duckworth)

MacIntyre, A. 'The Idea of an Educated Public', (Forthcoming)

Macquarrie, J. (1985) *Existentialism* (Harmondsworth, Penguin)

Margolis, J. 'The Reasonableness of Relativism', *Philosophy and Phenomenological Research*, Vol. XLIII, No. 1, Sept. 1982.

Matthews, M.R. (1980) *Marxist Theory of Schooling* (Sussex, Harvester Press)

Mill, J.S. (1974) *On Liberty* (Harmondsworth, Penguin)

Morris, V.C. (1966) *Existentialism and Education* (New York, Harper and Row)

Morris, V.C. 'Living Without Bridges', *Philosophy of Education*, 1980.

Norton, D.L. (1976) *Personal Destinies, a Philosophy of Ethical Individualism* (Princeton University Press)

Oakeshott, M. 'Education: the engagement and its frustrations', in: Dearden, R.F. Hirst, P.H., and Peters, R.S. (eds.) (1972) *Education and the development of reason* (London, Routledge and Kegan Paul)

O'Hear, A. (1981) *Education, Society and Human Nature* (London, Routledge and Kegan Paul)

Olafson, F.A. (1976) *Principles and Persons* (Baltimore, The Johns Hopkins Press)

Park, J. 'Education: Schooling and Informal', Philosophy of Education, 1971.

Parkyn, G.W. (1973) *Towards a Conceptual Model of Lifelong Education* (Paris, UNESCO)

Passmore, J. (1970) *The Perfectibility of Man* (London, Duckworth)

Passmore, J. (1972) *A Hundred Years of Philosophy* (Harmondsworth, Penguin)

Pateman, C. (1970) *Participation and Democratic Theory* (Cambridge University Press)

Paterson, R.W.K., (1979) *Values, education and the adult* (London Routledge and Kegan Paul)

Pedersen, J.T. 'On the Educational Function of Political Participation', *Political Studies*, Vol. XXX, No. 4, 1982.

Peters, R.S. (1966) *Ethics and Education* (Allen and Unwin)

Peters, R.S. 'John Dewey's Philosophy of Education', in: Peters, R.S. (ed.) (1977) *John Dewey reconsidered* (London, Routledge and Kegan Paul)

Popper, K. (1965) *The Open Society and Its Enemies* Vols. I and II (London, Routledge, and Kegan Paul)

Power, E.J. (1982) *Philosophy of Education: Studies in Philosophies, Schooling and Educational Policies* (New Jersey, Prentice Hall)

Pyong Gap Min. 'The Place of the Individual in John Dewey's Democratic Liberal Philosophy', *Philosophy of Education*, 1979.

Rawls, J. (1980) *A Theory of Justice* (Oxford University Press)

Raywid, M.A. 'More Criticism of Analytic Philosophy of Education', *Philosophy of Education*, 1980.

Reynolds, M. 'The Learning Environment and the Ideal of Participation', *Journal of Higher Education*,

5 (1), Spring, 1981.

Richmond, K. `The Concept of Continuous Education', in: Cropley, A.J. (1979)

Roberts, C. `The Three Faces of Humanism and Their Relation to Problems of Science and Education', in: Sloan, D. (ed.) (1979) *Education and Values* (Columbia University, Teachers College)

Roland Martin, J. `The Ideal of the Educated Person', *Philosophy of Education*, 1981.

Rorty, R. (1980) *Philosophy and the Mirror of Nature* (Oxford, Blackwell)

Rorty, R. (1982) *Consequences of Pragmatism* (Sussex, Harvester Press)

Rousseau, J.J. (1957) *Emile* (London, Dent)

Russell, B. (1953) *History of Western Philosophy* (London, Unwin)

Sabine, G.H. (1971) *A History of Political Theory* (London, Harrap)

Santayana, G. `Dewey's Naturalistic Metaphysics', in: Morgenbesser, S. (1977) *Dewey and His Critics* (New York, The Journal of Philosophy Inc.)

Sartre, J.P. (1982) *Existentialism and Humanism* (Harmondsworth, Penguin)

Scheffler, I. `Towards an Analytic Philosophy of Education', in: Scheffler, I. (1973) *Reason and Teaching* (London, Routledge and Kegan Paul)

Schiller, F.C.S. (1970) *Humanism* (Connecticut, Greenwood Press)

Schneider, H.W. `Morality as an Art', in Storer, M.B. (1980)

Self, D.J. `Inconsistent Presuppositions of Dewey's Pragmatism', *The Journal of Educational Thought*, Vol. 10, No. 2, 1976.

Simpson, J.R. `Towards a Humanist Consensus in Ethics of International Development', in: Storer, M.B. (1980)

Skager, R. (1978) *Lifelong Education and Evaluation Practice* (Oxford, Pergamon Press)

Skager, R. and Dave, R.H. (1978) *Curriculum Evaluation for Lifelong Education* (Oxford, Pergamon Press)

Skillen, A. (1977) *Ruling Illusions* (Sussex, Harvester Press)

Steiner, E. `Educology of the Free', *Philosophy of Education*, 1980.

Storer, M.B. (ed.) (1980) *Humanist Ethics* (New York, Prometheus)

Storr, A. (1960) *The Integrity of the Personality* (Harmondsworth, Penguin)

Suchodolski, B. `Lifelong Education — Some

Philosophical Aspects', in: Dave, R.H. (1976)

Telfer, E. 'Education and Self-Realization', *Proceedings of the Philosophy of Education Society of Great Britain*, 1972.

Trigg, R. (1973) *Reason and Commitment* (Cambridge University Press)

Tucker, D.F.B. (1980) *Marxism and Individualism* (Oxford, Blackwell)

Vinokur, A. 'Economic Analysis of Lifelong Education', in: Dave, R.H. (1975)

Wain, K. (1985) *Education and Participation* (The University of Malta Press)

Walker, J.C., and Evers, C.W. 'Epistemology and Justifying the Curriculum of Educational Studies', *British Journal of Educational Studies*, Vol. XXX, No. 2, June, 1982.

Wall, G. 'Moral Autonomy and the Liberal Theory of Moral Education', *Proceedings of the Philosophy of Education Society of Great Britain*, 1974.

Ward, S.E. 'The Philosopher as Synthesizer', *Educational Theory*, Vol. 31, No. 1. Winter, 1981.

Warnock, M. (1977) *Schools of Thought* (London, Faber and Faber)

White, F.C. 'Knowledge and Relativism I', *Educational Philosophy and Theory*, Vol. 14, 1981.

White, J. (1982) *The Aims of Education Restated* (London, Routledge and Kegan Paul)

White, P.A. 'Socialization and Education', in: Dearden, R.F., Hirst, P.H., and Peters, R.S. (1972)

Williams, A.J., and Foster, L.E. 'The Rhetoric of Humanist Education', *The Journal of Educational Thought*, Vol. 13, No. 1, 1979.

Wilson, J. 'Philosophy of Education: retrospect and prospect', *Oxford Review of Education*, Vol. 6, 1980.

Wilson, J. 'The Future of Philosophy in Education', *British Journal of Educational Studies*, Vol. XXXI, No. 1, Feb. 1983.

Wilson, J. 'Concepts, Contestability, and the Philosophy of Education', *Journal of Philosophy of Education*, Vol. 15, No. 1, 1981.

Wirth, A. 'John Dewey on the Relations Between Industrial Democracy and Education', *Philosophy of Education*, 1981.

Wittgenstein, L. (1972) *Philosophical Investigations* (Oxford, Blackwell)

Worsley, P. (1975) *Modern Sociology* (Harmondsworth, Penguin)

Yeaxlee, A.B. (1929) *Lifelong Education* (London, Cassell)
Young, R. 'Autonomy and Socialization', *Mind*, Vol. LXXXIX, 1980.